# PROFESSIONALISM AND ETHICS IN TEACHING

*Professionalism and Ethics in Teaching* examines the ethical issues in teaching. After discussing the moral implications of professionalism, the author explores the relationship of education theory to teaching practice and the impact of this relationship on professional expertise. He then identifies and examines some central ethical and moral issues in education and teaching. Finally, David Carr gives a detailed analysis of a range of issues concerning the role of the teacher and the management of educational institutions.

*Professionalism and Ethics in Teaching* presents a thought-provoking and stimulating study of the moral dimensions of the teaching profession.

**David Carr** is Professor of Philosophy of Education in the Faculty of Education at the University of Edinburgh. He is the author of *Educating the Virtues* (1991) and editor of *Education, Knowledge and Truth* (1998).

# PROFESSIONAL ETHICS
### Editor: Ruth Chadwick
*Centre for Professional Ethics, University of Central Lancashire*

Professionalism is a subject of interest to academics, the general public and would-be professional groups. Traditional ideas of professions and professional conduct have been challenged by recent social, political and technological changes. One result has been the development for almost every profession of an ethical code of conduct which attempts to formalise its values and standards. These codes of conduct raise a number of questions about the status of a 'profession' and the consequent moral implications for behaviour.

This series seeks to examine these questions both critically and constructively. Individual volumes will consider issues relevant to particular professions, including nursing, genetic counselling, journalism, business, the food industry and law. Other volumes will address issues relevant to all professional groups such as the function and value of a code of ethics and the demands of confidentiality.

Also available in this series:

# PROFESSIONALISM AND ETHICS IN TEACHING

*David Carr*

London and New York

First published 2000
by Routledge
11 New Fetter Lane, London EC4P 4EE

Simultaneously published in the USA and Canada
by Routledge
29 West 35th Street, New York, NY 10001

*Routledge is an imprint of the Taylor & Francis Group*

© 2000 David Carr

The right of David Carr to be identified as the author of this work has
been asserted by him in accordance with the Copyright, Designs and
Patents Act 1988

Typeset in Times by Taylor & Francis Books Ltd
Printed and bound in Great Britain by MPG Books Ltd, Bodmin

*British Library Cataloguing in Publication Data*
A catalogue record for this book is available from the British Library

*Library of Congress Cataloging in Publication Data*
A catalogue record has been requested for this title

ISBN 0–415–18459–2 (hbk)
ISBN 0–415–18460–6 (pbk)

# CONTENTS

# CONTENTS

# SERIES EDITOR'S PREFACE

Professional ethics is now acknowledged as a field of study in its own right. Much of its recent development has resulted from rethinking traditional medical ethics in the light of new moral problems arising out of advances in medical science and technology. Applied philosophers, ethicists and lawyers have devoted considerable energy to exploring the dilemmas emerging from modern health-care practices and their effect on the practitioner–patient relationship.

Beyond health care, other groups have begun to think critically about the kind of service they offer and about the nature of the relationship between provider and recipient. In many areas of life, social, political and technological changes have challenged both traditional ideas of practice and underlying conceptions of what professions are. Competing trends towards 'professionalisation' on the one hand (via, for example, the proliferation of codes of ethics, or of professional conduct), and towards challenging the power of the traditional 'liberal professions' on the other, have required exploration of the concepts of 'profession' and 'professional'.

The author of this volume argues a case for viewing the professions as moral projects; and teaching and education as genuine professions. He takes issue with views of teaching as simply competence based and of the teacher as technician. In the face of modern sceptical positions he explores the moral role of the teacher and the goals of teaching.

The Professional Ethics book series seeks to examine ethical issues in the professions and related areas both critically and constructively. Individual volumes address issues relevant to all professional groups, such as the nature of a profession and the function and value of codes of ethics. Other volumes examine issues relevant to particular professions, including those which have hitherto received little attention, such as social work, the insurance industry and accountancy. This volume makes a contribution to both aims of the series: the view of teaching presented here addresses both philosophical issues about how professions should be regarded and specific issues in contemporary debates about teaching.

# PREFACE

This volume represents an attempt, to the best of my ability, to draw together a decade of enquiries into the meaning of professionalism, the relationship of educational theory and practice and the nature of moral enquiry into a reasonably coherent whole. Although all these topics have interested me throughout my professional educational life, the path to this book can be traced back to an attempt in the summer of 1990 to assemble a full-length exploration of the moral basis of teaching and educational practice. This attempt was motivated mainly by a certain antipathy to prevailing tendencies, at least in some quarters, to technicist approaches to education, and by a concern to demonstrate the wider value implicatedness of education and teaching; in this respect, although this work is addressed to a rather wider set of educational, cultural and epistemological concerns, these original preoccupations should still be apparent in the present volume. In the event, however, the earlier enterprise proved premature and was abandoned following the completion of seven or eight draft chapters.

However, material from this earlier venture did survive in the form of two presently pertinent papers which were eventually published in late 1992. The first was published under the title 'Four dimensions of educational professionalism' in *Westminster Studies in Education*; the second appeared as 'Practical enquiry, values and the problem of educational theory' in *Oxford Review of Education*, and was later reprinted in W. Hare and J. Portelli (eds), *Philosophy of Education* (Detselig, 1996). Neither of these papers – with the exception of a paragraph or so from the second one – survives in original form here, but both were directly ancestral to the first two sections of this book. The first paper on educational professionalism was published at about the same time, more by coincidence than by design, as I found myself charged with co-ordinating and teaching two courses focused on professional issues – a cross-institutional module on professional values and a modular Master's course on professional knowledge and practice – in my employing institution. Over the years, these courses – as well as numerous invitations to present papers on various aspects of professional development to a variety of occupational groups – afforded unprecedented opportunities to explore issues raised in particularly the first two sections of this volume. In this respect, the *Westminster Studies* paper is a not too remote forerunner of many of the ideas discussed in Part 1 – as well as of a recent *Journal of Applied Philosophy* (1999) paper entitled 'Professional education and professional ethics', upon which Chapter 2 is based.

However, it seems that the second paper for *Oxford Review* provided an even more powerful springboard for further work throughout the 1990s on a variety of issues relating to the vexed educational problem of the relationship of theory to practice. Moreover, despite having written over the years on most topics of educational philosophy and theory, if I was asked to choose *one* paper which I would regard as having made a substantial contribution to the field as a whole, the 1995 *Journal of Philosophy of Education* paper, 'Is understanding the professional knowledge of teachers a theory-practice problem?' – upon which Chapters 4 and 5 are based – would have to be a strong contender. Notwithstanding that, so far as I can see, this paper has had next to no influence in the extensive literature of educational philosophy and theory (perhaps the less than prepossessing title did not help); where it has been noticed it has been seriously misunderstood, although it has more than likely been overshadowed by papers on the same theme by names more famous than mine, it still seems to me that it goes rather further in terms of basic analysis of this difficult problem than many if not most of its contemporaries. Be that as it may, as well as having clear ancestry in the earlier *Oxford Review* piece, this paper is also strongly related to critiques of the competency conception of teacher education and training which I mounted around the same time in several other places. Chapter 6, indeed, is effectively a revised version of a paper entitled 'Questions of competence', published in the *British Journal of Educational Studies* in 1993.

In brief, whereas Part 1 of this book is concerned to demonstrate the inherently ethical character of any distinctive occupational category of profession – to show that the standard professions are in a significant sense moral projects – and to defend the claim that teaching and education are genuine professions in this sense, Part 2 is concerned to show that the knowledge and expertise of teachers is essentially grounded in the kind of practical deliberation which Aristotle distinguished as *phronesis* or moral wisdom from *techne* or productive reasoning (though it is not denied that teachers and other professionals need both). Part 3, therefore, turns to the important task of defending – in the teeth of various kinds of contemporary subjectivist and relativist moral scepticism – the basic *objectivity* of moral reason and judgement. To this end, Chapter 7 develops themes which I have explored over the years in such educational philosophical papers as 'Education and values' (*British Journal of Educational Studies*, 1991), as well as in 'Moral education and the objectivity of values' – my own contribution to a collection entitled *Education, Knowledge and Truth: Beyond the PostModern Impasse*, which I recently (1998) edited for Routledge. In exploring the relativist connotations of a 'rival traditions' conception of educational thought with reference to the time-honoured educational theoretical dichotomy of traditionalism and progressivism, Chapter 8 also returns to a topic which has interested me at least from 'On understanding educational theory' published in *Educational Philosophy and Theory* (1985), to a more recent (1998) essay, 'Traditionalism and progressivism: a perennial problematic of educational theory and policy' in *Westminster Studies in Education* .

The main concern of Part 4 is to explore the ethical complexities of any serious reflection upon the aims and purposes of education, as well as to distinguish some of the key respects in which teaching is implicated in moral issues and concerns of human well-being and harm. To this end, Chapter 9 first distinguishes between the rather different levels of normativity at which teachers or teaching might be found derelict or wanting, before proceeding to explore the ethical grounds for regarding certain particular forms of institutional conduct or personal relationship as professionally suspect or inadmissible in educational contexts. Chapter 10 turns to the not inconsiderable problem of identifying positive goals for education – again in the face of influential postmodern scepticism about the very intelligibility of that knowledge-based notion of rational emancipation which was for post-war philosophical pioneers of liberal education the very cornerstone of educational endeavour. It is argued that it is crucial to the clarification of many contemporary confusions about educational aims that we observe a distinction between education and schooling. (This argument was more fully explored in my essay 'The dichotomy of liberal versus vocational education', in the American *Philosophy of Education Society Yearbook* of 1995.) Chapter 11 is concerned to examine different conceptions of the widely acknowledged moral educational dimension of the teacher's role and is essentially a revised version of a tract entitled *The Moral Role of the Teacher* which was first commissioned by the Scottish Consultative Council on the Curriculum for publication in their *Perspectives on Values* series (1996).

The two concluding chapters of Part 5 are expressly devoted to exploring particular ethical issues of education and teaching. Indeed, these are actually based upon 'case studies' presented for discussion to teachers in various Scottish schools by my colleague John Landon and me in the course of a project on values education, which was generously supported by the Gordon Cook Foundation of Aberdeen during 1991/92. A full account of this work may be found in a report submitted to the Cook Foundation in 1993, and a shorter version was published in a two-part co-authored (Carr and Landon) article for the *Journal of Beliefs and Values* (1998), entitled 'Teachers and schools as agencies of values education: reflections on teachers' perceptions'. However, apart from using the 'case studies' as a peg upon which to hang the final section, I have not here reproduced the substance of these reports (which were mainly critical appraisals of teachers' discussions), and have pursued the issues they raise in my own way.

It will already have been gathered, however, that the present work is not merely concerned with piecemeal exploration of particular ethical issues of education and teaching, but has the rather larger purpose of locating such issues within a more general theory of professional life and judgement into which education and teaching might be coherently fitted. It is mainly driven by the distinctive account of practical wisdom sketched in the first two chapters of Part 2 and is broadly consistent with the virtue-ethical conception of moral reason and sensibility which has also been a long-standing topic of interest to me. I first made a large-scale attempt to understand moral education in virtue-ethical terms in *Educating the Virtues* (Routledge 1991) and the co-edited collection *Virtue Ethics and Moral Education* (D. Carr and J. Steutel, Routledge 1999) represents a more recent (and I think more successful) effort in this direction. In this connection, by the way, it is possible that this book discloses the beginnings of arguments which would suggest that *only* a virtue-ethical account can give a full account of what is morally untoward about certain kinds of professional misdemeanour. However, since such arguments occur here only in embryonic form, we can be sure that plenty of work has been left for other occasions.

# ACKNOWLEDGEMENTS

As I have already indicated in the Preface, the following work draws upon a fair amount of previously published material. Whilst such material here occurs in more or less tailored, modified or revised forms, certain debts are substantial enough to warrant appropriate acknowledgement. In the first instance, thanks are due to Blackwell Publishers for permission to reproduce the substance of: (i) 'Professional education and professional ethics', first published in the *Journal of Applied Philosophy* in 1999 and here used as the basis of Chapter 2; (ii) 'Is understanding the professional knowledge of teachers a theory-practice problem?', first published in the *Journal of Philosophy of Education* in 1995 and here used as the basis of Chapters 4 and 5; and (iii) 'Questions of competence', first published in the *British Journal of Educational Studies* in 1993 and here used as the basis of Chapter 6. Chapter 11 is essentially a revised version of an essay entitled *The Moral Role of the Teacher* which first appeared in 1996 in booklet form in the *Perspectives on Values* series of the Scottish Consultative Committee on the Curriculum (SCCC). I remain deeply grateful to the SCCC for their kind invitation to contribute to this series. The key themes upon which Chapters 12 and 13 of Part 5 are built were originally developed in the context of research and development with teachers in Scottish schools during 1991/92, and supported by the Gordon Cook Foundation of Aberdeen – to whom thanks are also therefore due. In this connection, I should also record my gratitude to all the teachers in the various Scottish schools in which my colleague John Landon and I worked at this time, both for their unfailing hospitality and their inspiration to further thinking about the issues of this work. Thanks are also due to the many conference organisers from various professional sectors whose invitations to speak also provided vital opportunities and incentives to explore fresh conceptual pastures.

# Part I

# EDUCATION, TEACHING AND PROFESSIONALISM

# 1

# TEACHING AND
# EDUCATION

## Fundamental assumptions and basic questions

Any work on ethics and teaching written for a series on professional ethics would appear committed to certain key claims or assumptions. Basically, these are: (i) that teaching is a professional activity; (ii) that any professional enterprise is deeply implicated in ethical concerns and considerations; and (iii) (therefore) that teaching is also an enterprise which is deeply and significantly implicated in ethical concerns and considerations. I believe that all these assumptions are true and it is the aim of this volume to substantiate them. But at the same time, in the spirit of philosophical enquiry, these are assumptions which should not be allowed to go unquestioned, and we shall need to be ever alert in this work to the sceptical objections to which all these claims have been periodically subject. However, I think that there can be no better place to start with our assessments of these claims and counterclaims than with some basic analysis of the concepts of teaching and education. In Part I, then, we shall devote primary attention (via appropriate conceptions of profession and professionalism) to the following questions: (i) is teaching a professional activity?; and (ii) is education a profession?

Indeed, to begin with, it is worth asking whether the question of the professional status of *teaching* is identical to or different from the question of the professional standing of *education*. Certainly, teaching and education are not obviously one and the same enterprise. It seems excessive to suppose that education always requires teaching, it is arguable that not all teaching is educational in any robust sense, and I do believe that questions of the professionality of teaching and the professional status of education are significantly different. To that extent, as we shall see, I am inclined to respond (roughly) 'yes' to the question whether education should be considered a profession, allowing for an appropriately 'prescriptive' rather than 'descriptive' construal of profession, but 'not always' to the question of whether teaching is a professional activity. But even if education and teaching are not the same thing, they are clearly related in conceptually and practically significant ways, and it will therefore be a crucial task of this section not just to head off dangerous confusion of education with teaching (and such other closely related notions as schooling), but also to explore significant internal relationships between them. Moreover, it is pivotal to my argument that the more teaching can be shown to be implicated in the broader concerns of education, the stronger any case for regarding it as a professional activity is likely to be.

## Teaching and skill

Taking one step at a time, however, let us begin with the question of the nature and occupational status of teaching. What, roughly, is teaching? At the most general level of logical grammar, it seems reasonable enough to regard teaching as a kind of *activity* in which human beings engage. From this point of view, indeed, it is arguably important to distinguish both teaching and the larger project of education from various *processes* we merely undergo (such as socialisation and schooling); we are hard put to engage in teaching or benefit from education in the absence of witting or *intentional* participation or engagement. However, we should also note some ways in which talk of teaching contrasts grammatically with that of education; for example, whereas we might say 'please don't interrupt me while I'm teaching', it seems odd to say: 'not now while I'm educating'. Moreover, as already noted, education appears to be a rather larger and broader enterprise to which teaching may or may not contribute. But if teaching is an *intentional* activity, with what purpose do we engage in it? The answer, none the worse for obviousness, is that the purpose of teaching is to bring about *learning*; it is a significant consequence of this, of course, that it is not possible to define teaching other than by reference to learning: we need some understanding of what constitutes effective learning in order to see what it could be for teaching to constitute the sound or viable promotion of it.[1]

Moreover, any appearance of triviality notwithstanding, this point is a matter of some importance, since the surface grammar of

4

familiar talk about teaching is misleading and has been the source of some educational confusion. One source of trouble is that we talk of X teaching Y, where Y can be ambiguous between *persons* and *subjects*; hence, we speak naturally enough either of Mr Smith teaching mathematics or of Miss Jones teaching Sarah or 4B. It is important to see, all the same, that such ways of speaking are really contractions and that in fact the term 'teach' expresses what logicians would refer to as a 'three-place predicate'. To the extent that X teaches Y conceals a relation between not two but *three* terms, the true logical form of judgements about teaching is better captured by X teaches Y to Z, where Y represents some subject or activity, and Z stands for some particular pupil or group of learners. To see this, however, is to make nonsense of such familiar slogans as 'one teaches children not subjects' (or vice versa) – for there could hardly be any coherent notion of teaching which did not implicate both learners and something to be learned. In this respect, it is arguable that at least some of the vaunted differences between so-called traditional or 'subject-centred' and progressive or 'child-centred' educationalists have their source in simple grammatical error. Again, however, since it has always seemed to me to be a further mistake to regard traditionalists as at odds with progressives on exclusively pedagogical grounds, this would not take care of all such differences.

At all events, assuming it is basically correct to regard teaching as essentially a matter of the promotion of learning, what could we say about the general character of learning which might assist us to a clearer view of the nature of teaching as an activity? There has of course been considerable modern empirical scientific interest in learning, which some experimental psychologists have broadly characterised as a change in behaviour. Now whilst no such broad definition could be accurate, for there are clearly changes in animal and human behaviour which are not due to any kind of learning, it is nevertheless a persisting temptation to conceive of learning as a matter of the acquisition of knowledge, understanding and skills *behaviourally* construed. It is then but a short step to thinking of teaching as the mastery of further skills which are somehow causally effective in the production of learning so construed. Indeed, I would go so far as to argue that a conception of effective teaching as basically a matter of the acquisition of behavioural skills is the dominant political and professional educational paradigm of the present day.[2] But then, someone might well ask what other way of conceptualising teaching there could possibly be:

if teaching is to be a learnable occupation, how might it be learned except as a set of specifiable practical skills? However, it is this question – that of whether teaching as a professional activity is adequately characterisable in terms of the acquisition of skills – which takes us straight to the heart of the issues which will most deeply concern us in the rest of this work. A few general observations on this issue, therefore, may be appropriate at this point.

First, one should not generally assume that all qualities or capacities needed for the pursuit of a given occupation are acquirable as *learned* skills. It hardly needs saying that many activities and occupations require natural endowments, certain kinds of mental or physical potential, for their effective exercise and execution: without the right physique or mental capacity, for example, one's ambitions to become a proficient hurdler, dancer or theoretical physicist may be entirely in vain. In this respect, it is still something of a live question whether teachers are made or born. Indeed, few teacher trainers will be unfamiliar with situations in which a student's performance is deficient in certain crucial qualities of personality, expression or imagination which, though certainly apt for development if potentially there, can hardly be developed if they are not there even potentially. Second, however, certain key qualities would appear to be needed for professional or other occupational purposes, qualities acquirable by anyone of average physical and mental endowment, which are none the less not obviously or appropriately characterisable as skills. Precisely the problem with so much currently fashionable educational talk of 'caring skills' or 'listening skills' is not that there aren't acquirable qualities and capacities of caring and attention which we want people – pupils or student teachers – to acquire; rather, it is that it seems misleading to regard such abilities and capacities as learnable in the manner of *skills*. Once again, we should not generally say to a pupil, for example, 'You are not listening or showing enough care here, go away and practise your listening and caring skills'; indeed, it's not so much that we want teachers and pupils to acquire listening and caring skills, but that we want them to *pay attention* and to *care*.[3]

In short, to the extent that teaching seems to be an immensely complex and multifaceted activity, involving a wide variety of human qualities and attributes, certain well-nigh exclusive contemporary analyses of pedagogy in terms of skill and technique would appear to be dangerously and damagingly procrustean. However, although it seems far-fetched to maintain that teaching is entirely reducible to skills in the manner of a science-based technology, it would seem equally implausible to suppose that important questions of skill, technique and causal effectiveness *never* arise in connection with teaching, or that empirical scientific analyses of aspects of pedagogy are always inappropriate. Hence, it is perhaps worth devoting some space to a brief sketch of what the education profession urgently seems to lack – and what so far no one has gone very far towards providing – an adequate philosophical psychology of teaching.

## Towards a philosophical psychology of teaching

We may well begin by asking precisely what might be said for and against conceptualising teaching as a body of technical skills apt for identification or specification on the basis of objective scientific research into classroom practice. I certainly do not think we need doubt that there is some genuine mileage in this idea, or that there are aspects of lesson presentation, classroom organisation and pupil management which may be suitable to this sort of formulation. It seems possible to be more or less systematic about pedagogy, and some aspects of teaching do seem susceptible of rational improvement in the light of something approaching objective scientific research. On the other hand, however, there can be no doubt that this card has been considerably overplayed by modern pedagogical experts of a scientific bent. All else apart, teaching does not seem to be the sort of technical notion which requires sophisticated scientific enquiry to understand (like 'quark' or 'photon'). Indeed, it is not just that such terms as 'teaching' and 'learning' are learned at our mother's knees, but that there is a real enough sense in which anyone, even quite small children, both can and do teach.[4] The degree to which any kind of research-based know-how is actually necessary for effective teaching, then, is at least questionable, although there is no doubt something to be said for systematic attempts to improve our pre-theoretical pedagogical knowledge. Generally, however, it is arguable that hunch and intuition play as great a part in good teaching as technical rule following, and that good or inspired teaching may not be the most technically informed or systematic. Indeed, on extreme versions of this view, it could be suggested that a too technical approach to pedagogy leads only to mechanical, uninspired or lifeless teaching.

From this point of view, it is not uncommon for teaching to be regarded as an *art* more than a skill or a craft – at least in any technical or applied science senses of these terms – and there can be no doubt that there are significant thespian or dramatic dimensions to teaching which give it more the character of a performance art than a technical skill. In this respect, good teachers need, like artists, to bring qualities of expression, creativity and imaginative flair to their teaching – qualities which are not adequately captured by any idea of grasping causal generalities and observing invariable rules. There is no need, of course, to deny that such creativity and imagination can be taught or learned, and it may not be inappropriate to regard what is here taught and learned as *skills* – just so long as it is appreciated that one does not teach or learn imaginative teaching as one teaches or learns an organisational strategy of one kind or another. Hence, it again seems bizarre to advise a student to go away and practise teaching imaginatively, as we might advise him or her to practise her classroom organisation – precisely, I suppose, because there is a real sense in which what is imaginative is not readily susceptible of rehearsal in quite this way. Indeed, it is probably safe to say that imaginative teaching is something which is developed more than instructed – and, to the extent that its development depends on qualities and resources already in embryo in the personality of the teacher, this accounts for the difficulty teacher trainers often have in assisting dull and lifeless individuals to be more expressive and imaginative teachers, as it were 'from scratch'.

Indeed, there would seem to be two rather different respects in which qualities of pedagogical expression and imagination depend on personality and personal characteristics. First, although expression and imagination can be developed – it *is* possible to help realise expressive potential or to assist someone who is already imaginative to become more so – such development seems to presuppose an already given basis of sensibility, perception and insight: better jokes are largely impotent to enhance the comedial abilities of someone who lacks a sense of humour (or a sense of comedic pace and timing). But, second, such sensibility, perception and insight seem to be grounded in detailed situation-specific appreciation, which is probably as much a matter of sense and affect as cognition. Thus, just as a gifted comedian is one who can precisely adjust delivery and subject matter to the mood of the audience, so a good teacher is one who is able to perceive what is pedagogically or interpersonally salient in a specific educational circumstance. This aspect of the teacher's art brings us to a topic we shall need to revisit: that of the *particularity* of the craft skills of the teacher and the difficulty of generalising or codifying the skills of a teacher in a way that would render them applicable across the wide diversity of circumstances in which teachers may find themselves. Indeed, some recent educational philosophers[5] have finely honed this 'particularist' case precisely for the purpose of resisting educational *technicism* – the view that teaching is a kind of science-based technology which would enable anyone to practise it, irrespective of personal characteristics or particular circumstances.

But if teaching is not a science-based technology, it does not seem exactly right to regard it instead, or in addition, as some form of performance art. There are, for example, serious limits to the possibilities of originality and creativity in teaching – and a teacher, unlike an artist, is hardly free to do whatever might commend itself to him or her in a spirit of imagination or self-expression. Moreover, just as one can envisage technically effective ways of teaching which would be educationally suspect, so one can foresee creative and expressive ways of teaching which might also be pedagogically unacceptable. Indeed, charismatically attractive styles of teaching which leave audiences spellbound have clear corruptive potential, and educationalists will often come across students and teachers whose seductive personal style or character is an impediment rather than an aid to effective and purposeful teaching. Thus, on the most basic construal of teaching, it is arguable that there are normative or evaluative constraints on teaching, which are less technical and aesthetic, more moral or ethical. Good teaching is not just teaching which is causally effective or personally attractive, it is teaching which seeks at best to promote the moral, psychological and physical well-being of learners, and at least to avoid their psychological, physical and moral damage. That said, I think that there are weaker and stronger versions of this notion of the moral implicatedness of teaching. For although we would certainly be right to regard music or athletics coaches, for example, as professionally derelict for sexually abusing or otherwise corrupting their pupils, we should not normally – in so far as we take the be and end all of their role to be the teaching of certain prescribed knowledge and set skills – hold them accountable for having failed to improve the general characters of their pupils. On the other hand, it is common for parents, employers and politicians to hold teachers in schools to account for the moral development of pupils.[6] There is thus a broad and crude distinction to be drawn here between teaching in the more limited contexts of *training*, and teaching in the broader context of *education* – and, traditionally, the former has been deemed subject to weaker moral constraints than the latter.

Since it is with professional teaching in the stronger educational sense that we are mainly concerned in this book, considerable attention will be devoted in due course to the rather different levels at which education may be fairly said to be implicated in moral and ethical considerations. For the moment, however, we are concerned only to show that although what we have so far said about the inherent moral or ethical character of good teaching goes some way towards showing how *all* teaching must be bound by professional ties of accountability and responsibility to employers, parents, pupils, and so on, any deeper association of teaching with education must serve to complicate our view of the ethics of pedagogy yet further – precisely in so far as there seems to be widespread disagreement about what exactly *education* is. Moreover, it may be useful here to pursue an interesting and relatively uncharted insight into the extraordinary extent of this disagreement via the brief examination of different comparisons which appear to have been made, both explicitly and implicitly, between teachers and other occupational groups.

## Concepts of education: profession and vocation

### *Vocational conceptions*

We may begin by recognising a broad distinction between ideas of *vocation* and *profession*, since it is arguable that modern ideas of teaching reflect a certain vacillation between professional and vocational conceptions. These ideas are not, to be sure, entirely distinct, and it is not unusual for an occupation to be referred to in much the same breath as vocation and profession. But although both concepts are proteanly resistant to precise formulation, there are nevertheless significant and illuminating tensions, as well as interesting differences of emphases, between them. First, then, one consequence of regarding a given occupation as a vocation rather than as a profession turns on the idea of significant continuity between occupational role and private values and concerns. Thus, it is common for the incumbents of so-called vocations (the ministry, nursing and teaching) to regard themselves, rightly or wrongly, as people whose lives are totally given over to the service of others (parishioners, patients, pupils) in a way that leaves relatively little room for the personal or private – and has, indeed, in the case of more than one vocation precluded any possibility of marriage and family. In this respect, moreover, even if it should turn out that the time-honoured professions are able enough to match any traditional vocational devotion to service, the idea of profession does seem to be a more impersonally regulated one, and has often been constructed – in the alleged interests of clients – upon very precise separation of professional from personal concerns. From this perspective, the lawyer or doctor may for reasons of professional detachment precisely seek to avoid that affectively charged concern for the personal welfare of others which is often characteristic of a good nurse, or that devotion to the promulgation of partisan doctrines and values which may be the measure of a good priest.

Ironically, this idea of significant vocational continuity between personal and occupational concerns and interests has probably been one reason why traditional vocations have been less well financially rewarded than the professions. After all, if people have a genuine passion for spreading the Gospel, nursing the sick or teaching children – if these are the ways in which they find ultimate personal fulfilment, meaning or salvation – this should be in itself reward enough. It may even have been feared that raising the salaries of ministers, nurses or teachers would attract the wrong kind of people, those of a mercenary disposition, into the vocations. At all events, there can be little doubt that teaching has often been regarded as a vocation, that it has also been regarded as the kind of occupation which people enter for love rather than money, and that it has also frequently been woefully underpaid. But there are also different ways in which teaching has been regarded as a vocation – or, to put it another way, teaching has been liable to diverse vocational comparisons. Thus, to begin with, there is not much doubt that teaching, especially in the early years contexts of education, is regarded alongside nursing or midwifery as a 'caring' vocation, something which requires feminine or mothering qualities of affect more than cognition. Indeed, on extreme versions of this view (one such, emanating from central government sources under a recent British conservative administration, took the form of a proposal to recruit a 'mum's army' for early years teaching[7]) there may seem no need to train teachers in any sophisticated cognitive or theoretical skills for a task that is essentially little more than surrogate parenthood.

At a near opposite extreme to the caring vocation conception of teaching, however, we find a very much more exalted 'high church' vocational view, one which seems motivated more by comparison of teaching with the ministry or priesthood. On this view, probably deepest entrenched in the traditions of public, grant-maintained and grammar schools, teaching is regarded as a very high calling indeed. The teacher is conceived as the representative or custodian of a specific set of civilised standards and values predicated on a traditionalist idea of education as the transmission of culture – of 'the best that has been thought and said in the world'[8] – from one generation to the next. This perspective inclines to conceive the teacher as someone who can in principle be looked up to as an *exemplar* of the very highest culturally enshrined standards and values, and as someone who possesses a range of *virtues* more than a set of skills. Here, the contrast between vocational and professional views of teaching comes into sharp relief with respect to the ways in which teachers might attract criticism for failing to live up to the standards of their calling. For whereas professional conceptions might regard inadequacies of knowledge and skill as more of a cause for concern than purely personal or private shortcomings – assuming, of course, that such personal shortcomings did not interfere with pedagogical efficiency – shortcomings of personal character and value are liable to be weighted far more heavily on 'high church' vocational views. For example, whereas on the professional view it might be considered irrelevant to effective educational practice that a teacher was in private life an adulterer or a card-sharp, just so long as they possessed all the professionally approved teaching competences, the personal probity of a fumbling teacher might well be rated on the vocational view above the pedagogical efficiency of a lascivious bilker (which is not to deny, of course, that either conception would probably seek a happy mixture of both kinds of quality).

Still within the broad ambit of vocational conceptions, however, the traditionalist 'cultural custodian' view of teaching can be contrasted not only with 'child-minding' conceptions of education, but also with the social remedial or personal therapeutic educational approaches of many educational progressives and radicals. One reason for including such views among types of vocationalism, moreover, is that a certain anti-professional stance – as we shall see later in this book – has been a recurring theme of such radicals.[9] First, then, educational progressives and radicals are deeply critical of the educational bureaucratisation which follows in the wake of any professionalisation of teaching. This is on the grounds that: first, it conduces more to the self-serving interests of professionals than the needs of clients; second, it has the concomitant effect of depersonalising and dehumanising education. In consequence, educational radicals are, for much the same reason as social workers, distrustful of the idea of professionalisation because it opens up a chasm of mistrust between the suppliers and the receivers of a service – who may less easily perceive the professional as someone who is 'on their side'.[10] Hence, the alternative progressive and radical agenda – variously exhibited in private progressive institutions in the UK and elsewhere, in the 'Free school' movements of the 1960s and 1970s and from time to time in the primary and secondary sectors – is focused primarily on ideas of personal emancipation and social liberation from the indoctrinatory effects of conventional schooling. But then the progressive or radical would also be inclined like the nurse or priest, as well as their educational counterparts of 'cultural custodian' and 'child-minding' conceptions of teaching, to emphasise considerable continuity between personal and workplace aspects of teaching. On this view, teachers should above all avoid hypocrisy and be 'authentic' in their dealings with pupils; they should really practise what they preach, should *really* rather than merely apparently 'care', and be utterly and selflessly committed to the personal flourishing (however variously conceived on vocational conceptions) of their charges.

### *Professional conceptions*

However, although one need not doubt that most contemporary career teachers would readily identify and sympathise with at least some of these vocational priorities, it is arguable that there has over the years been a marked shift towards conceptions of education and teaching of more professional than vocational temper: conceptions, that is, which are more inclined to observe a fairly clear distinction between the private or personal, and the public or professional, and to define the occupation of teaching in terms of prescribed skills and rules of conduct. There are, moreover, some fairly weighty reasons for this. For one thing, there are legitimate concerns – reinforced perhaps by some of the worst excesses of radical and progressive attitudes in state schooling – about educational accountability to the practical needs and interests of parents, employers and the wider community. For another, however, there are substantial sociological reasons why it is difficult, if not impossible, to sustain even the non-radical 'cultural custodian' conception of education and teaching in the culturally pluralist conditions of modern liberal-democratic polity. The point is that whereas the cultural custodian view is tailor-made for circumstances of cultural homogeneity in which teachers are required not only to transmit but exemplify a commonly shared set of values or virtues, circumstances of greater cultural heterogeneity and value diversity conspire to render any such conception at best inappropriate and at worst invidious. The awkward question for teachers enjoined to be custodians of culture and values in a state school in, say, London, Glasgow or Manchester, is likely to be that of precisely whose values they are to transmit: are these to be the ostensible Christian values of 'British' culture – in which case, should these be Anglican, Catholic or nonconformist?; the secular-liberal values of many if not most people living in Britain?; or the Muslim or Hindu values of the British offspring of immigrant parents? It is for precisely this reason that the question of the *neutrality* of the teacher, and a corresponding perceived need to develop a conception of professionality which observes a clear line between professional obligations and personal commitments – in the interests, among other things, of avoiding indoctrination – has been a burning issue of post-war liberal philosophy of education.

In short, whereas the idea of educational professionalism seems to sit better than that of vocation with a 'thin' liberal-democratic notion of civil polity, the somewhat 'top-down' character of at least cultural custodian conceptions of vocation appears more consistent with paternalistic socialisation into 'thicker' traditonal values of communitarian conception.[11] That said, there would seem to be, as in the case of vocational construals of education and teaching, rather different available conceptions of educational or teacher professionalism. Having explored various possible comparisons of teaching with religious ministry, nursing and social work, it may be helpful to examine different conceptions of educational professionalism, via comparisons of teaching with other familiar occupations and services. In this connection, we may first observe an important distinction of modern treatments of this question between *restricted* and *extended* professionalism.[12] Although the distinction is usually observed in the interests of arguing in favour of the latter over the former, both notions of professionalism appear to conceive teaching as at heart a matter of the acquisition and practice of a range of skills of pedagogy and management in a contractually defined framework of professional responsibilities and obligations. The restricted version, however, conceives the skills and contractual obligations of the teacher somewhat more along the lines of trade expertise than professional knowledge – the expertise, one might say, of plumbers and electricians rather than doctors or lawyers. For the most part, restricted teacher expertise is taken to follow from familiarity with national or local policy guidelines and mastery, probably more in the field than the academy, of technical skills. The responsibilities of restricted professionals are therefore almost exclusively defined in terms of technical competence, and more or less direct accountability or conformity to the requirements of external authority. To this extent, although we may still speak of restricted teachers as more or less *professional* according to their conformity or otherwise to such requirements, restricted professionalism scores poorly on that criterion of occupational autonomy which is often held to be a key ingredient of the professional lives of doctors and lawyers. From this viewpoint, recent rationalisation of professional preparation according to competence models of training, and standardisation of educational provision through centrally imposed curricula, have been widely regarded as conducing to the 'de-professionalisation' of teachers, whose opportunities for individual and creative initiative and endeavour seem increasingly curtailed.

An 'extended' view of educational professionalism, on the other hand, aspires precisely to regard teaching alongside such traditional professions as medicine and law. On this perspective, teachers are to be regarded, along with general practitioners or legal advisors, as possessors of a socially valued specialist expertise which requires lengthy education and training – precisely because teaching requires educated capacities for independent judgement, rather than mere training in obedience to authority. Thus, just as we might well regard it as unacceptable for politicians or the general public – anyone other than those properly educated in complex issues of medicine and health care – to direct the decisions of doctors on important matters of medical policy and practice, so it could be considered inappropriate for politicians or employers to dictate to teachers what is or is not worthy of inclusion in the school curriculum, or what kinds of knowledge and skill are crucial for the professional conduct of teaching. Hence, although it has lately been fashionable for teachers to encourage a climate of positive 'partnership'[13] with parents and the wider community in the interests of a better diagnosis of children's educational needs and abilities, the 'extended professional' would still be a *senior* partner, the one with superior professional knowledge, in any such association. Indeed, his or her status might well be construed as a close educational analogue of the 'consultancy' role of general practitioners and legal advisors with regard to medical and legal care and assistance. On this view, the teacher should be regarded as someone who, by virtue of a sophisticated professional education, is well qualified to exercise a higher understanding of the nature of learning and pedagogy in meeting the particular and local needs of individual children in particular educational circumstances.

'Extended professionals', then, are inclined to resist the 'de-professionalisation' or 'de-skilling' of 'restricted professionalism' – which they may also take to be characteristic of narrow competence-based programmes of teacher training. Notoriously, however, recent general erosion of professional autonomy, and a marked shift to more centrally prescribed training programmes, has almost certainly been fuelled by mounting contemporary political and public mistrust of what has sometimes seemed an arrogant professional reluctance to acknowledge any public accountability. In this respect, however, an alternative strategy for bridling professional power, also a familiar feature of the recent political landscape of British and other liberal democracies, has involved surrendering control of professional activities to market forces. Ironically enough, such strategies for the control of professional monopolies in education and more widely were first proposed, in the form of voucher systems, by educational radicals of the 1960s. But such ideas have been given a more recent neo-liberal lease of life in the form of such proposals as local or devolved management, which make school funding crucially dependent upon attracting parental custom in a climate of educational market competition.[14] There can also be little doubt that the market conception of education has had an effect, for better or worse, on contemporary reflection about the nature of educational professionalism. One effect, for example, can be seen in the growing popularity of in-service courses for professionals focused upon more managerial, particularly economic-administrative, aspects of schooling. There would appear to have been a significant shift away from regarding headteachers as leaders of academic communities to a conception of them as managing directors of small businesses primarily concerned with packaging and promoting a product (via glossy brochures and syllabuses) in whichever way might best attract 'customers'.

## Analogies with teaching: similarity and difference

Thus, at the end of a line of more or less plausible comparisons between teachers and priests, nurses, social workers or therapists, plumbers and doctors, we come finally to a systematic political attempt to cast the teacher in the role of the small businessman. Which of these conceptions, one might ask, is correct? Clearly, the question is unhelpful. One reasonable response is that teaching is assimilable to *none* of these occupations, it is simply what it is – teaching. Indeed, the pioneer of post-war educational philosophy, R.S. Peters, makes this point when he distinguishes education from such other activities as care and therapy: 'the teacher's job is to train and instruct, it is not to help and cure'.[15] It is therefore important to bear in mind that any of these comparisons can be dangerously misleading, and that taking too seriously purported analogies between education and religious ministry, child-minding or salesmanship can have a distortive effect on our thinking about the distinctive character of teaching. However, as we saw in our initial exploration of the technical, aesthetic and moral dimensions of the activity of teaching, the educational project in which teaching is implicated is clearly a complex matter which might stand to be illuminated by *cautious* comparisons with some of these occupations. For example, there is clearly something to be said for the traditional 'cultural custodian' idea of education as the transmission of culture (evaluatively rather than merely descriptively construed). From this viewpoint, one would venture to suggest that an important lesson about educational professionalism is indeed contained in the custodial insight that the notion of an adulterous teacher is in its own way as professionally questionable as that of a drunken minister. Similarly, few can deny that teaching is an activity which is at least like nursing or midwifery to the extent that it involves a significant dimension of affective care and support; the good teacher is invariably someone who is able to win the confidence and trust of those in his or her charge. (It is also interesting to note that a comparison with midwifery is central to perhaps the first notable western philosophical exploration of educational initiation.[16])

Indeed, it might follow from this that the teacher–pupil relationship cannot be of *precisely* the detached clinical sort which characterises the professional involvement of, say, lawyers with clients. To this extent, educational progressives or radicals may also be onto something in claiming that the teacher needs to be perceived by pupils as someone who is 'on their side', and that too much emphasis on the 'formal' professional role of the teacher could serve to undermine the best quality of relationship between teachers and pupils, though some progressives have doubtless gone too far in wanting to purge education of *any* element of external authority. Moreover, even though the 'restricted professional' idea of the teacher as a glorified plumber, not to mention any associated notion that learning to teach might be achieved exclusively through 'hands-on' apprenticeship, is certainly inadequate to capture the conceptual and practical complexities of teaching (or even those, for that matter, of plumbing), it can hardly be doubted that teachers do need, in order to ply their trade with any degree of causal effectiveness, to acquire a range of crucial craft skills of communication, lesson presentation, organisation and management. Furthermore, even if there are considerable dangers in any overstated comparisons between the teaching world and the business world, there can be no doubt that the management of modern schools is a complex fiscal and administrative matter which may stand to profit (so to speak) from lessons from the business world. Moreover, there is much to be said for the view that schools do need to be more mindful than they may formerly have been of the best hopes and aspirations of parents for their children, and to be appropriately accountable to the practical needs and interests of the wider community and economy.

What then of the idea that teachers are to be compared to or included in the same category as such time-honoured professionals as doctors and lawyers? Although comparing teachers to doctors and lawyers is no less fraught with hazards than other analogies, I shall argue that the comparison is not entirely inappropriate – and, more importantly, that there is *enough* to the comparison to sustain a significant discourse of professional ethics with regard to educational practice. I do think, as we shall see, that there are difficulties about thinking of teaching in the same professional terms as medicine or law. It seems likely that teachers cannot realistically aspire, even in principle, to quite the same degree of professional autonomy as doctors or lawyers, and one reason for this is that, although the social and economic implications of the educational project seem to be as serious and significant as those of medicine or law, there is not the same degree of asymmetry between professional and lay expertise in the case of teaching as with medicine or law. Thus, although the general public have no less a vested interest in the state of health and justice than they have in the education of their children, they are less well placed than doctors or lawyers to pronounce authoritatively on the rightness or wrongness of this or that esoteric aspect of medical or legal practice. By contrast professional educational issues are much less inaccessible to non-professionals and there is more scope for joint lay–professional debate about educational issues between educated professionals and the educated public. Moreover, irrespective of expertise, members of the public are in another sense more entitled to their own perspectives in any disagreement with educational professionals. If, for example, a child is suffering from a serious medical condition for which the only clear remedy is surgical intervention, it would be irrational or irresponsible of a parent to take him or her instead to a faith healer. However, it may be neither irresponsible nor irrational of a parent to reject the verdict of an educational professional on what a child needs by way of knowledge or discipline, in favour of an alternative considered view of human flourishing. In short, the professional word does not seem as final in the case of education and teaching, as it clearly can be in matters of medical or legal practice – although again the line here is, as I shall also argue, by no means hard and fast.

Moreover, it will be central to the present case that the need for a high degree of ethical sensitivity on the part of educational professionals arises precisely from the essentially contested character of the educational enterprise: the fact that there is much debate and controversy about the point and purpose of education, and about what in the nature of human flourishing it should be concerned to promote. For irrespective of any and all reasonable points of comparison between teaching and such other occupations as the priesthood, nursing, social work, plumbing, medicine and commerce, it should also be clear that there are tensions and potential inconsistencies between such comparisons, and that there could be no possible reconciliation of all of them in one coherent conception of educational professionalism. For example, we have already noted a tension – not at all easy, as we shall see, to resolve – between the traditional 'cultural custodian' view that a good teacher should be a representative or exemplar of the virtues and values of a given culture, and the more modern 'professional' idea that a teacher should try to be 'value neutral', or to keep personal commitments separate from professional concerns. Moreover, even if it is possible to achieve some kind of general reconciliation of the vocationalism of cultural custodians with more recent conceptions of professionalism, there would still clearly be differences over matters of professional and other authority between any such position and that of educational radicals and progressives, for whom the very language of professionalism seems anathema. There is also clearly much potential for opposition between the market model of education and any traditional, particularly cultural custodian, conception of teaching; for being led by the market may not always be consistent with any eternal fidelity to 'the best that has been thought and said in the world'. Again, there are currently much debated tensions between ideas of restricted and extended educational professionalism: between any idea of teaching as largely a matter of conformity to the requirements of others, and any reflective practitioner account of teaching as a matter of the exercise of independent judgement. And so on, and so forth. These are some of the issues which we shall need to revisit in the following chapters. What is now required, however, is a closer look – with particular regard to questions of the professional status of education and teaching – at concepts of profession and professionalism as such.

# 2

# PROFESSIONS, PROFESSIONALISM AND PROFESSIONAL ETHICS

## Profession and professionalism: what's in a name?

Is it appropriate to regard teaching as a profession? It is tempting to suppose that this question is of little moment, if not actually meaningless. For one thing, it might be said (with some justice) that the line commonly drawn between professions and non-professions is a quite artificial one. For another, it may be also said (with even more justice) that an occupation does not have to be regarded as a profession in order to be the focus of moral issues; for that occupation to be, in other words, one to which questions of professional ethics are relevant. But although I think that there is something to both these claims, I nevertheless think that the question of the professional status of teaching is an important one, and that however we answer it has significant implications for our precise conception of the ethical issues which it characteristically engenders. Indeed, we are already able to see from the last chapter that different ways of conceptualising teaching – as a vocation like priesthood or nursing, a profession like medicine, or a trade like plumbing – can have significant implications for thinking about the character and extent of the moral and other responsibilities of teachers. Hence, in this chapter, we shall attempt to sketch a rough-and-ready account of what it might mean for an occupation to qualify for the status of profession – an account which, moreover, emphasises the centrality of ethical or moral concerns and considerations. And subsequently, in Chapter 3, we shall try to see how the occupation of teaching or the practice of education stands with respect to this account.

Always mindful that it would be vain to look for strict defini-tions, we shall all the same embark on our brief enquiry into the nature of a profession – in time-honoured philosophical fashion – with some observations on the common use of such terms as 'profession', 'professional' and 'professionalism'. Clearly, the term 'professional' has a number of different senses of greater and less present relevance. At one level, to describe a member of a given occupation as a 'professional' is to say no more than that they get paid for what they do; it is in this sense, for example, that we contrast a professional with an *amateur* footballer. However, there is also another fairly loose sense in which the term is used to indicate any job well done; thus, the plumber, joiner or electrician has done a professional job if it is efficiently executed or well finished, an unprofessional one if it is not – though it is important to note that any such evaluation of a plumber's or joiner's achievement does not in the least commit us to regarding him or her as a member of a *profession* as such. Indeed, there is clearly a third important sense of 'professional' which is intended to distinguish between the activities – well executed or otherwise – of different occupations. In this sense, professionality and professionalism are the requirements of a particular class or category of occupation which is usually taken to include doctors and lawyers, may well embrace teachers and clergymen (and other members of so-called vocations) – but traditionally *excludes* plumbers, joiners and other tradesmen.

It may be doubted, all the same, whether there is much substance to such general categorial distinctions between types of occupations. Indeed, it seems to be a fairly common sociological view that such distinctions reflect little more than differences of social or class *status* – perhaps a relic of medieval guild or other restricted practices. Whereas it so happens that certain occupational groups – doctors, lawyers, or whatever – have managed generally to corner the lion's share of authority, prestige or wealth in our society, this is a contingent social fact which might well have been otherwise; in some other society (perhaps one in which wood and water were in short supply) it might have been the hewers of wood and the carriers of water who were accorded higher status than the members of contemporary professions. Indeed, on a radically sceptical version of this view – which we shall shortly examine in a specifically educational version – the so-called professions are to be distinguished from other occupations almost exclusively in status seeking and self-serving terms.[1] However, to whatever extent it may be a socio-historical accident that some occupations have gained social ascendancy over others in this way, it may be doubted whether this could have been the *only* basis for familiar categorial distinctions between professions, vocations and trades; all else apart, some occupations have continued to be regarded as professions – teachers and religious ministers perhaps – despite having often attracted little in the way of either social prestige or economic prosperity. It therefore seems worth asking what might have served to distinguish those occupations commonly regarded as professions from other occupational categories.

Whilst different analyses of the idea of a profession are to be found in the literature, it should serve our purposes here to focus upon five commonly cited criteria of professionalism, according to which: (i) professions provide an important public service; (ii) they involve a theoretically as well as practically grounded expertise; (iii) they have a distinct ethical dimension which calls for expression in a code of practice; (iv) they require organisation and regulation for purposes of recruitment and discipline; and (v) professional practitioners require a high degree of individual autonomy – independence of judgement – for effective practice. It is also sometimes said that some occupations – such as medicine (doctoring) and the law – count as full professions by dint of fulfilling most or all of these criteria, whereas others – teaching or nursing perhaps – count merely as semi-professions[2] by virtue of satisfying only some of them. (Though, as we shall see, the force of this distinction may turn in part on whether the criteria are meant to be descriptive or prescriptive.) At all events, it is clear that an ethical dimension of professional practice features quite explicitly in the third criterion – as well as implicitly in others; moreover, once we begin to explore conceptual connections between the criteria, it should become clear that all are implicated in the ethical in ways which serve to lend a distinct character to professional as opposed to other occupational concerns.

## The ethical dimensions of professional engagement

How, then, do we begin to put all of this to work in distinguishing the idea of profession from other occupations and professional from other occupational concerns? We could start with a very basic observation about professional practice; namely, that it is precisely and primarily, like any trade, a matter of intelligent *practice*. Just as it is a plumber's task to achieve the practical goal of assisting drainage, so it is the task of a doctor to improve the health of patients. But one difference upon which a distinction between profession and trade might here be said to turn is – as indicated in point (ii) above – that professional training cannot be *solely* a matter of hands-on apprenticeship in the manner of carpentry or hairdressing; a surgeon or a doctor is rightly required to have mastered a good deal of complex – perhaps scientific – knowledge, information, theory and hypothesis before he or she is allowed to practise on patients. Moreover, there would appear to be a link – though by no means a straightforward one – between the theory implicatedness of professional practice and the need for professional autonomy (as specified in point (v) above). First, although theories certainly aim at truth they are also frequently provisional or speculative and function more to guide than strictly determine practice; second, since professionals are often confronted with unprecedented cases which competing theories may serve equally well to explain, much independent judgement is needed to match theoretical generalities to particular contingencies. Indeed, while it is because the professional is liable to encounter novel problems and dilemmas to which there are *not* established or cut-and-dried technical answers that he or she requires thorough acquaintance with the best which has been thought and said on such potential difficulties, professional theory is by the same token more often advisory than precisely prescriptive – and responsible professional decision depends in a large part on the quality of *personal* deliberation and reflection.

So (v) is connected to (ii) mainly via the idea that although the professional needs to act in the light of independent thought, this must mean thought informed by principles of intelligent professional practice. But now, in so far as thorough mastery of the theories, principles and skills presupposed to effective professional practice is likely to be a *sine qua non* of admission to full professional status, point (iv) would seem to be linked to (ii) – for, to be sure, it is often regarded as crucial to fixing the boundaries of what shall be counted as acceptable conduct, and to ensuring control over standards, that professions should be organised to restrict entry and deal with professional ineptitude; the British General Medical Council is an example of a professional organisation established to achieve these goals for the medical profession. All the same, this hardly serves to identify what is distinctive of *professional* organisation – since there were formerly guilds for achieving these ends for trades. The key idea regarding professional organisation would seem to relate more to the consideration that mastery of theories, principles and skills cannot be *sufficient* for fitness to practise, since it is quite possible – indeed, too often happens – that a professional with proper and adequate theoretical knowledge and skill nevertheless behaves inappropriately towards a patient or client. It is this consideration which brings us more directly to the idea expressed in point (iii) that there is an important *ethical* or moral ingredient to professional organisation, whereby someone may be judged unfit to practise professionally because, despite their possession of relevant theories and skills, they lack appropriate *values*, attitudes or motives. On this view, any profession worthy of the name ought to be governed by a code of professional ethics which clearly identifies professional *obligations* and responsibilities by reference to the *rights* of clients or patients.

What is a code of professional ethics? The Hippocratic oath, generally recognised as the earliest expression of such a code in relation to medical practice, seems to be built upon a simple basic principle to the effect that the doctor's first concern should be for the well-being of his or her patients above any personal interest or profit. From this point of view, doctors are enjoined to eschew abuse of their power or authority for the financial, sexual or other exploitation of patients. Thus stated, the idea may be regarded as a notable anticipation of the basic theme of a much later influential moral theory which claims that one should always treat people as *ends* in themselves rather than as means. Indeed, Kant's[3] distinction of the morally grounded categorical imperative from the hypothetical imperatives of instrumental agency seems tailor-made to distinguish the endeavours of professionals from those of tradesmen or salespersons. Although we should not for a moment deny that there are virtuous tradesmen or salespersons, or that the moral dimension of service to others is often acknowledged in nonprofessional occupations, it is arguably not as centrally implicated in such spheres as it is in professional practice – or, if it is, this might well be a reason for elevating what have hitherto been regarded as trades to the status of professions. For one thing, although a builder renowned for the effectiveness of his skills may also be honest and fair, he is not less likely to be highly rated *qua* builder on the grounds that he short-changes or sleeps with his clients – whereas these would be reasons for regarding doctors, lawyers or teachers as bad exemplars of their respective occupations. Again, whereas a good professional is one who is scrupulous in observing and meeting what he or she takes to be the exact needs of patients – giving, as it were, full value for money – the automobile or snake oil salesman of the year might just be the one who manages to sell the shoddiest goods for the highest profit to the largest number of gullible customers (although a good salesman is for purely commercial reasons also likely to want to avoid a reputation for this).

Thus one might conclude that, whereas a good tradesman or salesperson is first and foremost someone who is procedurally skilled – irrespective of any other virtues – a good professional has also to be someone who possesses, in addition to specified theoretical or technical expertise, a range of distinctly moral attitudes, values and motives designed to elevate the interests and needs of clients, patients or pupils above self-interest. On such a view, any full professional initiation must require, *alongside* training in theoretical and technical knowledge, some explicit instruction in the moral presuppositions of professional involve-ment – possibly extending to systematic initiation into current formal theories of deontic usage. In the event, there appear to be different ways in which those responsible for professional education have recently sought to acknowledge and accommodate the ethical dimensions of professional engagement. First, it has become increasingly common to encounter 'bolt-on' courses in ethical theory mounted by professional ethicists – perhaps moral theorists from neighbouring faculties of philosophy – in programmes of professional preparation for doctors or nurses. Second, as we shall shortly consider more closely, the competence models of training which have recently overtaken professional preparation in such occupational spheres as teaching and social work aim to combine instruction in the technical skills of good practice with the cultivation of a range of attitudes and values (more often than not apparently secondary to the specification of technical skills) reflecting the top-down decisions on what is or is not acceptable in the way of proper professional conduct of central and local authority guidelines. In short, either professional ethics is conceived as an extra theoretical component in courses of professional education, or the ethical aspects of professionalism are reduced to just so many extra practical competences to be quasi-technically acquired through training. Some attention to the only criterion of professionalism which we have not yet considered, however, may serve to cast suspicion on both these ways of incorporating the ethical into the professional.

On the face of it, criterion (i) above – that professions provide an important public service – seems trivial to the point of vacuity. After all, there could hardly be any occupation which does not count as an important public service in *some* circumstance or other. Indeed, if my kitchen is flooded because of a burst water pipe, it is likely to be a more urgent matter that there is a plumber near to hand than that there is a doctor or lawyer in the vicinity. So the first criterion clearly stands in need of some filling out if it is going to do much in the way of serious conceptual work. One possible way of giving greater content to this dimension of professionalism, however, is to recognise that the services provided by professionals – adequate health care, legal access, educational provision, and so on – appear to constitute human necessities of a kind that the services of a hairdresser, joiner, electrician or builder do not. Of course, we should probably distinguish here between different kinds of necessity: given *basic* human needs for food, shelter and clothing, those trades and services which supply these are to that extent essential. But beyond problems of house-less heads, unfed sides and looped and windowed raggedness, human flourishing is also clearly liable to be undermined by the absence of an adequate health service, educational or judicial system – or what we might call *civil* necessities. Indeed, it is hardly an exaggeration to characterise access to such services or their lack as life or death matters: one may be quite literally staring death in the face if one is a citizen of a society in which no medical help is readily forthcoming in the event of serious illness, or in which health care is inadequate to prevent the spread of lethal epidemics; any guarantee of the secure pursuit of one's life is forfeit if one is a citizen of a state where one may at any time be arrested for no crime, accused without evidence and condemned, perhaps to death, without legal appeal – or in which there is no police protection from the incursions of brigandry; and so forth with regard to a range of other professional services.

In this connection, it is significant that the kind of services that professionals are in business to provide have increasingly come to be regarded as human *rights*; thus, just as post-Enlightenment philosophers have been prone to speak of *basic* human rights to life, liberty and freedom of thought and association, so many of the services now under the control and direction of the more or less established traditional professions – health care, legal aid, arguably education, and so on – are apt to be characterised as *welfare* rights. And, while the moral and metaphysical status of rights continues to be a matter of serious philosophical dispute, there can be no doubt that talking of rights to education, health care and legal access seems to make more sense than talk of rights to good plumbing, hairdressing, car maintenance or an annual holiday abroad. Indeed, as already noted, perhaps the best philosophical handle we are likely to secure on the righthood of health care, education and legal redress is in terms of a notion of what is *necessarily* or indispensably conducive to overall human flourishing; whereas it is, one might say, merely contingent to such flourishing whether one has a new car, a Swiss watch or a decent manicure, it is something close to a necessary truth – something true, as some philosophers would say, in all possible worlds – that human life *per se* is bound to be impoverished in circumstances where disease, injustice and ignorance are rife and their remedies in short supply.

Moreover, despite recent philosophical emphases on the circumstances of social and cultural pluralism and on the way in which moral differences are all too often the cause of serious divisions between human constituencies, there would appear to be remarkable cross-cultural *agreement* – it would be surprising if there wasn't – that freedom from disease, injustice and ignorance are unqualified human goods. It is presumably in the spirit of some such consensus that Aristotle[4] maintained we deliberate in practical matters about the *means* rather than the *ends* of action; thus, in principle at least, the physician deliberates not about whether but how he should heal, the lawyer not about whether but about how he should promote justice, and so on. But, of course, in another sense – a sense which is precisely connected with our uncertainties about appropriate means in just such spheres – it is exactly about these otherwise agreed preconditions of human flourishing that we *do* deliberate. Here again, moreover, the services provided by the traditional professions appear to be in a somewhat different case from those provided elsewhere; by and large whereas the basic ends and goals of plumbing, joinery, catering and hairdressing are fixed and the main questions are technical ones about the effective achievement of these fixed ends, the basic nature, ends and goals of good medicine, law and (arguably) education are deeply *contested* and matters for serious public debate. Thus, though no sane person could doubt that it is a bad thing to be diseased, oppressed or ignorant, very sane and sensible people do debate about what constitutes genuine or adequate education, justice or health care. Again, we may raise the point about the contentiousness of professional as distinct from other concerns by noting that although we can attach real sense to the idea of a *philosophy* of law, health or education, we should be hard put to make much of a going concern of any philosophy of plumbing, hairdressing or cooking – and this is precisely because serious questions arise in the former but not in the latter cases about what these concepts actually *mean*.

## Professions as moral projects

Since professional services purport to conduce to human flourishing via the promotion of health, legal entitlement, social security or whatever, they are philosophically problematic in the manner of *moral* concepts – precisely because they *are* themselves moral projects; thus, professionals are from the outset involved in the practice of activities and endeavours whose ends and purposes are matters of genuine ethical controversy. Appreciation of the ethical, in short, must lie at the heart of any professional understanding and deliberation worthy of the name. But if we are right in taking this to be a direct implication of our enhanced construal of the first criterion of professionalism, it must have consequences for our understanding of other criteria. Consider, first of all, criterion (ii): that professional competence cannot be merely practically acquired but requires significant theoretical knowledge. It is widely assumed, I suspect, that theoretical knowledge in the context of professional training means some kind of scientific or evidential knowledge which has direct technical application to practice – in the way, perhaps, that physiological and anatomical knowledge may serve to assist a surgeon to find his or her way without undue collateral damage to a patient's appendix. But aside from the consideration already adduced that any idea of a straightforward link between theory and professional practice is itself problematic – since competing theories may well lay claim to our allegiance in a given professionally problematic situation – the very *idea* of professional theory seems prone to ambiguity. Such ambiguity is, as we shall see, perhaps most apparent in ordinary talk about *educational theory* which, whilst sometimes taken to refer to a range of natural or social scientific disciplines of psychology, sociology, history, learning theory, and so on, is just as readily used in connection with such particular evaluative perspectives on the socio-cultural ends and goals of education as traditionalism, progressivism and child-centredness.

Clearly, however, principled reflection on such perspectives is not theoretical in anything like the same sense as natural or social scientific theory; indeed, in the spirit of an important distinction pioneered by Aristotle,[5] we may observe that what is here called theory is often enough a matter for normative or evaluative rather than scientific or theoretical reflection, focused on the pursuit of what is *good* rather than upon the discovery of what is *true*. Again, as we shall later try to show, this is not to endorse any strict post-Humean distinction between fact and value – for clearly human values and the success of our projects must be in some sense influenced by considerations about how things are in a world independent of our wills; but, because human goals and aspirations are often practically inconsistent, the evaluative or normative is considerably underdetermined by the evidential in human affairs and inferential relations between theoretical or truth-focused reflection and evaluative deliberation are far from straightforward. Thus, to take a possible educational example, whatever past policy-makers may have thought, it would not follow from evidence that some children are (innately) more intelligent than others that one should devote a larger share of available educational resources to the more intelligent – for we might have cause on the basis of such evidence to argue in any of at least three ways: that more should be given to those who have; that more should go to those who haven't; that we have no warrant, on the basis of such considerations, to advantage one more than another. But just as educational deliberation involves highly complex interplay between the evidential and the evaluative, so it appears on closer scrutiny do forms of theoretical reflection in such areas of professional concern as medicine and law. Hence, we may include among fundamental professional questions (for example): what are to be counted as genuine illnesses for the purposes of institutionalised medical treatment, what should be regarded as conduct to be criminalised for the protection of society rather than as personal preferences of more private than public concern – as well as, arguably, how we may justly frame educational policy in the light of individual differences of ability. But though these are questions to which the facts of the matter are clearly relevant, and upon which theory and evidence may be brought to bear, they cannot be decided by the application of theory (in this sense) in any straightforward instrumental or technical way.

But these observations on criteria (i) and (ii) must also have considerable implications for others – especially for any attempts to conceive the ethical dimension of professionalism in reductive or 'bolt-on' ways. First, consider the cruder competence conceptions of professional preparation. Whereas competence conceptions of non-professional trades and services are usually little more than lists of skills to be mastered, competence models of professional training, especially in such areas as education and social work – where there has been much central pressure to adopt them – have generally acknowledged both the significance of theory for professional practice and the need for some kind of moral preparation via the cultivation of right attitudes and values. Nevertheless, it is common for such models to conceive professional expertise as a matter of the acquisition of a kind of technology – of a repertoire of skills based upon the findings of value-neutral social-scientific research – to which some notion of the cultivation of right interpersonal attitudes and values is added as an apparent afterthought. Indeed, since it is the whole point of a competence model to try to identify *uncontroversial* skills and attitudes which are likely to be needed by any professional come what may, it is hard to see how such a model could proceed otherwise. But from what has already been said about the essential contestability of the goals of most professional conduct, it seems implausible to view professional expertise in this technicist way – and, as we shall see, it is rare to find anything much in the way of detailed specification of value-free technical skills in lists of professional competences for teachers. What one more often finds are very *imprecise* indications of areas of professional concern which are highly value-laden: thus, teachers will be advised that they need to be able to interest children, to 'manage' classes, to set high standards of achievement, and so on, with little apparent recognition that there are widely different and competing educational conceptions of discipline, interest and standards. Indeed, skills of teaching and discipline appear to be context-dependent to the extent that what counts as such a skill on one educational conception might not so count on another. Moreover, lists of professional attitudes and values – honesty, devotion to duty, respect for others – are also offered as though there are completely uncontroversial and agreed interpretations of such qualities and dispositions.[6]

But to separate *professional* skills and values in this way and to treat them simply as different kinds of behavioural dispositions to be mastered via schedules of professional training is – no matter how otherwise congenial to the aims of those policy-makers who incline to competence models – to ignore the crucial interplay between the evidential and the evaluative in professional knowledge and expertise and, thereby, the essentially contested nature of professional goals and purposes. Moreover, in pretending to a professional consensus which does not really exist, it discourages healthy professional disagreement about aims and methods, which is vital both to the development of professional autonomy – that mature independence of judgement mentioned in criterion (v) – and to wider informed debate about matters of general public concern. But is this not precisely a case for the introduction into programmes of professional preparation of specific professional ethics courses in which ethical specialists can explore with trainee professionals the complexities of professional dilemmas? To be sure, since much is likely to turn here upon the nature of such courses – particularly perhaps upon their relationship to other parts of the professional curriculum – the idea of such specific ethical components should not perhaps be condemned outright. But there can also be little doubt that such ways of dealing with the ethical implications of professional involvement are liable to be distortive or misleading in a not entirely dissimilar way to the reductive strategy of competence models.

First, for example, the not infrequent curricular dissociation of such courses from the more theoretical or technical parts of professional training may serve to reinforce the idea that the latter are value-neutral and that ethical problems arise in professional contexts only in relation to a more restricted set of concerns affecting the rights of patients or other clients; however, we have already seen reason to doubt that this is so, since all aspects of professional conduct – theories and skills as well as contractual obligations and responsibilities – are value-laden in ethically relevant ways. Indeed, one of the problems about courses of professional ethics which operate ancillary to the theoretically or technically orientated parts of professional programmes is that they may be restricted to consideration of those more contractual aspects of professional development of a kind emphasised in codes of professional ethics. But to the extent that these are given to the articulation of considerations of a fairly commonplace 'don't sleep with the patients' variety, there is always a risk of trainees coming to regard them as at worst trivial and at best secondary to the 'serious' business of acquiring theoretical understanding and technical expertise – again without sufficiently recognising that professional theories and skills are themselves deeply implicated in ethical issues.

## 'Bolt-on' versus integral professional ethics

At this point in the argument, I would concede something to the complaint that I have attacked little more than men of straw; surely, someone will say, no respectable course of professional ethics *is* likely to be confined to the airing of such trivialities, and most if not all such courses do engage in serious exploration of the wider implications for human flourishing of various kinds of professional theory, technology and conduct. Even so, this raises further awkward questions about what need there might be for any separate course in professional ethics over and above what should otherwise be contained in a programme of professional education and training concerned with initiating trainees into the complexities – including, by implication, any ethical dilemmas – likely to arise in a given form of professional life. And if it is now replied that a course in professional ethics – some sort of formal introduction to the main past and present theories of ethics – is required to equip professionals with the means to clarify, systematise, articulate or justify their response to a given professional dilemma, it is still not at all clear how this would precisely serve such professional purposes. Or, to put it another way, it may seem clear only on a rather suspect conception of the relationship of formal ethical theory to actual practical moral concerns – a conception which may indeed lurk not very far below the surface of much latter-day fashionable talk of 'applied ethics'. There can certainly be little doubt that some past moral philosophers have entertained highly instrumental conceptions of moral enquiry as primarily concerned to identify specific modes of moral deliberation apt for the quasi-technical solution of moral dilemmas. There cannot be much doubt that the principal architects of utilitarianism were driven by some such conception of moral enquiry – and, nearer our own time, some of the non-cognitivist heirs of Kant seem to have held an essentially problem-solving view of moral deliberation. Again, by far the most influential moral educational theory of modern times – Kohlberg's stage theory of moral development[7] – seems to have been driven by an explicitly pragmatist dilemma-resolving view of the uses of moral reason.

Whatever the appeal of such crude instrumental or technicist conceptions of moral enquiry as a rational procedure apt for the solution of moral problems, however, they should be resisted. Such perspectives on the nature of moral dilemma almost certainly rest on serious misconceptions of the causes and sources of such dilemmas in our lives; indeed, to put the matter at its most basic, if a problem did turn out to be resolvable in the way in which some moral theorists have supposed, that could only be because the problem was, after all, a *technical* rather than a genuine moral problem. In fact, several different but connected dangers hove into view over the possible exploration of formal theories of ethics in relation to professional dilemmas. In the first place, ethical theories clearly conflict to the point of contradiction; conduct disallowed by Kantian deontologists may be endorsed by utilitarians, and vice versa. But, consequently, if it is given as a reason for teaching formal ethical theories to professionals (as would sometimes appear) that they need to be equipped with resources for the principled justification of their conduct, then there is a distinct danger – in so far as almost any conduct may be justified in the terms of some ethical theory or other – of moral deliberation degenerating into expedient casuistry or rhetoric. And if it is now protested that one of the main aims of a professional ethics course should be to encourage the principled fidelity of students to *one* particular conception of moral problem solving – Kantian deontology, utilitarianism, virtue theory or whatever – rather than the adoption of a promiscuous pick-and-mix approach for reasons of personal convenience, one may reply that it is nothing short of bizarre to suppose that it might be a reasonable goal of any such course to produce professionals whose ethical reasoning was moulded in such an inflexible way.

The problem with such classical analyses of the mechanics of moral deliberation as Kantian deontology and utilitarianism, of course, is not so much that they are mistaken as that they represent *partial* accounts of the logic of moral discourse. Thus, utilitarianism is not wrong because we never argue utilitarianly – there are bound to be occasions upon which sane and sensible people will put the reduction of harm or pain above the observance of absolute principle – it is only mistaken in maintaining that the promotion of happiness or the reduction of suffering is our *only* criterion of moral deliberation; likewise, deontology is not mistaken in claiming that moral argument involves obedience to principle – there will be many occasions upon which it is appropriate to put observance of absolute principle even above the reduction of harm or pain – it only errs in holding that such observance is our *only* moral criterion. But in that case it is natural to ask where and when it is appropriate to reason utilitarianly or deontologically. And the only *general* answer to this question is that this has to be determined *contextually*. The key players in major moral debates over such crucial questions of individual and social human well-being as abortion, capital punishment, euthanasia and divorce are not deontologists, utilitarians or other professional ethicists but the advocates of often fine-grained competing systems of evaluative priority such as Catholic Christians, Fabian socialists, liberal humanists, free-marketers and Darwinian evolutionists – and, of course, ordinary pre-theoretical moral agents. Of course, these are people who often argue deontologically and utilitarianly – but on the basis of rival interpretations of principle and utility embedded in and conditioned by quite different conceptions of human flourishing.

This point takes us into some fairly familiar territory of recent moral and social theory. It has been the persistent theme of a motley alliance of communitarians, post-analytical social philosophers, virtue theorists, ethical realists and feminists that enlightenment ethics – by aspiring to prescind processes of moral deliberation from the contexts of evaluative priority which fix the moral horizons of socio-culturally attached human agents – has seriously distorted our understanding of moral life. From this viewpoint, significant moral disagreements reflect differences of culturally conditioned social practice enshrining rival conceptions of human well-being or flourishing which admit of no neutral or independent rational arbitration.[8] Indeed, under the influence of a certain 'postmodern' amalgam of pragmatism, post-structuralism and neo-Hegelianism, there has been a recent marked tendency to give a relativistic interpretation to such considerations – and it hardly needs saying that such an understanding must spell ultimate ruin for the prospects of any objective discussion or evaluation of professional or other moral questions. But it is not necessary that it be so construed – and, indeed, we are not normally inclined to infer from the fact of rival value perspectives that one is as *morally* good as any other; to take a rather worn example, Nazi war criminals are not generally exonerated from their crimes against humanity on the ground of their allegiance to a different value system. So the fact that there is no value-free process of moral deliberation which might enable us to decide from some elevated position of neutral rationality between the claims of competing moral perspectives does not mean that there are *no* criteria at all on which we might largely agree that the ideas and actions of Nazis or Klansmen are beyond the moral pale. There may be much disagreement about what exactly these criteria are – but this is as often as not against a background of civilised agreement that certain forms of conduct are downright wicked. The point is more that intelligent exchange between individuals who have been thoroughly initiated into traditions of reflection with developed resources for addressing moral issues offers a better model of the nature of moral ratiocination than the application of a moral algorithm or ethical decision procedure developed according to some view from nowhere.[9]

## Professional autonomy and the dangers of technicisation

But then why should what is generally true of moral judgement and understanding not also be the case of professional ethics in particular since, to a large degree, a thorough understanding of some moral professional concern is simply a deeper or more sophisticated appreciation of issues of health, legal entitlement and education which are clearly of broader public interest? Indeed, this point is worth emphasising in the light of contemporary pressure to technicise professional expertise. It cannot be doubted, of course, that professional training in such areas as medicine and law involves the acquisition of often complex skills and techniques; doctors and nurses may be required to utilise state-of-the-art hardware, and lawyers, teachers and social workers will often require quite sophisticated levels of administrative, organisational and procedural skill. But one also suspects considerable professional pressure to 'scientise' or technicise aspects of practice which may not be really technological at all – perhaps for mainly territorial purposes. I believe that there is hardly a better example of this than the way in which matters of curriculum design and implementation – especially in the wake of recent national curriculum developments – have lately been made to appear a matter of specialist knowledge and skill acquisition and the sole preserve of such educational experts as curriculum authorities and teachers. In fact, however, such specialist *techne* invariably amounts to little more than the repackaging of commonplaces about knowledge, understanding and learning in a form of impenetrable professional jargon which serves mainly to avoid serious engagement with genuine evaluative issues of general public concern about the nature of educational provision.

This on a broader social, political and moral front has a twofold anti-democratic effect: first, it discourages parents and other interested non-professionals from engaging in discussion of urgent curriculum issues – since any lack of understanding on their part may be taken as a sign of their own incompetence; second, it deburdens professionals themselves of any responsibility to address such issues – since, in their new role as mere operatives of a technology of pedagogy (allegedly grounded in scientific research), they assume any wider evaluative reflection on the socio-cultural point and purpose of education and schooling to be someone else's (perhaps the politician's) business rather than their own.[10] We have here, then, a perfect expression of the professional tendency against which we have been inveighing in this work to separate the theoretical and technical from the evaluative (which is then more often than not reduced to a set of simple behavioural prescriptions) and to treat professional procedures as though they are somehow insulated from wider public concerns. But this, as well as seriously mislocating the real difficulties and complexities of professional engagement, more than likely reflects some confusion between concepts of difficulty and technicality; indeed, it is possible that teachers, for example – all too often held for various reasons in low public esteem – are drawn to a certain technicisation of their work because it makes it appear more difficult, and therefore more professionally exalted to outsiders.

But matters that are technical need not be difficult, and matters that are difficult may be all the more so precisely because they are neither technical nor susceptible of technicisation; indeed, the difficulties of moral life are a case in point – they are difficult precisely because they require the kind of sensitivity, experience and fine judgement which cannot be captured or codified in the terms of some technical system. But from this perspective any expertise which might assist a teacher, for example, to engage in useful professional reflection about the curriculum, or make wise decisions about the educational development of his or her pupils, seems radically misconceived as the acquisition of some incomprehensible quasi-technical jargon of curriculum development – perhaps combined with some pseudo-moral technology purportedly apt for the solution of ethical dilemmas. The effective professional educationalist is not someone who speaks a language of teaching and learning which his or her pupils and their parents *cannot* understand; on the contrary, he or she is someone who – by virtue of deeper professional reflection on diverse conceptions of the point and purpose of education and wider practical experience of particular problems of teaching and learning – can clearly communicate to parents, in a language which they are able to understand, what exactly the evaluative and practical difficulties are in the particular circumstances which affect their child, and who can also make a case for a reasonable set of evaluative and practical priorities in these circumstances.

This is because any meaningful professional language of education and teaching should be significantly *continuous* with the ordinary experience of teaching and learning as essentially pre-theoretical and non-technical notions; indeed, once educationalists and teachers begin to speak of teaching and learning as technical concepts we may be sure that something has gone awry. But we start to get rather ahead of ourselves. Indeed, someone might protest that it rather begs the question – in a chapter concerned to explore a concept of professionalism which might be used as a yardstick to judge teaching by – to employ examples drawn from educational practice in the very definition of that concept. I hope to show in the course of this work, however, that there is good reason to believe that education is of its very nature one of the best available sources of insight into the nature of profession as a special occupational category – in the 'moral project' senses of 'profession' and 'professional' on which this chapter has focused. From this point of view, it is likely that there is much to be learned about the professional status of doctors, nurses, lawyers and social workers from due reflection on education and teaching (rather than vice versa). The chapters to follow, then, will be concerned with a deeper exploration – precisely in relation to education and teaching – of the various relations between ethical or moral deliberation and professional practice.

# 3

# TEACHING AND PROFESSIONALISM

## Professional status and the elitist objection

The main concern of this chapter is to consider the appropriateness or otherwise of regarding teaching and education as professional enterprises in the sense highlighted in Chapter 2 – a sense which does give grounds for distinguishing occupations such as medicine or law as *professions* from trades, manufacturing industries, mercantile enterprises, at least some kinds of vocation, and so on. It is important to emphasise here that this sense is focused upon the idea that enterprises such as medicine, law and (arguably) education are implicated in questions and considerations of a *particular* ethical or moral character which are not to the forefront of, for instance, plumbing, joinery, auto-repair, wholesale or retail and hairdressing,[1] although they are also not well typified by the more intimate personal transactions into which individuals may enter with their religious confessors or psychotherapists (despite the fact that such relationships will also invariably exhibit clear professional dimensions). It may therefore be wise at this point to head off several possible kinds or sources of misunderstanding of this basic distinction.

The first would rest on the charge of *elitism* – of regarding some occupations, such as medicine, law or teaching, as of greater social importance than others. However, this charge would appear vulnerable to immediate conceptual difficulties, not only in the present instance, but generally. In the first place, of course, it makes little sense to regard some occupations as more important *as such* than others. Indeed, it would be merely foolish of someone to value the services of their doctor, lawyer or teacher over those of their grocer, plumber, refuse collector or hairdresser *per se*, and clearly there are going to be tides in the general economy of human affairs when shortfalls in auto-repair or joinery are likely to weigh as heavily, in terms of plain inconvenience, as any professional (in our more rarefied sense) inadequacies. Still, a second shot at this complaint might claim that any such response perversely or obtusely misses the point. The real point is that any occupational distinctions of a professional/non-professional kind are little more than social fictions anyway, so that any attempt to distinguish (in whatever terms) some occupations as professions could not have its source in anything other than the ambition of such occupations to gain an unwarranted social or economic edge over others. But this, too, seems less than coherent. In the first place, how could occupational distinctions as such have any consequences *whatsoever* for their social standing – unless the distinctions actually registered features upon which social and economic differentials might be constructed? The objection, in short, has things the wrong way round: we do not judge this occupation to be different from that one because we regard the one as more important than the other, but assess relative importance on the basis of perceived differences.[2] Hence, it seems more sensible to suppose that we esteem or reward (if we do) medical practice more highly than night-club hostessing because we regard the former as a more humanly serious and responsible occupation, than that we regard the former as more serious and responsible than the latter only because we are inclined to esteem it more.

But second, it is not clear that the broad distinctions here observed follow the (also divergent) fault lines of social esteem and economic reward. In terms of our distinctions, some occupations apt for consideration as professions, such as religious ministry and teaching, probably attract far less social esteem or economic advantage than others which are not on our account professions – such as, for example, those of a fashion designer or professional footballer. There are also callings which might, for present purposes, fall into very much the *same* sort of occupational category – such as airline pilot, chauffeur and bus driver – which are subject to significant social and economic differentials. (Compare also differing social perceptions of restaurant waitress and airline hostess – occupations which nevertheless do not differ much for present purposes.) Moreover, of considerable and sensitive present concern, it is notorious that different kinds and levels of teaching and education have long been a source of marked social and economic differentials – the basis, indeed, of a discernible educational pecking order. Hence, university lecturers probably regard themselves as considerably superior to lecturers in further education, lecturers in further education see themselves as a cut above secondary teachers, it is not unknown for secondary teachers to look down on primary teachers (as well as upon each other – according to whether they teach in independent, grammar or grant-aided or comprehensive schools), and there is at least a common public perception of upper primary school teaching as more the real educational McCoy than infant and nursery teaching. Yet all of these may, for the purposes of our argument, be regarded as belonging to one teaching profession.

If anything, indeed, it would be entirely consistent with the key thesis of this work to regard the activities and concerns of primary and early years teachers as *more* professional (in the present sense) than those of many academics in universities. It is not just that there is evidence that some of the attitudes underlying just noticed educational prejudices are now changing, particularly in view of overdue contemporary recognition of the enormous importance and complexity of early years education, but that in so far as they are involved more (if not entirely) in research than teaching, many university academics are hardly typical of professionals in our sense at all. But is not the problem here precisely that 'profession' and 'professional' are *in our sense* radically revisionary terms of art, which are hopelessly at odds with ordinary usage? As indicated in Chapter 2, however, our account is only revisionary to the extent that ordinary usage is itself a hopeless and not especially reputable tangle of diverse distinctions enshrining different senses of 'profession' and 'professional'. Hence, we are not denying that it makes good sense to regard the activities of university academics, plumbers, airline pilots, footballers, and so on, as professional or unprofessional, in the handy evaluative senses in which these terms are commonly used; the point is rather, in the light of the different senses of 'professional' marked in the previous chapter, that such talk does not in the least license regarding plumbing, footballing or even air pilotry as professions in that more specific sense which serves to distinguish medicine, law or (arguably) education from trades, industry or merchantry. Moreover, although we are wont to fix this difference in terms of the *special* place of ethical issues and considerations in the professional lives of doctors, lawyers and (arguably) teachers, this is not to deny that there are crucial ethical dimensions to other activities; plumbers, airline pilots and footballers, no less than doctors, lawyers and teachers, can all be more or less virtuous and ply their trades more or less honestly and responsibly. It is, however, with certain significant *differences* of ethical character between human occupations – rather than with differences of power, class, social standing or economic edge – that this present work is primarily concerned.

To this end, it will be the concern of later chapters of this work to try to give more precise substance to these differences – to identify the principal respects in which the peculiar ethical and moral nature of practical professional engagements serves to define the distinctive character and structure of professional expertise and deliberation. In the rest of this chapter, however, we need to say a little more about education as a profession in this more particular sense: more, to be precise, about why it might be appropriate to regard teaching and education as closer in crucial respects to such enterprises as medicine and law than to some of the other vocations, trades and services with which, as we saw in the last chapter, they have sometimes been (explicitly or implicitly) compared. In this connection, it seems promising to pursue two main strategies. First, we shall examine teaching and education in relation to the general criteria of profession explored in the previous chapter, with particular regard to how they score (so to speak) on this familiar scale of professional measurement. Second, however, we shall briefly examine the arguments of those who would want to claim that teaching and education are precisely *not* appropriately compared to such established professions as medicine and law – or who would argue, still more radically, that professional status or professionalisation are not anyway respectable or legitimate occupational aspirations for teachers (or anyone else).

## Teaching, education and professional criteria

To begin, how do teaching and education measure on the criteria of professionalism considered in Chapter 2? On the face of it, this might seem to be a straightforward matter of employing the five criteria as a checklist against which education and teaching might be passed or failed. Indeed, it would appear that the issue has sometimes been approached in this way in the sociology of professionalism; thus, as already noted, social theorists interested in this question have inclined to regard some occupations as professions by virtue of their meeting most or all of these criteria, to deny professional status to other occupations on the grounds that they meet few or none of them, and to regard others – such as, for example, teaching – as 'semi-professions' on the grounds that they satisfy some key criteria but not all.[3] Clearly, however, any such strategy is a simplistic one, and ignores certain crucial complications. In the first instance, any such procedure rides somewhat roughshod over an important distinction between the *prescriptive* and *descriptive* aspects of professional normativity. Thus, for example, although it may well be that the various commonly cited criteria of a profession all serve to identify desirable features or qualities of professional life, there might be purely contingent historical reasons why such features have failed to achieve full institutional recognition or embodiment. It could be, for example, that any true profession should be organised on a self-regulating basis for purposes of registration and discipline, but also that some occupations warranting such professional organisation have not as yet, for a variety of contingent historical reasons, achieved such a degree of regulation. Moreover, if organisation analogous to that of the British General Medical Council is taken to be evidence of such professional regulation, it may also be that education and teaching score better in some places than others; thus, whereas bodies designed for much of these professional purposes certainly exist in some quarters – the Scottish General Teaching Council may serve as an example – they are elsewhere either in embryo or not as yet conceived.

There are also, as we have already seen, potentially awkward questions about proper interpretation of the criteria. Even in the case of professional organisation, it has been questioned whether the Scottish Teaching Council provides an appropriate or adequate example of a truly autonomous professional body.[4] One might ask, for example, whether this organisation has appropriate professional authority and power and whether it is sufficiently independent of central government, or of such other potential controlling agencies or pressure groups as trades unions or parents' associations. Indeed, related considerations are clearly going to affect the more general question of how well teaching and education score on the matter of the autonomy of individual professionals. It is a principal complaint of those currently given to speaking of the growing 'de-professionalisation' of educational practice that recent central pressures have greatly undermined teachers' powers to determine – in the light of something like informed professional knowledge, understanding and conscience – what they shall teach and how they shall teach it: that, in short, government mistrust of teacher professionalism has reduced teaching to the mere mechanical execution of other people's (i.e. politicians') educational designs. But it is possible to respond to any such objection to regarding teaching as a profession in either (or a mixture) of two ways. On the one hand, one can set out to resist what one regards as recent moves to erode teacher autonomy on the grounds that since education *is* a profession, teachers *should* be given more autonomy; it is on such grounds, for example, that I believe teachers are right to resist central pressure to more pragmatic models of teacher training. On the other hand, however, there also seems to be a case for some redefinition of what is meant by professional autonomy in the case of education and teaching – on the grounds that, given certain reasonable considerations regarding the contribution of public education (or at any rate schooling) to civil flourishing, there are bound to be constraints on teacher freedom of a kind that may not similarly apply in other professional spheres.

Even though the professional eligibility of education and teaching cannot be simply ticked off against a list of professional criteria, we do need to be able to say a little more here – in anticipation of the following section – about why education is the kind of enterprise, and teaching the sort of activity, which calls for intellectual and moral capacities of a broadly similar sort to those also arguably required in medicine and law. From this viewpoint, I believe that the first and second conditions of important public service and significant theoretical expertise are key notions for understanding the professional status of education and teaching. Indeed, the status of education and teaching with respect to these considerations should help to clarify the extent to which these are the sorts of enterprises for which the other professional trappings of individual autonomy, professional organisation and code of practice are appropriate – irrespective of whether these are widely in place in the realms of education and teaching. This would, moreover, be the presently recommended procedure for any other occupational candidate for professional status. It seems quite the wrong way round for any occupation to seek professional status by first establishing the machinery of professionalism – professional organisation, code of practice, and so on – in the hope that a professional climate of practice might follow in its wake. Indeed, to the extent that much of this machinery is now a feature of trade and commerce, it could hardly be sufficient to distinguish profession from trade. The proper way to proceed seems rather to ask whether a given occupation exhibits the general features of professional engagement – which is more a matter of greater clarity about the kinds of issues and problems it raises, the qualities of reflection and judgement required for dealing with such problems, and the sort of education and/or training practitioners would need to address these issues effectively.

## Human flourishing and educational theory

As previously seen, education scores very well on a robust version of the important public service criterion. Thus, although we observed that on a trivial construal of this criterion any occupation is likely to pass muster as a profession (even, as it were, the oldest of so-called professions), the sense in which such traditional professions as medicine and law count as important public services is that in which they provide basic mainstays of any decent level of civil flourishing. It is the very measure of a civilised polity that its citizens are provided with significant and systematic insurance against such evils as disease and injustice. But an evil which looms as large as disease and injustice, and whose widespread incidence is just as prone to impair proper individual and communal civil functioning, is widespread ignorance in all or any of its forms. Thus, one's chances of leading a flourishing life are liable to be as seriously curtailed if one lacks access to even basic educational means to literate and articulate self-expression, or to the skills required to earn one's daily bread, as they would be in circumstances where there is no medical help available in prospect of disease, or no legal defence against injustice. Seen from this stance, medicine, law and education are arguably the 'big three' civilised bulwarks against the time-honoured human curses of pestilence, injustice and ignorance.

So far so good. But what of the second – 'professional theory' – criterion, as applied to education and teaching? It is here that quite serious questions are sometimes raised about the knowledge and expertise of teachers as compared to doctors or lawyers. As we saw in the previous chapter, what is distinctive about the idea of professional knowledge is that although it is practically focused it should also involve, perhaps for purposes (as it is sometimes said) of application to practice, some degree of *academic* or *theoretical* understanding. What might count as such knowledge, however, in the case of teacher education and training? Certainly many teachers (though not all) require academic or theoretical knowledge of what they are in business to teach. But such knowledge often amounts to little more than what well-educated non-professional persons might have come to possess in the course of their own general education. Indeed, one source of 'vocationalist' mistrust of the very idea of teacher professionalism (even among 'cultural custodians' of the independent and grammar school traditions) is fuelled by a certain scepticism about whether teaching does require anything more in the way of specialised expertise than an enthusiast's passion for a given subject and the ordinary virtues, decencies and sensibilities of a civilised person. But, in any case, much of the subject knowledge required for primary and early years teaching need not run very deep, especially on more 'progressive' conceptions of primary teaching which conceive the teacher (rightly or wrongly) less in the role of repository of information and more in that of some sort of 'facilitator' of enquiry. On this view, it may not be plausible to claim much extensive subject expertise for levels of teaching below upper secondary or for remedial education. Moreover, with increasing central prescription of the structure and content of the curriculum through national curricular initiatives, the curriculum development role of ordinary classroom teachers may seem less and less expressive of passionate personal interest and enthusiasm, and more a matter of routine delivery of packages designed by others.

It might be claimed, however, that a far better candidate for the professional theoretical expertise of the teacher is what has generally been referred to in teacher education and training as 'educational theory'. Indeed, it is likely to be complained by modern-day educational professionals of their 'vocational' colleagues in the independent and old direct grant sectors (many of whom may have entered service without benefit of postgraduate professional training) that such teachers, precisely in so far as they have not been properly initiated into a complex understanding of the theoretical mysteries of learning and motivation, or the esoteric professional skills of pedagogy and management, are ill-equipped to cope with the educational demands of all but a few able and privileged young people. With regard to this, moreover, modern training colleges have done a fairly brisk trade in those academic disciplines of educational philosophy, psychology, sociology, history, curriculum studies, and so on, alleged to be the theoretical *sine qua non* of effective professional development. But while it is certainly one aim of this book to vindicate the place of such studies in the professional development of teachers, I believe that the card of academic theory has often been overplayed in the rhetoric of teacher education, and that the proper professional role of such enquiries has been widely misconstrued. In this connection, indeed, it is impossible to ignore the frequency with which the professional relevance of such studies is called into question – by, for example, politicians and both practising and trainee teachers – and it is certainly far from clear how one might hold such theory to be directly applicable to educational practice in anything like the same way anatomy or physiology is obviously so applicable to medical practice.

Might it not be, however, that the professional knowledge of teachers consists for the most part in a kind of craft knowledge, the acquisition of a range of teaching styles, communication, management and organisational skills, which – though certainly articulable as and underpinned by academic principles – are nevertheless best apt for acquisition as practical skills? Some possible objections to this idea, however, have already been touched upon. In recent discussions of this question, for example, one cannot ignore a currently fashionable particularism about the nature of practical knowledge in teaching and elsewhere (drawn largely from a modern communitarian reworking of Aristotelian notions of practical reason) which maintains that educational skills are simply not codifiable in any way which might give much bite to the idea of applied science.[5] In this sense, teaching is viewed more like an art than a science: a rich and vigorously shaken cocktail of personality, character, intuition and knack which develops with on-the-job experience, is not readily transferable from person to person, and is resistant to codification in the form of general or precise rules and principles. Any such view of teaching as an art would certainly imply that pedagogical craft is something which needs to be acquired personally, through hands-on classroom experience. In another gear, however, it may only be an extreme instance of a more general idea that professional expertise is little more than the acquisition of practical skills – which also *includes* the applied science view of professionality. For, of course, even if there are generalisable skills of teaching which are grounded in scientific research and enquiry, there is as yet no compelling reason why field professionals would need any sophisticated intellectual or academic grasp of the scientific rationale of such skills, of how and why they worked, so long as they had causally effective mastery of them. In short, an applied science understanding of professional knowledge, no less than a particularist art and craft conception, is entirely consistent with the idea of an essentially field practical, rather than academic or theoretical, acquisition of professional teacher expertise.

Thus far we do not seem to have come up with a convincing candidate in the case of educational practice for a necessary body of theoretical knowledge which would justify the regarding of teaching as a truly professional practice. It will be a key claim of the present work, however, that we have so far failed to look in the right place. I believe that the commonest error with respect to this issue lies in an over-simple construal of 'theory' as the product of research-based and empirically-focused natural or social scientific enquiry. Hence, although it would be rash to deny that proper acquaintance with relevant empirical research and enquiry does contribute, in some part, to the education and training of professionals in general and teachers in particular, it does so only as part of a larger principled understanding of human practical concerns which is not primarily (empirical) knowledge, or even *truth,* focused at all. In this respect it is important to recognise that a general medical practitioner is not to be regarded as someone of professional standing and expertise solely in virtue of the possession of a body of *theoretical* knowledge, for the possession by laypersons of such knowledge would not in and of itself equip them for professional medical practice. Moreover, it may be a mistake to suppose that professionality increases in direct proportion to the depth, specialism and lay inaccessibility of academic or theoretical knowledge; it is not obvious that someone possessing the theoretical knowledge and skills of some esoteric branch of surgery thereby counts as *more* professional than a general practitioner whose day-to-day diagnoses may seldom draw on anything more arcane than what is on hand in a copy of *Home Doctor*. Indeed, there seems to be some case for arguing the other way about: that in so far as the more specialised, esoteric knowledge of surgeons is focused upon a very narrow field of remediation involving the application of finely-honed techniques to precisely defined medical problems, so much the less is professional judgement required of them – at any rate, in any sense which might serve to contrast professional practice with the activities of such high-level technicians as airline pilots or civil engineers.

I would argue that professional expertise is to be distinguished from many other highly regarded forms of occupational knowledge, precisely because it *cannot* be understood in terms of straightforward application to practice of skills or techniques directly derived from empirical research and enquiry, although this is not also to imply (absurdly) that professional expertise *never* involves technical application of empirical knowledge. The point is not just that one cannot *sufficiently* account for professional expertise in terms of any such technical application of theoretical knowledge, but (more strongly) that there would be no need for professional – medical, legal or educational – judgement if one could. This point is not a notably original one and has been widely made by others. However, I shall try in subsequent chapters (especially in Part II) to make it in my own way, not least because it also seems to me that the logical geography of the professional theory–practice problem has not yet, especially in relation to education and teaching, been adequately explored. But what requires present emphasis is that the problem of the relationship of professional theory to practice is crucially linked to the issue of the contestability of professional enterprises broached in the last chapter. It is because there is inherent uncertainty and significant public disagreement concerning the purposes and aims of medicine, law and education, and about their contribution to human flourishing, that there can be no straightforward technical or technicist construal of professional practice and professional deliberation. Indeed, as I shall argue in more detail, it is for this reason that there cannot even be any uncontroversial account of what empirical evidence, or which technical skills, are professionally relevant to educational and other practices. In what follows, then, we shall need to locate the *heart* of professional knowledge, expertise and deliberation elsewhere than in theoretical or technical knowledge and understanding, in a way which should considerably serve to clarify the respects in which the problems and deliberations of teachers are analogous to those of other professionals. On the basis of this account, moreover, to whatever extent teaching as a professional practice can currently claim to be patterned on (some substantial interpretation of) the third, fourth and fifth criteria of professionality explored in the last chapter, I believe that a strong *prescriptive* case may be made for its being so modelled in most or all of these respects.

### The case against educational professionalism

At this point, however, we should also acknowledge that the case for the professionalisation of education and teaching is controversial and has been disputed. Everything said so far seems to assume that professionality and the aspiration to professional status, including the bureaucratic trappings of professional organisation, is a good or desirable thing. Indeed, it appears to be assumed on what we might call the orthodox or *conventional* view of profession that professionalisation does significantly *improve* the quality of a given service. Those in favour of professional organisation argue that it serves to concentrate the minds of professionals upon the rights of clients or consumers, and upon the obligations of professionals with respect to them. On this view, the advantages of a more professional approach are measurable in terms of greater commitment to public service and enhancement of standards of provision, both of which cannot but be of benefit to the client or consumer. However, in earlier explorations of different concepts of education and teaching, particularly of the various vocational conceptions, we have already tapped veins of scepticism about this orthodox view. For example, even on the otherwise traditional 'cultural custodian' conception of education there is more than a hint of disdain for any regulated or contractually defined conception of teaching of the kind characteristic of modern professionalism. Thus, there seems to be some tension between the 'gentleman scholar' view of educational practice as a matter of personal ideal and aspiration – as mythologised by the 'Mr Chips' or 'Miss Jean Brodie' portraits of life in independent or old grammar schools – and a conception of teaching as a matter of the acquisition and exercise of specified competences in accordance with contractually defined obligations. But at the other more radical end of the vocational spectrum, opposition to teacher professionality extends far beyond any *de haut en bas* public school disdain for the vulgarities of state-sector career teaching, to a positively hostile view of professionalisation in general and of the professionalisation of education in particular.

According to what we might call radical vocationalism, the very idea of professionalism is anathema.[6] It is not just that a professional conception of education offers a more prosaic, impoverished or less than ideal picture of the practice of medicine or education, more that – since professionalisation is directly contrary to the very spirit of these and other enterprises – any aspiration to professional status cannot but be deeply corrosive. Radical theorists go to some lengths to show that far from enhancing and improving the quality of a public service in the interests of clients or consumers, the professional mindset is conducive more to the provider's exploitation of them. To begin with, the bureaucratic trappings of professional organisation, in particular the regulative machinery of restricted entry and practice, serve more than anything else to insulate professional activities from wider public scrutiny and accountability. In this respect, much is made of the deliberate adoption by most professions of a specialist professional discourse or jargon which is for the most part impenetrable even to educated outsiders. Indeed, one distinguished contemporary ethical theorist has persuasively argued that the rapid modern rise of such specialised professional discourses has been one reason why it has become nowadays all but impossible to characterise education in terms of the cultivation of a common framework of educational reference and sensibility.[7] The pretext for the development of such specialised discourses is, of course, that professionals require a non-vernacular occupational terminology to discuss the highly technical issues with which they have to deal – issues which ordinary resources of usage are inadequate to express. But whatever truth there may be in this, and it would be rash to deny that there are professional issues and problems which do call for new conceptual coinage, any case for the unavoidable use of professional jargon does seem to be overstated, if not infrequently bogus. Even in the more technical reaches of medicine and law there seems to be much obfuscation for its own sake – the obscuring of fairly straightforward and readily comprehensible issues in pseudo-scientific terminology – and in such less technical fields as social work and education, it is often difficult to see what purpose much quite ugly and distorting professional jargon might serve other than to keep the public nose out of professional business.

Moreover, there is more to the radical complaint than the point that professionals do not like the public to know what they are up to: the heart of the criticism is that they do not want this known because they are up to no good. In this connection, radicals rest their case on substantial evidence of professional exploitation and abuse of public trust and confidence, even of little more than monopolist racketeering. Indeed, some traditional professions, such as law, are popularly renowned for the promotion of professional benefit at the expense of clients, and it is well nigh a piece of folk wisdom that the only people to profit or benefit from any association or involvement with lawyers are lawyers themselves. Hence, if it is proper to characterise professions, in the spirit of the last chapter, in terms of a root concern with the promotion of such higher social goals as health, learning and justice – and a corresponding reduction of disease, ignorance and injustice – then the last of these purposes seems not to be especially well served by an adversarial system of civil and criminal law which enables highly paid lawyers to get known miscreants off the hook and to blacken the characters of innocent witnesses. But it has also been argued that a professionally regulated medical profession is no less open to serious self-serving abuses on the part of medical practitioners who, despite Hippocratic pretensions, can often be seen to put personal career advancement or financial reward before any concern with promoting wider human health care.[8] A striking example of such self-interest relates to medical professionals in the straitened circumstances of Third World economies, who – aspiring to the power and reputation of their counterparts in more developed economies – have been known to corner scarce public resources for more personal status-enhancing purposes. Thus, medical funds which could be deployed in improving the water supply or other basic aspects of health and hygiene in slums or undeveloped rural areas – investment which might save many thousands of lives – may be diverted for the development of well-equipped clinics or laboratories in expensive hospitals, for the study of rare medical conditions of relatively uncommon incidence, but internationally high research profile.

However, points of a similar nature have also been made by radical critics of the professionalisation of education and teaching. To begin with, there are general points to the effect that the very existence of a teaching profession is predicated upon or tied to an essentially bankrupt conception of education: that the teaching profession of modern compulsory schooling is a priesthood in the service of an empty theology of personal emancipation which has no real contemporary relevance, other than the preservation and perpetuation of that social and political elite from whom the teaching profession is itself recruited.[9] On Marxist or neo-Marxian versions of this radical critique, indeed, the education profession is no more than an instrument of class domination and oppression, expressly designed to ensure the educational success of the few and the failure of the many in the interests of maintaining an unjust *status quo* of minority privilege and mass exploitation. Such critiques, then, reject lock, stock and barrel any notion that occupations might be improved or made more effective via professional establishment, and they invite radical reappraisal of popular associations of hospitals with health, schools with education, law courts with justice. It is not just, they argue, that the institutions *need* not go with the practices, but that the institutions actually *impede* proper conduct of the practices. Just as it is sometimes claimed that whatever religion is, it is not likely to be found in churches, so radical critics argue that hospitals, law courts and schools are the last places in which one might hope to find real health, justice or education. Indeed, it is noteworthy in this connection that such radical critics of education have commonly gone under the name of 'deschoolers'.

Moreover, even at a less uncompromising level, one which is less inclined to dismiss the general social value of schooling, or a distinct occupational class of teachers *tout court*, one encounters similar criticisms of the *bureaucratic* accretions of educational professionalism. It is characteristic of professions to embody career structures designed for the systematic reward, via promotion and financial incentives, of deserving practitioners. However, two (not entirely consistent) points are often made here. First, it is argued that whereas it would be reasonable to expect a system of professional advancement that actually benefited the client to keep successful teachers in the classroom, the existing system is one which forces such teachers out of the classroom into administrative posts. In the interests of better pay and higher status, then, good teachers have usually to move away from the 'chalk-face' of classroom engagement. Indeed, those who through choice or necessity remain in the classroom throughout their careers may well be regarded as professional failures by their colleagues who have 'got on'. At the same time, however, it is often claimed that the ladder of professional promotion more often favours classroom 'yes men' than educational innovators: that one is much more likely to 'get on' by blind obedience to the policies and protocol of headteachers and other superiors than via any display of the sort of individual initiative which might rock the institutional boat. But it is also complained by even more mild-mannered critics of the system that the discourse of teacher professionalism seems seldom concerned with improving the quality of service, more often with protecting the salaries, working conditions and career prospects of educational professionals.[10] Teachers like other workers, it is said, are more inclined to invoke the rhetoric of professionalism in support of claims to better pay or shorter hours, than in connection with proposals or policies which might substantially increase their professional burdens – even when such burdens apparently conduce to 'client' advantage. To be sure, it may be claimed that there is little more than *emotive* or *prescriptive* force to such terms of evaluation as 'professional' and 'unprofessional' – terms which find most frequent use as counters in markedly partisan disputes, usually between workers and employers. Hence, educational employers will refer to teachers as 'unprofessional' when they threaten to strike for more pay, and teachers may speak of threats to their professionalism when employers attempt to impose unwelcome workloads or schedules of accountability on teachers.

## Towards a more balanced conception of professionalism

The principal difficulty of assessing such critiques of the language of professionalism and professional aspiration, especially in relation to education and teaching, is that they are evidently not of a piece. There are clearly different claims here of varying strength and plausibility (not to mention more or less radical implications) which require very careful sorting. Broadly, however, we might distinguish between the *stronger* claims which entirely repudiate notions of educational or other professionalisation, and those rather *weaker* claims more concerned to identify current shortcomings of professional organisation. I believe that the stronger claims, those committed in the case of education to some radical alternative to institutionalised schooling, are vulnerable to insuperable theoretical and practical difficulties. To begin at the conceptual level, although deschoolers are correct to draw a distinction between schooling and education, they appear to draw it in quite the wrong place to potentially disastrous effect. In the event, whereas deschoolers appear to identify with schooling what modern liberal educationalists have generally regarded as 'education' – a broad initiation of individuals into those forms of rational knowledge and understanding crucially transcendent of merely local and particular concerns[11] – they seem to identify education with what liberals are more inclined to regard as (vocational or other) training. Certainly, those modern liberal educational accounts which have identified education with schooling have not been free from confusion either, since schooling is concerned with many forms of socialisation and training besides (in their sense) education. But it should be clear enough that any proposal to deny young people rational access to a wider understanding of their world and broader cultural inheritance in the name of initiation into more 'relevant' social or occupational 'survival' skills, is not just conceptually problematic, but also potentially subversive of any genuine radical emancipatory ideals.

The related practical problem, however, is that deschoolers and other radicals so far appear unable to have come up with any alternative practical educational proposal – at any rate, any proposal which would appear to be at all feasible in contexts of modern post-industrial economy. Proposals for community-based 'learning webs'[12] which would replace the school-based instruction of full-time educational professionals with something more like part-time apprenticeship to practising masters of this or that occupation, have been reasonably dismissed as utopianly unsuited to the individual, social and economic requirements of modern industrial and technological societies. Indeed, they may appear merely expressive of reactionary nostalgia for a pre-industrial golden age which has long gone and is unlikely to return. It is true that neo-liberal free-marketers have recently reworked the deschooling notion of educational 'vouchers'[13] for the purpose of generating educational competition between schools – in the interests, allegedly, of raising standards. All the same, such neo-liberals never seem to have doubted that such voucher systems should operate *within*, rather than outside or instead of, existing frameworks and contexts of institutionalised schooling and teacher professionalism. Moreover, one should not overlook previously indicated dangers of even modified attempts, via vouchers or whatever, to hand the quality control of education and teaching over to market forces. The difficulties of running educational institutions as businesses may come to a very real practical head, as we shall see, in tensions between what parents as customers want from schools and what professionals may regard it as crucial, in the name of proper fidelity to professional principle, to provide.

What, then, of those rather weaker criticisms of teacher aspiration to professional status which are not entirely dismissive of the idea that teaching should continue to be a particular and distinct professional specialism? Such critiques are nevertheless prey to some ambivalence. On the one hand, there can be no doubt that they have often seemed to suggest that *any* use of the language or 'rhetoric' of professionalism is bogus and self-seeking in a manner guaranteed to undermine the integrity of all and any who allow themselves to be seduced by it: that, in short, there is something inherently and ineradicably debilitating about professional regulation and bureaucratisation or any aspiration to professionality. The trouble is, of course, that it is difficult to characterise any such loss of integrity other than in terms of betrayal of a particular set of occupational ideals. It is barely coherent even to claim that there are *misapplied* emotive or prescriptive senses of 'professional' or 'unprofessional' unless one has some inkling of how such terms might, at least in principle, be literally or *correctly* applied. Hence, weaker objections to any educational use of the language of professionalism more often seem to amount to the charge of *hypocrisy* – of educationalists failing to live up to occupational ideals, which may all the same have genuine authority, and to which teachers might nevertheless be held accountable or encouraged to aspire. In short, it is not clear that the weaker critiques identify anything more than failures of individual attitude and institutional structure which might, notwithstanding, be susceptible of revision and improvement through better professional education and some institutional reform. Assuming that this is so, we shall in the following chapters continue to develop further the case for regarding education and teaching as professional enterprises demanding fidelity to a range of ideals and principles of a not merely dishonest or self-interested kind.

# Part II

# EDUCATIONAL THEORY AND PROFESSIONAL PRACTICE

# 4

# EDUCATIONAL THEORY
# MISAPPLIED?

## Some basic questions about educational theory

In Part I we saw that theory-dependence is generally taken to be a key criterion of professional engagement – and I believe that there is everything to be learned about the distinctively 'professional' character of such engagement from a clearer understanding of the relationship of professional theory to practice in general, and of educational theory to practice in particular. Despite the fact that much ink has been spilt on this question in post-war literature of educational philosophy and theory, however, it is arguable that this issue still requires some very elementary ground-clearing conceptual analysis. This might of course be thought a surprising – if not audacious – observation; after all, it might be said, have there not been several influential papers from leading post-war educational philosophers devoted precisely to examining the issue of the relationship of theory to practice and to identifying different accounts of this relationship?[1] But whilst I am far from unapprecia-tive of such interesting and valuable work, I nevertheless fear that the problem has not yet been addressed at quite the required ground-floor conceptual level; and, to that extent, some of the fundamental questions we need to ask may have been begged rather than answered in previous literature. Indeed, attempts to identify different models of 'the relationship of theory to practice', or to argue for one model over another, may be in thrall to a question-able assumption that the term 'theory' has a single coherent sense in popular educational discourse: that, in short, one and only one thing is or can be intended by talk of theory's relationship to practice. Any such procrustean assumption, however, risks missing the range of complex logical relations between diverse forms of so-called educational knowledge and understanding – at the expense of a dangerously simplistic and lopsided view of the relevance of such reflections to practice. This and the next chapter will therefore be concerned with a rather more basic sorting out of some of the different things that educational theory has commonly been taken to mean – together with some basement exploration of how these might be held to interrelate in a larger and more complex picture of principled professional expertise.

We shall begin by looking at what might be the most simplistic or primitive conception of the relationship of theory to practice, or, more generally, of thought to action; indeed, we might first ask why theory and practice, thought and action, have been regarded as at all separate – and in what sense action requires thought. Arguably, the root idea here is that there can be action – or at least movement – in the absence of anything worth dignifying with the term thought. Most natural entities exist, move and have their being without benefit of reflection – which is, all the same, still needed to explain the existence and movement of non-reflective things. It has therefore appeared to many great philosophers that what sets human beings apart from the rest of creation is their capacity for rational or principled understanding of the world in which they find themselves – the abilities of human agents to deliberate, form intentions, entertain purposes, make plans and theorise. This basic thought, moreover, has drawn such great philosophers as Plato[2] and Descartes[3] to forms of psycho-physical dualism: to one or another version of the idea that whereas we may account for the rest of nature, even non-human animate nature, more or less exclusively in natural scientific terms, human nature requires to be understood as a composite of mutually irreducible psychological and physical attributes. From this viewpoint, it is significant that although there can be scientifically explicable but non-rational or thoughtless human agency – conduct that is habitual, compulsive, reflex, careless, inattentive, and so on – what is needed to turn otherwise blind physical human behaviour into rational action is the addition, as it were, of thought or theory. It seems to some such an idea which grounds an *applied theory* conception of rational human agency.

## Education and applied science

Indeed, it is but a further refinement of the *applied theory* conception of rational agency – to which such great rationalist philosophers as Plato and Descartes have no doubt contributed – to conceive rational agency as a kind of applied *science* or *technology*. This is, as we shall proceed to argue, a rather one-sided conception of rational action, but it is also clearly a significant one for any attempt to understand problems of the relationship of theory to practice in professional and other contexts – not least because it has had a powerful influence on popular thinking about such matters. Indeed, the thought is now that no professional or other practice may be regarded as having come of full rational age until it can be grounded in scientifically reputable evidence and principles. In this connection, we may need look no further than to medical practice for what would generally be regarded as a professional technology of this kind; it seems fairly safe to assume a common conception of medical practice as the application of scientifically attested theoretical knowledge to particular contingencies of medical need – as well as a more general understanding of practices as professional or otherwise in proportion to their scientific grounding. On this view, such trades, arts or crafts as dry-stone walling, animal husbandry, chicken-sexing or carpentry which rely largely on experience, practice or intuition would not qualify as professions in so far as they do not require agents to apply knowledge of a proven scientific kind. On the other hand, such practices as psychological counselling and midwifery, which once lay in the realms of guesswork and folk wisdom, might nowadays be regarded as candidates for professional status precisely in the light of scientific developments in psychiatry and obstetrics. At all events, in view of a conspicuous modern trend towards construing professional status largely in such applied science terms, it would be somewhat surprising if no similar attempt had ever been made to construe teaching in some such 'scientistic' way.

Attempts to systematise pedagogy certainly go back a very long way. For example, despite Socrates' apparent hostility to the technicist educational pretensions of the sophists in Plato's dialogues, there is evidence in the *Meno* that that greatest of systematisers, Plato himself, had more than a passing interest in pedagogical technique.[4] However, despite apparent denials of interest in this direction from major educational progressives,[5] it may well be that close attention to technicalities of pedagogy – often in the context of psychological theories of child development – really takes off in the so-called progressive educational tradition from Rousseau onwards.[6] At all events, the possibility of a scientifically-grounded programme of pedagogical research finally hoves into view in the twentieth century with the alleged coming of age of an experimental science of psychology explicitly focused on the study of human and non-human animal learning. It is noteworthy in this connection that John Dewey and Bertrand Russell, both of whom sought to develop progressive or experimental approaches to education, were among the first educational theorists to welcome behavioural psychology as the potential scientific grounding for educational practice for which so many had long hoped.[7] There is also much to be said (as I have done so elsewhere[8]) about the largely lamentable influence of reflex psychology on modern theory and practice of education. The point of present concern, however, is that early claims (albeit inflated and premature) to have discovered an experimentally-grounded basis for the practice of education and teaching was undoubtedly heartening to any and all who may have aspired to an applied science conception of teacher professionalism.

Moreover, spurred on by the prospects of a behavioural science of pedagogy, twentieth-century educational theorists have increasingly appealed to the findings of such social sciences as psychology, sociology and anthropology in pursuit of a reputable scientific basis for professional practice – so that it is nowadays not uncommonly assumed that the *only* kind of research relevant to knowledge growth in the field of education is social scientific enquiry of an empirical data-collecting kind. From this viewpoint, it is striking that although the academic faculty-based view of professional teacher education which underpinned post-war development of professional teaching degrees in the UK and elsewhere – qualifications which sought to root the professional preparation of teachers in a systematic initiation into the disciplines of psychology, sociology, philosophy, curriculum studies, and so forth – was largely the brainchild of educational philosophers,[9] it was seldom seriously questioned that the educational disciplines were essentially forms of rationally systematic science whose findings might be applied to educational practice in a more or less technical way. With this in mind, it is noteworthy that post-war pioneers of analytical philosophy of education often rejected what they regarded as an outdated conception of educational philosophy as broad initiation into the educational theories of such major philosophers as Plato, Rousseau and Dewey, in favour of a view of educational philosophising as concerned more with the cultivation of a range of analytical techniques for the detection of fallacies in educational documentation and discourse.[10]

There can also be little doubt, however, that this widespread conception of professional preparation as a matter of initiation into a repertoire of theoretically-grounded expertise or technique – apt for application to a field of practice construable as otherwise unprincipled, non-rational or untheoretical – has, down the years, been a source of much serious embarrassment to those charged with the task of the professional education and training of teachers. It has given rise to numerous bizarre questions about what should be the *balance* of educational theory to educational practice in training, and about whether there might not be too much theory and too little practice – for, of course, if 'theory' simply means having a rational or principled understanding of what we are doing, how could there be a question of whether there is too much of it, or about whether we might have more ignorance instead? However, when theory and practice are respectively taken to mean 'college study' and 'school experience' – as often seems to be the case in issues about balance – the question invariably comes down to that of whether there is too much academic study in relation to experiential school-based learning. To be sure, it may sometimes be quite sensible and coherent to ask how much theory in this sense is required for professional preparation, and, in the medical field, for example, a very general answer to this question would be: as much knowledge as a general practitioner or surgeon needs to do the job. If human lives are not to be put at grave risk, we cannot have doctors entering the field of medical practice who have not mastered an instrumentally indispensable body of anatomical, physiological or bio-chemical knowledge, in whatever time it takes to do so. However, the question of the balance of academic knowledge to experience in professional preparation for teaching arises in an especially virulent form, because of at best wide disagreement and at worst widespread scepticism about the significance for professional practice of much if not most of the academic study that trainee teachers are required to undertake in college courses of teacher education.

## The practical relevance of educational theory

The rise and fall of theory in post-war teacher education in the UK serves well enough to illustrate this difficulty. It is now fairly common knowledge that post-war educational theorists and policy-makers sought as part of a general programme of social and economic reconstruction to put the conduct of teaching on a surer professional footing by extending the duration and improving the quality of teacher education and training. Imposing more rigorous academic demands on entry to teaching, with the ultimate aim of producing an all-graduate profession, was a major goal of this project. To this end, during the 1960s and 1970s most college courses of teacher education required systematic initiation into what were regarded as the principal educational disciplines of philosophy, psychology, sociology, history and curriculum studies, and – though it remained an ideal to recruit teacher trainers who were able to combine academic expertise with experience of school teaching – it was not unusual for those employed in teaching these disciplines to be drawn from the academic ranks of philosophical, psychological or sociological scholarship, rather than (or as well as) from those of school experience. It was of course seldom if ever seriously supposed that such courses might suffice in and of themselves to turn trainees into practically effective teachers – and teacher colleges continued to provide teaching methods courses and opportunities for school experience alongside programmes of educational theory. But a certain disillusionment, not unfamiliar to teachers of educational theory, soon set in. Teacher trainees continued to complain of their inability to see the relevance of philosophical or psychological studies to actual classroom practice, and there seemed to be no obvious connection between such academic learning and expertise in teaching. Indeed, it was by no means unknown for academically poor students to turn out to be practically good teachers, and for students excelling in academic studies to make practically inept teachers.

The new academically-based courses of professional educational preparation emerged in a climate of post-war economic expansion and social optimism, but with the economic downturn of subsequent decades, professional doubts about the value of any such theory-based teacher education were gradually reinforced by wider public and political scepticism. Indeed, politically right-of-centre lobbying for the reform of teacher education, emphasising reduction (if not elimination) of the academic elements of teacher education in favour of school-based, hands-on training, was a conspicuous feature of the twilight years of the Conservative governments under Margaret Thatcher and John Major – and such thinking has undoubtedly left its mark on current political thinking about professional teacher preparation. Thus, in contrast to a conception of educational theory as necessary (if not sufficient) for professionally effective teaching, we encounter at the other extreme a view of professional preparation which places paramount importance on the acquisition of practical teaching skills and competences, in relation to which theory is regarded as a hindrance more than a help.[11] From this point of view, it would appear that there could hardly be any other professional field in which there is as wide disagreement about the purpose, value and utility of theory in professional training as there is in the field of teacher education and training. Moreover, this is so notwithstanding that professional (as opposed to public or political) consensus would appear to repudiate both the 'sufficiency' and 'redundancy' conceptions of the professional value of theory in favour of some notion of a 'right balance' between the two.

The trouble with the idea of a right balance, of course, is that it simply returns us to the question of what any such right balance could be – which clearly depends, in turn, upon what one takes to be the purpose of professional theory; we are back, in short, to square one. By and large, however, it would seem that the prevailing professional consensus on balance – focused since the late 1970s and 1980s on the idea of a 'professional degree' – turns upon a particular ideal of effective teaching as *applied* theory. On the one hand, such consensus rightly rejects the redundancy account of educational theory and the pure apprenticeship model of training on the grounds that this must lead to a hopeless narrowing of both the professional vision and the practical experience of educational practitioners; on the other hand, however, it would regard any earlier academic faculty conception of professional preparation as inappropriate to the extent that it encourages student engagement with such disciplines as philosophy, psychology and sociology 'for their own sake', with insufficient attention to their practical relevance. In short, the 'applied theory' view of professional preparation appears to regard theory – at first sight plausibly enough – as *necessary* but not sufficient for effective professional practice; theory is to be regarded as integral to professional teacher training in so far as it can be shown to have real relevance to classroom practice. This account has the additional benefit of reinforcing a traditional and fairly reasonable, though increasingly challenged, view of the division of professional training labour between academy and school; whereas it is the job of the academy to provide the theoretical expertise that students need for professional practice, it is that of schools to provide contexts for the application of theory in professional experience. But whatever the appeal of this account as a solution to the theory–practice problem of teacher preparation, especially in its avoidance of extreme 'anti-theory' and 'theory-only' stances, it simply raises afresh the initial problem of what counts as professionally relevant theory, and there are clearly more or less generous construals of this.

## Problems with the 'applied' conception of educational theory

If, for example, one takes seriously the idea of classroom application as one's main criterion of practical relevance, then it is clear that we may dispense with much of the philosophy, history, sociology, and so on, previously taught in the context of academically-based courses. Indeed, as I have noted elsewhere,[12] there would appear to have been – in the context of many professional degrees – a recent gradual erosion of such disciplines as philosophy, history and sociology of education in favour of newer and more instrumentally conceived courses in management, pedagogy, curriculum studies, and so on. Since many of these studies appear to draw on (or to be pragmatic descendants of) that discipline of experimental psychology which we earlier observed to have set the modern ball of educational theory rolling, it is noteworthy that what seems mainly to have survived into contemporary professional education and training is a conception of theory as applied to educational practice in much the same way that we might regard anatomical or physiological science as applicable to medical practice. In fact, I believe that this idea is even more deeply entrenched in latter-day 'action research' attempts to shift the burden of theory-generation from professional educational researchers to field professionals.[13] The idea that professionals should themselves take responsibility for the quasi-scientific testing of the effectiveness of their practice against self-generated theories and hypotheses rests ultimately on an inherently instrumentalist conception of theory.

In the cold light of day, however, it has never seemed particularly plausible to regard even experimental psychology or 'learning theory' – in any of its modern forms – as providing a scientific-theoretical basis for a kind of technology of pedagogy. First, as previously noted, although it may be reasonable to articulate some aspects of teaching in terms of general techniques or strategies, the prospect of conceiving teaching as more a context-specific non-generalisable art than a scientifically-grounded technology points to the limits and dangers of any such overall conception. This is one way, to be sure, in which any such *techne* may not even be *necessary* for effective teaching. Another such consideration, however, relates to the fact that even if we correctly supposed effective teaching to depend upon the development of some such scientifically-grounded technology, it would be hasty to suppose that modern psychology has to date provided any such basis for pedagogical science. Thus, for example, despite their continued influence on behavioural objectives models of educational assessment and competence models of professional training, it is highly unlikely that psychological learning theories are suitable for direct classroom application. This is, of course, no reason for discontinuing college instruction in them – we have good reason to acquaint students of education with (even mistaken) theories of human learning as part of their general professional education – but it is misguided to suppose that we might teach these with a view to their direct application to classroom practice. Much the same, moreover, goes for more sophisticated 'cognitive' accounts of knowledge acquisition; while these may afford insights into certain general features of human understanding, the theories of a Piaget or Bruner are far too general to be of much particular educational utility. But in any case, even if we were to develop a scientific theory of learning which could be given direct classroom application for the effective production of some generally desirable human learning, that would not be in itself sufficient to warrant its use, for, of course, there are familiar *moral* problems about the employment of such learning technologies in the human case. It is possible, for all I know, that brainwashing is based on scientifically impeccable principles which explain how people can be psychologically conditioned for certain instructional purposes; but, of course, it does not follow that it would be appropriate to use any such technology in the context of education. So, at the very least, the notion of theory application sends out seriously misleading signals about what should be learned and why – or included and excluded – in programmes of professional education and study for teachers. Furthermore, since the applied theory view seems confused at the conceptual level, it is only to be expected that it should also at the practical level be unsatisfactory as an account of the respective roles of training institutions and schools in professional training; in this connection, there is currently much dissatisfaction with the view of division of labour implied by such an account.

## Rationality and skill

The problems of relating so-called educational theory to practice encountered so far would seem to follow, at least in part, from regarding practice as essentially a matter of blind behaviour, in itself quite innocent of rationality and intelligence, until informed or guided by the theorising operations of the mind. It seems beyond doubt that much common professional thinking about the relationship of theory to practice continues to enshrine certain assumptions, well embedded in ordinary usage, regarding the mind as a sort of 'ghost in the machine' – a source of essentially intellectual reflection and motivation – in the absence of which no human conduct or practice could be regarded as intelligent. It was against precisely this intellectualist legend, deeply rooted in both traditional philosophical rationalism and empiricism, that such important modern philosophers as Ryle[14] and Wittgenstein[15] so persistently inveighed. Both were concerned to show that there are forms of essentially *practical* reason which are not reducible to theoretical reason, so that whilst reason is implicated just as much in cookery or carpentry as it is in effective scientific or historical theorising, it is not necessarily so in the manner of conscious deliberation. As Ryle put it, we do not have to suppose that in order to be considered rational or intelligent human practical conduct has to be preceded by an episode of intellectual reflection or that each exercise of knowing how requires a prior exercise of knowing that. All the same, the basic insight here is that human conduct can hardly be conceived as other than informed or guided by rational principles or rules, because the ordinary pre-theoretical discourse of practical life is inherently *normative*. But in that case, it might also seem reasonable to suppose that initiation into such familiar forms of rational human practical activity as plumbing, gardening, engineering, hairdressing, medicine or teaching is precisely a matter of the grasp of forms of *practical* more than of theoretical reasoning. Hence, it has become fashionable of late to try to understand problems of professional educational knowledge and reflective practice – and, indeed, of the actual procedural thinking of teachers – in terms of a distinctively practical mode of rationality.[16]

At first sight it might well seem that the idea of practical rationality offers us a very neat and conceptually economic way of understanding the difference between proficient and incompetent professional practice, which to a large degree by-passes the theory–practice problem. This seems especially so to the extent that we may regard the practical rationality inherent in a given form of human conduct as logically quite independent of any sort of theorising. What, we might ask, defines a competent hairdresser? Presumably he or she is a person who is able to trim or style hair intelligently – that is, in accordance with certain recognised procedural rules and principles. It is very important to grasp, on this view, that competent hairdressers are *not* those who apply rules in any loaded sense of this treacherous term. Certainly, they are not bound to be conscious of the rules they are following in plying their trade any more than one may need to be conscious of grammatical rules in speaking grammatically. But we should beware particularly of any connotations of 'application' which suggest the independent existence of a body of theoretical principles apart from the procedural rules the hairdresser is following. For why should we have to suppose any such thing? What sense could we really make of a theory of hairdressing, and what substantial conceptual work might any such notion do?

What such considerations suggest, of course, is essentially the *competence* conception of occupational expertise which has proved so popular in recent theorising about the nature of vocational education – and about which we shall in due course have more to say. The basic idea here is that many human practical occupations can best be understood in terms of the acquisition of a repertoire of rational *skills* – skills which can be exercised well or badly, wisely or foolishly – but which do not depend for their intelligent exercise on the sophisticated mastery of theories. But however much it may be tempting to seek such conceptual economy in thinking about the nature of professional training in other areas of human practical concern, an idea which appears plausible in relation to the pursuit of certain crafts or trades begins, for all sorts of reasons, to look rather far-fetched in relation to the practice of various higher professions. For example, although a surgeon may not be consciously applying a theory when he excises a tumour, he is nevertheless utilising a technique which presupposes a good deal of scientific knowledge of the human body; in short, the practical skills of a competent surgeon are by no means independent of theory since they represent the essentially technological application to practice of scientific knowledge which could not be had independently of an intelligent grasp of theoretical research and enquiry.

## Theory and practical reason

To make this point slightly clearer, let us consider how a simple pattern of practical inference might be exhibited in the practical reasoning of members of different occupations. A particular tradesman, a joiner, is anxious that he should not splinter the wood. He reasons that if he is to avoid splintering the wood he should not plane against the grain – and concludes, correctly, that he should not plane against the grain. A particular professional, a doctor, is concerned to anaesthetise the patient effectively. He reasons that for effective anaesthesia he should locate a major vein – and concludes, correctly, that he should not miss the vein. Clearly, though the form of the reasoning is identical in the two cases (p, p only if q, therefore q), the content of the reasoning differs markedly from case to case – notably with respect to the content of the conditional premises. In the case of the joiner the conditional premise embodies the kind of pre-theoretical or experiential knowledge which requires expertise, but not sophisticated scientific understanding, to master. In the case of the doctor, however, the conditional clearly does embody knowledge of a complex theoretical kind derived from extensive scientific research and enquiry. Thus, the practical reasoning embedded in the competences of a surgeon cannot be regarded as logically independent of theoretical knowledge of a scientific temper and may be understood only in terms of the direct technical application of that scientific understanding. It is not, of course, that the exercise of knowing how needs, at the level of psychological description, to be preceded by an episode of knowing that – more, at the level of logical presupposition, that the skills of surgery themselves make little rational sense apart from a background understanding of scientific knowledge concerning the human body. Thus, we might explain the difference between a trade such as hairdressing and the medical technology of surgery by saying that whereas it is not necessary for a hairdresser to be a hair scientist as well as a pruner of hair, a surgeon does need to be a body scientist as well as an amputator of body parts.

The trouble is, however, that both these accounts of the operations of practical rationality in human affairs – the theory-independent and theory-dependent conceptions of professional competence – seem to boil down once again to those practical craft and applied science notions of professional knowledge, whose appropriateness to education and teaching we earlier saw some reason to doubt. For what should we now say of teaching by comparison with hairdressing or surgery? On the one hand, it would appear to make teaching resemble surgery to the extent that we *do* want to say that substantial bodies of social scientific and other knowledge are of genuine relevance to a proper understanding of educational practice. On the other hand, however, it makes teaching look rather more like hairdressing to the extent that we ought *not* to want to say that competent teaching requires a thorough grasp of academic psychology or sociology in quite the same way and for the same reason that effective surgery depends on a thorough knowledge of anatomy or physiology. One way to put this is to observe that it would be very much less disconcerting to encounter a practising classroom teacher who had never heard of Piaget, Bernstein or Stenhouse than it would be to discover a practising surgeon who had little or no knowledge of anatomy or physiology. In short, we have reason to be sceptical about regarding teaching as *either* a mere craft or trade like hairdressing, *or* as an applied science or technology like surgery.

To sharpen these points further, it would appear that while the trouble with a theory-independent conception of professional knowledge as applied to teaching is that it *is* theory independent, the trouble with a theory-dependent view is that it precisely re-opens all those old wounds about an actual gap in practice between educational theory and practice. For example, the trainee surgeon is unlikely to experience difficulties understanding the relevance to his or her training of lectures on anatomy and physiology of quite the same order as those of which trainee teachers frequently complain with regard to their lectures on sociology or psychology. In medical school teachers of theory and teachers of techniques can pursue their diverse enquiries with reasonable confidence that their separate contributions ultimately conduce to a common goal of health promotion; whereas the theories which trainee teachers are taught so often appear to them to be remote from, out of touch with, even irrelevant to, the real-life business of classroom teaching. This is presumably what lies behind those frequent calls for teacher trainers to display a degree of street credibility in the form of recent and relevant experience in schools.[17] However, if the sciences of psychology and sociology had the same clear relevance to educational practice as the sciences of anatomy and physiology have to surgery, then the only real issues with respect to their teaching ought to be those of how well they are taught and whether they are *true*. In this regard, how would practical experience of classroom teaching in schools be likely to improve a tutor's theoretical grasp and ability to communicate an understanding of psychology or sociology? It is as though teachers are saying to their college tutors of theory – as surgeons would not have to say to their anatomy teachers – show us how this experimental work with rats can assist us to promote learning in the classroom. Moreover, on the assumption that teaching is theory dependent in much the same way as the profession of surgery, this is not an unfair question.

I believe, incidentally, that it is largely on just such an assumption that teacher trainers are perennially inclined to resort to various operational strategies which might appear to plug the embarrassing gap between theory and practice.[18] Thus, for example, one might re-locate the theoretical activities of the college tutor in the school context, encouraging him or her to focus on only those aspects of his or her theories which might have immediate relevance to the particular features of that educational situation. Or, again, one might even transfer responsibility for theory-generation from professional researchers to teachers in schools themselves, by promoting the currently fashionable cause of action research among classroom practitioners. Surprisingly, however, it rarely seems a reason for disquiet among teacher trainers inclined to these and other similar strategies that they clearly tend towards an unfortunate diminution of both the intellectual and practical horizons of teachers; whereas the former strategy inclines towards a radical reduction of any serious and substantial intellectual and academic content in courses of teacher education from which only pseudo-disciplines like curriculum studies, pedagogical science and management theory emerge relatively unscathed (and we already appear to have reached the stage, at least in some places, at which theory means little more than the largely uncritical study of official reports), the latter encourages excessive concentration on such less elevated aspects of daily classroom life as time management, desk organisation and furniture arrangement.

In short, it would appear that recent emphases on the idea of practical rationality as the key to understanding reflective practice have not infrequently taken forms which actually narrow rather than broaden scope for serious intellectual reflection, thereby offering hostages to the fortunes of those who have a vested political interest in proclaiming the irrelevance of educational theory to professional educational practice.[19] The problem with the theory-independent view of teacher expertise as a repertoire of professional competences is that it inclines to an implausible view of practice as related only contingently to theoretical and other principled reflections about education; they may be useful to justify and underpin rational practice, but practice may be rational in the absence of any explicit acquaintance with such reflections. The problem with the theory-dependent conception of practical deliberation in teaching, on the other hand, is that it inclines to insist upon something like a necessary connection between educational theory and practice – which, because such necessity is rarely if ever to be found, must radically narrow the scope of what could possibly count as relevant intellectual reflection in the context of teaching. In short, whereas in one case the connection between theory and practice is too loosely conceived, in the other it is construed as too tight; what is required, then, is a conception of practical deliberation according to which the connection between theorising or other forms of principled reflection and practice is *neither* necessary *nor* contingent. Is such a conception available? It is, but only via rejection of the predominantly or excessively instrumental reading of practical deliberation to which many theorists of reflective practice have been, explicitly or implicitly, inclined. But this must also mean, I think, considerably playing down the actual importance which theories and theorising as such have been given in relation to the question of what constitutes principled understanding of professional practice.

I believe that although the practical deliberation presupposed to intelligent professional engagement is rightly understood as a form of practical wisdom, such wisdom is expressible neither in scientific theoretical laws or principles apt for quasi-technical application in experience, nor (in retreat from any such principles) in some purely experiential form of practical initiation – but rather in that constellation of capacities, sensibilities and qualities of character which Aristotle referred to as *phronesis*. Thus, in any attempt to find a coherent way between the theory-dependence and theory-independence views of professional practice, it is crucial to appreciate that there can be meaningful construal of and/or reasonable responses to the particularities of professional experience which are neither matters of technical application of the causal generalities of scientific theory, nor of intuitive non-deliberative engagement with unconceptualised or unconceptualisable practical experience. In this respect, it has been arguably one of the most serious mistakes of recent theorising about the educational theory–practice relationship to suppose that there can be no observation, perception or interpretation of experience which is theory- or value-free. Indeed, directly under the influence of philosophical views hailing from pragmatist and neo-Hegelian sources, it has of late been more or less taken as read that there can be no meaningful grasp of experience which does not involve some kind of theoretical interpretation. As I have argued elsewhere,[20] and shall argue here, however, whereas such views are rightly concerned to preserve the insight of Kant's first *Critique* that there is no such thing as *concept-free* experience, this is *not* the same as the idea that there is no *theory-free* experience; thus, whilst it may be that making sense of experience is conceptualising it in some way, it seems nevertheless misleading to suggest that we invariably do this by applying theories. In the next chapter, then, we shall need to look more closely at the nature of non-theoretical deliberation in professional contexts of education and teaching.

# 5

# DIFFERENT FACES OF EDUCATIONAL THEORY

## The practical wisdom of *phronesis*

Notwithstanding that in the grossly pragmatic and instrumental times in which we live it is ever tempting to construe all rational conduct in technical terms – as a matter of the practical application of certain kinds of (preferably scientific) knowledge to the solution of one human problem or another – it is a mistake to think that technical deliberation is the only or even the primary mode of practical discourse. This point has, of course, been widely acknowledged by contemporary educational philosophers, as attested by the enormous recent interest in Aristotle's account of intelligent or reflective conduct as *praxis* informed by *phronesis*.[1] Thus, in the *Nicomachean Ethics*, Aristotle first distinguished practical deliberation from theoretical deliberation as primarily concerned with pursuit of the *good* more than pursuit of the *truth*;[2] whereas in physics or geography we are mainly concerned with understanding or explaining how the world *is*, in politics, arts or crafts we are concerned rather with bringing about certain changes in the world in the light of our desires and interests – changes which we will regard, under some description or other, as good. However, since the basic logical form of human action is exhibited in the idea of taking means to ends, particular actions can be evaluated as good or bad in a variety of ways – for example, from the point of view of the desirability of the ends or the efficiency of the means. Indeed, Aristotle regards reasoning about actions which is mainly focused upon establishing effective means to chosen goals (*techne*) as *technical* or productive reasoning, but refers to reasoning which is primarily directed towards the discernment of right ends – what to value as such – as moral wisdom (*phronesis*).[3]

Aristotle would also appear to have held that moral or evaluative reasoning is logically presupposed to technical or productive reasoning – or, at any rate, that there can be no reasoning about means to ends except in the light of certain assumptions about what is or is not humanly worth pursuing. Moreover, deliberation is also evidently implicated in moral and evaluative enquiries in two main respects – reasoning *about* values and reasoning *from* values. With regard to the latter, in so far as it concerns deciding what is to be done in various problematic circumstances, reasoning from values resembles technical reasoning. There are also, however, certain crucial logical differences between these two sorts of practical deliberation, and perhaps the most significant of these is that whereas technical deliberation involves reasoning between means and ends conceived as only *externally*, contingently or causally related, means require to be construed as *internally*, logically or constitutively related to ends in the case of moral or evaluative deliberation. Hence, moral or evaluative reasoning is sometimes distinguished from the simple means–end reasoning of technical deliberation as 'constituent-end reasoning'.[4]

This distinction between moral or evaluative and technical deliberation is of utmost moment for educational and other professional spheres of concern, and a failure to observe it is the source of much confusion in educational debate. The crucial reason why questions of education are inherently open-ended, questions which raise further questions rather than inviting straightforward or unequivocal answers or solutions, is that education is at heart a *moral* practice which is deeply implicated in values and conflicts of value – rather than a technological enterprise directed towards the efficient achievement of agreed ends. Some examples may help to make the point. On the one hand, if my car comes to a dead stop because of a broken timing chain, it may be a complex and expensive business to dismantle the car and replace the chain; but given that I need the car and want it repaired no problems need here arise about what I should do other than *how* to get it done (and/or whether I can afford it). On the other hand, however, if I want to exercise discipline over an unruly class and have discovered that wiring the children's seats to the national grid and administering painful shocks to recalcitrants secures the necessary order, the discovery of this straightforward pragmatic solution to a practical educational problem hardly concludes matters, but rather raises considerable further problems about what on earth I am up to in educational terms. This rather outlandish and overdrawn illustration of the point at least serves to bring into focus what is really at issue in the debates which have actually raged – and still from time to time resurface – about the legitimacy or justification of physical and other sorts of punishment in schools. Far too many teachers have assumed that because the strap or the cane has seemed to be a working practical solution to a range of discipline problems in many schools, the matter is actually settled in favour of its continued use. But this is precisely a case of mistaking a moral or evaluative issue for a technical one, and of seeing further educational debate as terminated rather than occasioned by the discovery of a particular instrumental means to a purported educational end.

Of course, someone might say, is not the means in this case – the just flogging of offenders – justified by the reasonable and rational end of the establishment of good order for learning in the classroom, just as the dismantling of my car is justified by the reasonable and rational goal of establishing the good running order of my car? However, we must again reply negatively to this objection because the analogy is predicated, once more, on the mistaken idea that means are related to ends on the discipline issue in a technical rather than a moral way. Whereas the means are related to the ends of car maintenance *externally* or as cause to effect, the means to moral ends – such as the appropriate discipline of children – are related *internally* or constitutively; moral means contribute qualitatively to the character, in this case of human discipline, of the goals they produce. Presumably we will not be satisfied with *any* sort of order of discipline in the classroom, but a particular sort of order and discipline. We ought not to want (as good liberal democrats) order which is based on fear, resentment and abuse, because presumably confidence, security, trust and respect are also (among other things) some of the qualities we wish young people to acquire – and it is at least arguable that these qualities as well as their opposites are best acquired through experience and example. Discussions of physical and other punishment in education have thus all too often been vitiated by a failure to distinguish, within the logic of practical discourse, the moral from the technical. Advocates of physical punishment will say that it works, and their opponents will say that it doesn't – and they will often rest their respective cases on empirical evidence one way or the other. Such arguments and the evidence to which they appeal clearly cannot conclude matters, however, since it is quite intelligible to maintain that even if beatings do serve in every case to deter or control offenders, the practice should nevertheless be discontinued because it teaches children that it is in the last resort appropriate or permissible to enforce one's will or get one's own way by the exercise of violence. It is also intelligible to argue, moreover, that even if corporal punishment does *not* deter or reform in all or even the worst cases of maleficence, it ought still to be deployed in the interests of justice construed as simple tit for tat reciprocity. This is to my mind a dubious argument – but it is at least the *right sort* of argument in which to engage when discussing matters of educational procedure, because it is addressed to the moral and evaluative dimensions of the issue.

Hence, if my concern with securing order in the classroom was merely a technical one I might be free, at least in principle, to employ *any* available method which might achieve the desired goal – including various more or less radical forms of psychological manipulation or physical coercion. But to regard the problem of school discipline as a moral or ethical one is to recognise that disciplinary conduct is subject to certain proper constraints with respect to such basic principles of civilised association as respect for persons, and so on; not every means causally productive of good order in the classroom can be regarded as constitutive of or consistent with the broadly ethical goals of any activity we should properly wish to regard as educational. At the same time, these observations regarding the logical dissimilarity of moral and technical reasoning are quite consistent with recognising that they often go together in practice: that having established via moral deliberation what conduct is consistent with a given value, more technical concerns with discovering the most effective way to achieve what is desired can then take over. But to leave matters thus would be to risk presenting a very partial – not to say misleadingly instrumental – picture of the nature of moral reason as primarily concerned with deciding what to do in the light of values we happen to have already. For, of course, questions about what is to be done in particular circumstances are logically dependent upon more basic reflections, in the light of our general knowledge and experience of the world, about what it is to live well or otherwise as individual or social human agents – and practical deliberation is required for the discernment as well as the expression of human values.

From a logical point of view, however, it is notoriously difficult to discern the true character of the relationship between our knowledge of the world – including of our human place in it – and our practical goals and projects as moral agents. Thus, at extreme ends of the spectrum, two philosophical accounts of the logic of moral or evaluative reasoning are fairly familiar. According to one view about the nature of moral argument,[5] an unbridgeable logical gulf is fixed between facts and values, which also means – since evaluation is conceived as ultimately dependent on prescription – that one cannot rightly derive an *ought* from an *is*. According to another familiar view,[6] however, since one can reach conclusions about what is morally or otherwise good or bad for human beings from considerations about how things are (that, for example, pain can be reasonably regarded as bad given that human beings find it unpleasant and are inclined to avoid it), one can legitimately infer conclusions about what is morally right from descriptive premises. But it is important to see that to whatever extent these two accounts logically conflict at points of particular detail, they are not in general mutually contradictory – since, of course, they are both *false*. The first view, associated with certain modern forms of non-cognitivist ethics, seems to go wrong in assuming that since there is a logical gap between is and ought there must also – because evaluation is a function of prescription – be such a gap between fact and value. The second view, associated with certain familiar forms of ethical consequentialism, wrongly assumes, to the contrary, that because certain observable facts about the human condition have a clear bearing on the way human interests, values and preferences must go, one must therefore be warranted in deriving conclusions about what one ought to do from purely factual or descriptive premises.

## Moral reason and moral inference

These two apparently opposed ethical perspectives, then, make the common mistake of conflating the fact–value and is–ought distinctions, and of assuming that if there is (or is not) a gap between the one there must also be (or not be) a gap between the other. But the fact–value distinction precisely relates to questions of evaluation, and construed as a denial of the logical possibility of deriving values from facts, it seems mistaken. For, from premises exclusively concerned to describe natural characteristics of objects, and observations concerning the actual goals and purposes of human agents, one clearly *can* argue that such objects have value for such purposes; precisely, from the facts that object O exhibits features x, y and z which are satisfactory for purpose $\varphi$, and A has purpose $\varphi$, one *can* conclude that O must be of value to A. It does not thereby follow, however, that from premises describing natural properties of objects and statements identifying the value of them for certain purposes, one can logically conclude that a given human agent should *have* such purposes. From the fact that tomatoes have features x, y and z which make them good for eating, I cannot infer that I *ought* to eat such tomatoes because, *inter alia*, I might not like tomatoes or might, for another purpose entirely, wish to have tomatoes with properties a, b and c.[7] So, although there may be legitimate inference from descriptive premises concerning features of natural objects and actual goals and interests of human agents regarding those objects to conclusions about the value of those objects for agents, there cannot be similarly straightforward inference from descriptive and evaluative premises to prescriptive conclusions.

This is not, of course, to deny that there is such a thing as practical *inference* or reasoning; but such reasoning normally proceeds from descriptions of objective circumstances and expressions of intention or purpose to prescriptive conclusions. From a given aim $\psi$ and the observation that $\varphi$ing constitutes a satisfactory means to $\psi$, one can reason, all things being equal, to $\varphi$ing as a prescription. The *ceteris paribus* clause is of the highest significance here, however, given the generally contextualised nature of practical deliberation. It now becomes of some importance, of course, to distinguish practical *reasoning* from practical *inference*. Patterns of practical inference are essentially abstractions from the deliberative contexts of human life, and are as such entirely subject to certain requirements of formal validity. Thus, it formally follows from considerations about the basic means–end character of human action that if Y is desired and X is a means to Y, then one should, all other things being equal, do X. But practical reasoning is, of course, an essentially agent-centred and situation-relative activity which in normal circumstances means that many different and conflicting aims and purposes may be brought to bear on a given context of decision making. To be empowered as rational human agents with genuine choice between alternative courses of action presupposes not only the freedom to do other than we do, but also the possibility of conflict and contradiction between our wants and values. Without freedom we have no alternatives, but the appreciation of alternatives brings with it responsibility to choose in the light of available knowledge what might practically be for the best – although such present knowledge can never be sufficient to ensure in the teeth of future contingency what that best might *be*.

Some of these points are captured, rather more technically, by referring to practical arguments – primarily those of a moral or evaluative kind – as *defeasible*;[8] there can indeed be valid practical arguments to prescriptive conclusions, but, unlike theoretical arguments, the addition or suppression of extra factual or other premises can subvert or falsify an initial practical conclusion. Such arguments are, of course, a familiar feature of legal and judicial debate and controversy; a given body of facts based on eye witness accounts may indicate in the context of a given penal code that this is a criminal act which ought not to go unpunished – but the entry of further evidence about the accused's unstable mental condition may counsel a more lenient verdict. A rather less technical way of putting this point, however, might be to say that whilst our practical decisions are not dictated or constrained by our theoretical or factual knowledge of the world or the human predicament, they are nevertheless *informed* by that knowledge.

Thus, because factual or theoretical knowledge of our nature as human agents must have a bearing on the sort of interests and desires we can entertain as partakers in that nature, connections between either description and evaluation, or the premises and conclusions of practical arguments, cannot be merely *contingent*. However, because of the crucial element of freedom in human affairs which allows scope for different agents to pursue diverse interests or conceptions of the good, we are not in practice forced to value exactly the same things – and so the relationship of prescriptive conclusions to practical premises cannot be strictly *necessary* either. But although from a technical perspective human freedom may be constrained only by what it is practically *possible* for people to do, there are obviously limits to what human beings can entertain as morally worthwhile or acceptable in the light of our ordinary pre-theoretical conceptions of human flourishing; we cannot, for example, coherently regard the murder, torture or enslavement of other human beings as genuine moral goals without serious self-deception or corruption. (This is a point, of course, about what ought properly to count as a correct grasp of the logic of moral discourse; it is not a denial of the obvious fact that people can often behave badly, while still regarding themselves as moral agents.)

None the less, although moral reasoning is susceptible of rational appraisal, and there are clear enough normative constraints upon what can count as valid moral arguments, since moral imperatives often conflict and people are inclined to give weight to different imperatives, particular moral judgements and perspectives are often (though by no means always) liable to debate and controversy. Hence, even though moral deliberation is quite properly apt for construal as a species of practical discourse, it should not thereby be assumed that its only point is to guide action towards the solution of moral problems. Indeed, since it is not especially in the nature of genuine moral problems to be satisfactorily resolvable, moral reason might well be said to be more centrally concerned with the discernment or identification of problems and questions concerning the human predicament – for the important practical purposes of understanding better the complexities, trials and vicissitudes of human association, and the building of human character in response to them. Moreover, one presently relevant point of labouring these somewhat formal considerations concerning the logic of moral and evaluative reasoning is that it seems reasonable to distinguish certain complex practical occupations on the grounds that they are primarily focused on moral rather than technical deliberation. This may well be a matter of degree, since even the simplest technical occupations cannot be entirely characterised without reference to ethical and evaluative considerations; but certainly some practical occupations – precisely the so-called professions – would appear to be much more focused upon moral or ethical than on technical outcomes.

## The moral character of professional deliberation

Moreover, although the professional status of teachers has often been belittled – especially in comparison with doctors and lawyers – I think it would be hard to doubt that teaching is a prime example of the sort of activity in which almost all the important decisions which need to be made at a practical level are more of a moral than a technical nature. Since teachers are essentially concerned with guiding the development of young people, with encouraging particular forms of positive human association, and with promoting the intellectual and moral virtues required for such association, they are unavoidably professionally implicated in profound questions about the moral ends and goals of human life. Thus, in the interests of a better understanding of the way in which the professional knowledge and reasoning of teachers impacts upon their professional practice, it is crucial to grasp not only the way in which they exercise moral wisdom in their actual practical dealings with children, but also the way in which their moral and evaluative deliberations are informed by a wider understanding of the world, human nature and society.

From this viewpoint, however, a significant advantage of grounding professional knowledge and understanding in the idea of moral or evaluative deliberation is that it is thereby centrally located in *neither* theory *nor* practice as these have commonly been construed. For, although on this view professional knowledge does require engagement in a form of practical deliberation, the deliberation in question is of that kind concerned primarily with serious *evaluative* reflection upon the moral ends of that important aspect of human flourishing known as education, not deliberation of the mere 'how to do' variety associated with procedural reasoning and/or the mastery of skills. On the other hand, however, although practical moral wisdom requires to be widely informed by different sorts of reflection upon the nature of human life and association, it is nevertheless not in and of itself a form of *theoretical* reasoning focused upon the discernment of *truths*, but a form of *practical* reason concerned with pursuit of the *good*. Thus, on this account, the problem of professional knowledge for teaching is not that of resolving a dualism of theory and practice – of understanding how a kind of scientific knowledge can be given technological application. It is more that of appreciating the role in human affairs of an inherently principled form of practical reflection concerned: first, with the rational articulation of educational values in the light of all we know of ourselves and the world; second, with the proper expression of such values in civilised conduct. To a large extent, then, to relocate the problem of the relationship of professional knowledge to professional conduct in this way is to undermine the dualism which aligns a principled understanding of educational issues with academic theory, and good educational practice with the cultivation of craft skills. The primary concern of professional understanding can now be seen to lie with the articulation and expression of professional educational values, and with theory or techniques only in so far as these inform or are informed by practical wisdom.

The point that the professional understanding of teachers should properly be focused upon the development of practical wisdom is in itself, of course, hardly original – and many recent educational philosophers have sought to explicate professional practice in terms of Aristotle's notions of *phronesis* and *praxis*. It is also arguable, however, that other accounts along these lines have not been as resolute as might be wished in observing the distinction which

Aristotle was clearly at great pains to draw between the moral and technical aspects of practical deliberation, and that this crucial distinction is in particular seriously blurred by those who are inclined to characterise principled educational enquiry and practice in the terms of moral or practical science.[9] Indeed, I believe that it is impossible to regard the idea of a moral or practical science as other than thoroughly anomalous in Aristotelian terms, since it precisely rides rough shod over the distinctions between theoretical enquiry, technical conduct and moral wisdom which Aristotle himself took so much trouble to observe; for a science, at least in the sense in which it will nowadays be inevitably construed – as a mode of theoretical knowledge focused upon the discovery of truth by observation and experiment – is just exactly what *phronesis* is not for Aristotle. I am concerned to defend these distinctions between theory and practice, not out of blind devotion to Aristotle, but because, as I have already suggested, they serve to indicate important differences between the occupational understanding of teachers or other professionals and other forms of occupational expertise.

From this perspective, the association of *phronesis* and *praxis* (or practical wisdom and judgement) with ideas of moral or practical science becomes even more problematic when it is also linked, as it has lately been, with notions of action research into education and teaching.[10] One might express the central problem in the form of a dilemma. On the one hand, if the professional understanding of teachers is to be regarded as informed by the outcomes of certain kinds of quasi-scientific empirical observation and experiment, then there would appear to be little to prevent the collapse of practical reason into the technicism of applied science. On the other hand, however, if we insist that the scientific findings of action and other educational research do not determine educational conduct in any technicist way, but are liable to be influenced, even rendered irrelevant, by moral and evaluative considerations, then we are back to observing Aristotle's clear distinction of *phronesis* from both *theoria* and *techne*, and it can only be misleading to characterise moral wisdom in the terms of either moral or practical science. Thus, I believe that the best way forward is to embrace fully the Aristotelian view that practical wisdom is significantly distinct from both theoretical and technical enquiry, and to eschew ideas of moral or practical science as dangerously liable to give serious hostages to the fortunes of the would-be educational technicist. This is not to say, of course, that one can or should regard the

moral and evaluative enquiry at the heart of professional understanding as entirely independent of either theoretical understanding
or technical considerations; indeed, we have already conceded that
moral deliberation in the context of educational practice is
informed by the former and informs the latter. The difficulty is
rather that of seeing clearly how moral and evaluative enquiry is
conceptually connected to theoretical and technical considerations,
in a non-technicist way – and, for obvious reasons, this primarily
requires clarification of the relationship between theoretical
understanding and evaluative enquiry. When we begin to examine
closely the relationship between theoretical and evaluative
deliberation in education, however, we encounter some very
interesting, even surprising, results.

## Technicist and non-technicist educational deliberation

From a logical point of view, there would appear to be three main
levels at which theory talk is implicated in educational discourse.
First, there is the level of what might generally be regarded as
straightforward social scientific research and enquiry. However,
whilst it has of late been almost an article of faith among teachers
and other professional educationalists that the sort of investigations
carried out by sociologists and psychologists into aspects of
individual development and social conduct must have direct
implications for our educational policy-making, it is no less true
that such research has often been considered highly problematic by
educational (and mainstream) philosophers. Thus, with regard to
social scientific enquiries of a more theoretical and speculative kind,
it has been part of the stock-in-trade of recent educational
philosophers to argue that far from providing a secure foundation
upon which to construct a body of educational practice, many if
not most alleged scientific theories of human behaviour are actually
grossly distortive of our ordinary pre-theoretical conceptions of
individual conduct and social relations.[11] In so far as such social
scientific work is illuminating in relation to educational practice,
then, it is so only to the extent that it can assist teachers to a critical
view of how *not* to understand the individual and interpersonal
behaviour of pupils in their classrooms. Indeed, what may
principally help to inform a teacher's practice here is the recognition of a certain degree of conflict or inconsistency between
theoretical and pre-theoretical (or ordinary moral) understandings

of the nature of human life. Of course, at the level of more straightforward statistical research, it may be useful for teachers to know (for example) that too many valuable hours of schooling may be wasted due to widespread failure of teachers to appreciate the limitations of average pupil attention span. But even here it is important to see that such statistical findings do not unequivocally dictate practical policy – that, in short, one cannot get an *ought* from an *is*. (Thus, in the light of such knowledge, one might well ask whether teachers should try to teach within existing pupil attention span, or try to expand the capacities of pupils by teaching beyond it.)

The second level at which it is not uncommon to hear people speaking of theory and theories in relation to education is with regard to what I have previously referred to as the pseudo-disciplines of curriculum studies, pedagogical science, management theory and so forth. The virtue of such disciplines is usually held to lie in their apparently clearer relevance to the actual business of educational policy-making and practice. The price of any such relevance, however, is that it becomes difficult in any serious way to regard such disciplines as genuine branches of theoretical enquiry, as we can see when we examine one or two significant examples. In the first place, we may consider the so-called theory of pedagogy which is all too often presented to student teachers as some sort of scientific enquiry concerned with the observation, description and analysis of so-called teaching styles. But whatever our success in selling the theory of pedagogy to the epistemologically naïve as a paradigm of objective scientifically-grounded enquiry into the nature of teaching, it is really no such thing. In fact, the analysis of teaching styles is a prime example of the constituent–end reasoning characteristic of *phronesis* which involves an exclusively *a priori* conceptual unpacking of what can readily be understood about teaching in pre-theoretical terms. Thus, we do not discover by neutral and disinterested empirical observation and experiment that exposition, enquiry, discussion and activity are the main elements of educationally acceptable instruction (otherwise why do we not also come up with brainwashing?); the point is that these are, on mature reflection, the only features of teaching consistent with the commonly acknowledged moral aims of education.

But, second, we may consider the business of so-called curriculum theory – again often sold to both students and teachers, especially in policy documents from official sources, as a quasi-scientific enterprise apt for the technical solution of certain problems about the content and transmission of education. Again, it is not uncommon for curriculum theory to proceed by the listing of principles of curriculum design and development which will, if faithfully followed (so it is alleged), lead to the construction of the rational scientific curriculum. But, as I have argued elsewhere,[12] such principles of curriculum design as balance, breadth, coherence, continuity and progression are not instruments for the technical solution of problems, but *labels* for problems, which, once again, clearly await exercise of the sort of constituent–end reasoning characteristic of *phronesis* for any meaningful application. It takes little thought, for example, to see that different conceptions of the needs of individuals and society with respect to the purposes of education can issue in quite different curricular interpretations of balance, breadth, coherence, continuity and progression.

In sum, it would seem that both these examples (to which many others, such as competence-based approaches to questions of authority and discipline in education, could be added) of currently fashionable attempts to bypass the traditional academic educational disciplines of sociology, psychology, and so on, in favour of more practically-orientated enquiries focused upon central professional concerns of teaching and curriculum development, acquire greater apparent relevance to educational practice only at some cost to their theoretical credibility. At the heart of all these analyses of teaching, curriculum and other aspects of educational practice lie evaluative deliberation and moral controversy regarding issues which cannot be resolved by the technical application to educational problems of the results of quasi-scientific research and experiment. Indeed, it seems reasonable to suggest that the familiar discourse of curriculum, pedagogy, discipline, and so on, is not in any significant sense a form of *theoretical* discourse. It is nothing short of fraud for self-styled curriculum theorists, pedagogical scientists, management consultants and the like to suggest that the language of learning and instruction, knowledge and understanding, discipline and punishment, and so on – learned at our mothers' knees – expresses precise terms of art belonging to esoteric sciences accessible only to the professionally initiated. Indeed, this seems truly the royal road to the technicist elitism and obscurantism which I believe it is in the best interests of both teachers and those whom they serve to resist. Teachers may properly be expected to communicate with parents on the topic of education precisely in so far as the way of talking about teaching and learning into which they have been professionally initiated is continuous with that in which others have ordinarily been accustomed to speak about the same issues. Of course, teachers may also be expected to converse in a much more informed manner about such issues than parents, just because they have reflected more deeply upon them and have had more practical experience of the formal conduct of education. The mistake to be avoided here, however, is that of assuming that if a matter is not *technical* it must be *simple* – and conversely, that if it is not simple it must be technical; but, clearly, achieving a higher level of educational understanding is not simple – but that is *not* because it is technical.

But there is yet a third time-honoured way of speaking of theories in relation to education: that by which certain approaches to education have come to be classified as traditional or progressive. Is it not basic to a student teacher's theoretical understanding of educational possibilities to grasp the difference between, for example, subject-centred and child-centred theories? However, despite the fact that at least one substantial educational reputation has been established in academia on the basis of an attempt to test empirically which of these two traditionally opposed educational theories best works in practice,[13] it ought to be clear that any such experimental programme can only rest on a mistake about the status of traditionalism and progressivism as educational views. To begin with, as we shall see, it should be clear that traditionalism and progressivism are entirely misrepresented as scientific theories – and so it makes next to no sense to suggest that we might test empirically between them, or to suppose that one or the other might be applied in practice on the grounds of its greater technical effectiveness. Indeed, these so-called educational theories are probably better regarded as shorthand accounts or characterisations of essentially moral or evaluative perspectives, enshrining particular educational aims and specifications of procedures considered constitutive of, or consistent with, such aims.

## Need we be afraid of theory talk?

But might not my denial that traditionalism and progressivism are properly construable as theories be held to turn on a terminological quibble, to rest merely on the observation that they are not *scientific* theories? Why, however, would this rule out our calling them, for example, moral theories? But although we are to some extent free to call them what we like, it behoves us in discussions of such serious matters as education to employ our terms with care; if the discourse of educational theory is precisely to do any useful theoretical work, it is wisest to deploy it in a way which conduces to the best discernible conceptual advantage. Clearly, in this connection, one good reason *for* adopting the more generous or permissive use of the term theory (against which I have been arguing) in relation to any and every educational perspective, is to resist certain political and other philistine approaches to thinking about education which might seek to construe good practice as a matter of uncontroversial common sense – which hardly requires us to bother teachers unduly with high-flown ideas. But an arguably *more* persuasive reason for *resisting* the indiscriminate characterisation of any and every educational view as a theory is in the interests of halting the widespread contemporary drift towards educational technicism. The trouble is that thinking generally of educational perspectives in terms of theories tends inevitably and inexorably towards an understanding of education as a sort of causal process susceptible of explanation in terms of essentially scientific concepts and categories, apt for technical analysis and application in the light of empirical observation and experiment. Indeed, if theories are assumed to embody testable hypotheses which scientific research may prove for once and all true or false, on any assumption that educational claims embody such hypotheses, they might also be shown to be true or false, and all further public debate can then be closed with respect to them.[14]

On the other hand, however, construal of differences between educational views and perspectives in terms of moral or evaluative debate and controversy serves to remind us that far from identifying opposed theories which require testing for their truth or falsity, the distinction between traditionalism and progressivism turns primarily upon tensions between different goals of education, which have equally serious claims on our educational allegiance. Indeed, to understand properly any such distinction is not in the least to suppose that one perspective is true and the other false, but rather to recognise in the requirement to do justice to both authority *and* freedom, instruction *and* discovery, received knowledge *and* personal interpretation, certain intractable evaluative problems about the very nature of our educational goals and purposes. Moreover, it soon becomes clear to student teachers worth their salt, as they progress ever more deeply with their educational studies, that traditionalism and progressivism represent mere caricatures of crucial evaluative questions about the nature of education – mere starting points on the road to clearer thinking about such issues. Hence, it is better to think of professional initiation into educational enquiry as a matter of acquiring capacities to ask ever more complex and sophisticated evaluative questions about that important aspect of human flourishing called education, than to think of it in terms of a search for cut and dried theoretical explanations which might underpin an effective technology of pedagogy – though there are doubtless further problems about the nature of this evaluative enquiry to which we must shortly return.

But there remains another extremely important reason for resisting that conceptual devaluation which may accompany the characterisation of any and every perspective on education as theoretical, and this follows precisely from the point upon which we have continued to insist in this work, that it is not at all plausible to regard all principled understanding of education as anyway theoretical. To begin, overemphasis on the role of theory in our understanding of the nature of education blurs an important distinction between theoretical and *pre-theoretical* or *non-theoretical* understanding. In consequence, however, it also overestimates the value of theoretical studies in professional education for teaching, and seriously underestimates the value of non-theoretical studies. But the importance of a pre-theoretical understanding of education, and of non-theoretical studies, should not be underestimated for a host of reasons. First, as previously indicated, it is against our pre-theoretical knowledge of or intuitions about ordinary human moral association that we are able to test and reject some of the more far-fetched revisionary claims which have been advanced in the name of much so-called educational theorising. Second, however, it is a cause for considerable regret that heavy 'scientistic' emphasis on theoretical studies has led to the virtual exclusion from the professional education of teachers of many kinds of study – which may be of just as much if not more benefit to trainee teachers' understanding of education and teaching, than the social and other scientific theory they are presently constrained to learn. From this point of view, I have long been convinced that students may have far more to gain from a sympathetic reading of Dickens, Orwell and Lawrence in relation to their understanding of education, than they are likely to get from studying Skinner, Bruner or Bloom's taxonomy.[15] In the current climate of both theoretical and anti-theoretical thinking about education, however, one is liable to attract the reputation of an educational Neanderthal for even hinting at this possibility.

# 6

# TEACHING AND COMPETENCE

## Knowledge and professionalism

As has already been noted, notions of competence and competence models of professional expertise have occupied a central place in contemporary debates about the sort of professional preparation which might best conduce to improving the practical efficiency and effectiveness of teachers in schools, and it is worth taking a closer look at the details and difficulties of such models. There can be no doubt that the idea of competence, which began to exercise serious training influence in the UK in thinking about national vocational qualifications,[1] is now generally on the agenda of educational debate[2] and entrenched in official teacher education policy-making in particular.[3] In brief, competence-mongers argue that we need educational field professionals who are not only knowledgeable or well informed about education, but also capable of giving expression to their knowledge: in short, teachers who are *competent* by virtue of intelligent application of educational theory, knowledge and understanding to effective practice. Now since competence is a matter of conduct in accordance with established occupational standards, and conduct appropriate to professional and other occupational practices is publicly observable and accountable, it ought to be possible, in both principle and practice, to specify in detail what counts as competent conduct for purposes of objective professional prescription.

To this end, moreover, usage licenses talk of competence not only with respect to performance in general, but also in relation to particular episodes of performance. A competent joiner exhibits overall mastery of his or her trade in such particular competencies as hammering nails straightly, planing smoothly, sanding finely, and so on. In this case, indeed, it may seem safe to assume that a joiner's overall competence is effectively no more than the sum of those individual items of practical knowledge, skill and ability acquired during apprenticeship. But then, why should we not assume that the same is true of any human enterprise or activity – plumbing, hairdressing, nursing, general medical practice, teaching – for which the question of overall competence is a serious issue? That being the case, it should be possible for us to identify and specify a range of practical competencies presupposed to any satisfactory initiation of trainees into the technology, art or craft of effective teaching. This line of reasoning, of course, also sits fairly well with some modern proposals to make teacher training essentially a matter of extended experience in schools, of learning, as it were, on the job.[4] If the particular competencies which contribute to or constitute overall competence are essentially items of knowing how or practical skill, albeit theory informed, it seems plausible to maintain that these are best acquired in the way practical abilities are invariably acquired: through 'hands on' practice more than academic instruction. Predictably, this is just the route which many teacher education and training policy-makers have been inclined to pursue; one which leads not only to school-based training, but also less directly to intern schemes, mentoring programmes and the like.[5] In addition, though present purposes preclude detailed exploration of the particular difficulties of such strategies, I suspect that many of them follow from much the same basic confusion of the perfectly proper idea of teacher competence with an improper notion of competency which I now propose to examine.

## Concepts of competence: capacities and dispositions

I believe that a fairly discernible ambiguity or equivocation lies at the heart of this confusion. The ambiguity is not, of course, of the ordinary kind whereby a single term has come to connote quite distinct concepts; it is not that the term 'competent' as in 'x is a competent teacher' and 'y was a competent lesson' varies in meaning as, for example, the term 'bank' in 'Toad has just robbed a bank' and 'Ratty lives in the bank' does. From a logical point of view, it might often be quite legitimate to derive conclusions about more general competence from observations of more specific competencies – and vice versa; the connection between the senses in question is sufficiently close to license many general inferences of this nature. But the notion of competence seems nevertheless to be a complex 'family resemblance'[6] concept in which rather diverse dimensions of evaluation are interwoven in intricate ways – in consequence of which the term is liable to have variable implications for different contexts of professional discourse and concern.

Indeed, the main ambiguity or instability of sense to which the term competence is prone is one which it shares with such other key terms of practical discourse as, for example, 'skill' and 'creativity'. First, it is clear that all these terms have significant *normative* content; talk of a person or a performance as skilled, competent or creative, presupposes the application of criteria or standards of accomplishment – some appraisal of agents and actions according to goals of achievement or aspiration. But second, such terms also have more modest connotations of causal efficiency or effectiveness; to speak of an action or item of conduct as skilled or competent may be to assess it only in terms of routine proficiency. The significance for practical discourse of such equivocation is of the very highest moment, however, precisely because these different senses of skill, competence, creativity, and the like, have sometimes been held in some philosophical opposition. We might call the first sense *teleological*; it requires understanding in terms of higher level goals, purposes or, in Aristotelian terms, 'final causes'.[7] The second sense, however, could be called *aetiological* or *causal*, since it courts explanation in the more quantitative or statistical terms of natural science and 'efficient causality'. More familiarly, if more misleadingly, we might think of the former sense as implicated in the prescriptive language of *values*, and the latter as explicable in terms of the descriptive language of *facts* (or, perhaps, events). In this connection, it is noteworthy that the study and discussion of such topics as skill and creativity has of late been hijacked by modern empirical psychologists who are widely given to speaking and writing quite unproblematically of value-neutral 'processes' of skill and creativity. (Just as they also speak, as Wittgenstein insisted we should not, of the 'process' of understanding.[8])

Whatever might be said for or against the psychologist's pursuit of 'creative processes', however, it seems clear enough that both skill and competence have both teleological and causal dimensions – and that these stand in need of reconciling in some conceptually satisfactory way. Indeed, the senses of competence as they might occur in 'x is the more competent commander' and 'y was a competent shot' are sufficiently different to require some account of their relationship, yet sufficiently similar to engender significant confusions about the nature of professional practice in the event of any failure to grasp the complex inferential relations between them. So, how is the more normative sense of competence, implying aspiration to and achievement of higher level goals, related to the more technical sense of causal efficiency and effectiveness? We might first try to characterise the difference between the senses a touch more precisely. The broader evaluative sense by which we assess individuals as more or less successful in realising the aims and goals of a given professional activity – the sense in which we might judge one doctor to be more competent than another – we may call the *capacity* sense. The narrower sense by which the term is used to label particular abilities, or mark episodes of efficient causality with respect to these abilities, we may call the *dispositional* sense.

Broadly speaking, we may regard dispositions as those inherent tendencies or causal powers which enable agents or objects to perform certain specifiable functions, either by training or natural endowment. Dispositions include skills, habits and faculties; we have visual perception by virtue of our physical and biological constitution, we greet by shaking hands as a result of social conditioning, and we read fluently having been taught or trained to do so. The value of dispositional accounts of human and other activities, however, is that they purport to account for the effects of natural and acquired powers by relating their typical manifestations or expressions to (physical or other) features of ourselves or the environment in terms of causal generality;[9] we do thus and so because we have this or that sense organ, or because we have been causally conditioned in this way or that by our physical, social or educational circumstances. Capacities, on the other hand, are more than abilities in any such simple sense of causal power. Unlike dispositions, capacities are not just formed in us by the operations of causality, and hence explicable in terms of (natural or social) scientific law; on the contrary, in so far as they presuppose voluntary and deliberate exercise of principled judgement in accordance with rational knowledge and understanding, capacities are actually epistemically constituted. To construe conduct as expressive of capacity is therefore to regard it as not so much causally conditioned, but more as consequent upon the voluntary rational exercise of this or that sort of (not necessarily scientific) reflection. Hence, there is a certain intelligible (though not literal) sense in which, whereas our dispositions exercise us, it is we who set out to exercise our capacities.

Thus, to whatever extent they are related, there are differences between the competence of capacity and dispositionally conceived competencies; whereas dispositional outcomes are for the most part particular exercises of ability, power and causal effectiveness, the conduct of capacity is expressive of autonomous agency, of voluntary choice and aspiration to the values and standards of higher level goals. Whereas the discourse of disposition turns on considerations of technical effectiveness, that of capacity is more focused on the wise ordering of our affairs according to rational values and principles. All the same, as already noted, these two distinguishable levels of competence talk are inextricably interwoven in the web of our general practice; we naturally and normally regard capacity competence as constituted by dispositional competency, and take dispositional competency to be included in capacity competence. However, in the interests of a coherent account of professional preparation for teaching (and other occupations), I believe that a good deal hangs upon which sense of competence is allowed to gain ascendancy.

## Some views of dispositional competence

It is obvious that teachers and other professionals do require the dispositional competencies which contribute to competence in the capacity sense; the crucial issue is that of how such qualities of practical efficiency and causal effectiveness are to be rightly conceived. First, whatever the temptation to try to reduce the workaday or 'craft' skills of the teacher to some inventory of simple 'single-track' dispositions – abilities to mark registers, set out jotters, write clearly on the blackboard, and so on – any such fine-grained behavioural analysis of educational professionalism seems wildly far-fetched.[10] It is highly implausible to suppose that the practice of education is so devoid of occasions for the exercise of rational judgement and principled decision that it might be carried on by human teaching machines programmed to perform entirely routine tasks. Moreover, those who have argued for some kind of competency analysis of educational professionalism invariably deny that this sort of crude behaviourism is what they have in mind. What they more often appear to be arguing for is a specification of the required craft skills in terms of more complex or principled 'multi-track' or generic dispositions which resist any such simple correlation of precisely determinable behavioural responses with the circumstances of their exercise.[11] Thus, most contemporary competency analyses of professional conduct are inclined to focus on so-called *generic* competences. The goals of professional training at which they aim – effectiveness in the pedagogical and/or managerial spheres of planning, organisation, communication, class control, and so on – are not the mechanical single-track dispositions of old-fashioned behaviourism, but complex multi-track dispositions which are alleged to allow scope for principled and flexible responses to the diverse practical contingencies of teaching. Indeed, advocates of the idea of generic competences sometimes claim support for their more sophisticated conceptions of competency from the empirical scientific researches of cognitive as opposed to behavioural psychology. Despite the rich and varied accounts of generic competence to be found in the literature, however, I believe that the idea is flawed from the outset.

I believe that the idea of generic competencies remains problematic to whatever extent it is intended to warrant the pre-specification and/or discrete itemisation of a range of dispositions apt for characterisation and appraisal first and foremost in terms of causal effectiveness. The difficulty is that any attempt to construe teaching skills in this way seems to leave only two options open – namely, interpretation of dispositional qualities in terms of either *actual* or *potential* conduct. Thus, on the one hand, if one construes the desired dispositions in terms of *actual* conduct, one can hardly avoid the requirement to specify or itemise the intended conduct in terms of hypothetical or law-like connections between types of behaviour and the occasions of their exercise – and, along with it, the familiar language of behavioural outcomes and objectives. But, of course, it was just this kind of reduction of professional competences to an unlimited inventory of occasion-specific dispositions which we sought to avoid by invoking the idea of generic competences. This can only lead us, on the other hand, to construe the sought-for dispositions in terms of *potential* conduct – states or powers 'within' the agent which might allow for behaviour of the required complexity and flexibility. Thus, for example, we might here invoke the familiar educational distinction between process and product, and argue that it is the *process* more than the product which should be regarded as the goal of professional training in dispositional competences.

The difficulties with this suggestion are, however, quite fatal to the idea of generic dispositions. I have argued elsewhere that the distinction between process and product is itself a quite misbegotten one which we would do well to purge entirely from the discourse of educational theory and practice.[12] It would seem to rest, as best one can tell, upon a modern, quasi-scientific, cognitive, psychological restatement of what is arguably little more than a fundamentally indefensible Cartesian psychology. In the present connection, the process–product distinction promises to reap the full grim harvest of confusions by identifying the normative, evaluative or principled aspects of professional judgement with certain highly speculative and dubious 'inner' processes of mind or brain. For one thing, this threatens to put the project of assessing and evaluating the behavioural expressions or outcomes of such processes in serious jeopardy – for how are we to know that this product which we can observe is the expression of that privileged process which, by definition, we cannot? More seriously, however, construing dispositional competences in terms of 'inner' potentialities in the fashion of mental or physical processes merely obtains by fraud what it cannot gain by honest toil. It tries to eat the cake of the causal effectiveness or dispositional sense of competences, at the same time as it holds on to that of capacity competence. In this connection, it cannot be too strongly emphasised that there is a fundamental and irresolvable *tension* between the idea of process – understood as some sort of principled understanding – and any tendency towards the pre-specification or discrete itemisation of professional dispositions in measurable quasi-behavioural terms.

Educational philosophers have long been suspicious (rightly in my view) of any educational discourse of generic abilities and competences,[13] and it would seem that objections to the kinds of general abilities formerly paraded in statements of aims of education[14] apply just as much to the generic competences of more recent professional discourse. For just as educational goals expressed in terms of the promotion of generic abilities of communication and problem-solving can make next to no sense apart from those precise contexts of knowledge and understanding in which such abilities find particular application, so professional educational goals of planning and organisation are barely intelligible apart from the sort of theoretical and evaluative frameworks which would enable us to judge that this behaviour is good rather than bad, effective rather than ineffective, innovative rather than routine, teaching activity. The precise trouble with the notion of a generic competence is that it confuses the idea of a capacity with that of a disposition; it mistakes a condition whose normativity is a complex practical expression of sophisticated forms or knowledge, understanding and value, for one whose normativity is a function of its place *within* a framework of (essentially causal) regularity. It is a conceptually bastard notion, riven with irresolvable contradictions.

It is therefore arguable that any attempt to reduce those highly important and rightly valued professional competencies – that repertoire of practical skills, sensibilities and aptitudes which is indeed required by teachers for the successful prosecution of their profession – to some inventory of discretely specifiable, causally effective dispositions, courts a quasi-behaviourist caricature of the more general capacity sense of professional competence. In short, to try to understand educational professionalism from the direction of discretely specifiable competences is essentially to start from the wrong end of things. Indeed, it is liable to distort not only our grasp of competence as capacity, but also our understanding of competencies as individual practical expressions of capacity.

## Professional capacities and practical knowledge

An alternative strategy for understanding the particular professional competencies required by teachers and others, however, is precisely to start from the end of what might be meant by a capacity sense of professional competence. We might reasonably start from the idea of teacher education and training as a matter of systematic initiation into a particular mode of normative, evaluative or practical discourse concerned with the principled articulation and formulation of educational issues and problems in the light of competing concepts of human flourishing. Such initiation would locate professional competence directly in a serious appreciation of civilised educational practice as a function of informed and responsible professional interpretation of local and particular educational needs and problems in the terms of more general educational principles and purposes. On this view, the emphasis would be more upon equipping trainees with the intellectual resources needed to identify clearly and respond rationally to the practical challenges and problems of education, than upon requiring obedience to some top-down pre-specification of educational needs and requirements. Basically, then, to approach educational competence from the direction of capacity rather than disposition is to begin from the idea of knowledge and understanding, rather than of skill or ability. But does this not simply return us to the problem about professional effectiveness – the problem of the shortfall between knowledge and performance in educational practice – which the talk of competences was designed to overcome? And this is the problem, we may recall, which is invariably laid at the door of too much theory and too little practice in teacher training.

Rightly understood, I believe that it need not – for appreciating that teacher competence (of capacity) is rooted in knowledge and understanding should not commit us to the view that teacher training is a matter of students mastering academic theories, *rather than* practical expertise. For a start, we should remember that the knowledge and understanding characteristic of professional capacities is not of a *primarily* theoretical kind; indeed, as we saw earlier, the notion of competence (in either the capacity or the disposition sense) is basically a concept of *practical* rather than theoretical discourse. Hence, any distinction between capacity and dispositional senses of competence is not well illustrated by the difference between having a knowledge of scientific hypotheses about human behaviour – for example, Piaget's view of child development – and actually helping a child to learn to read in the classroom (as the theory–practice caricature so often goes). On the contrary, it is rather closer to the distinction between acting from an informed, principled and reflective sensibility, and performing efficiently or effectively *according to* some verifiable canon or standard of acceptable performance. Moreover, it should be clear that although these two aspects of competent performances ideally ought to go together, it is certainly possible for them to come apart: on the one hand, a reflective practitioner may nevertheless perform badly in terms of causal effectiveness; on the other, an efficient practitioner may perform routinely well according to the dictates of others, rather than on the basis of individual (principled) initiative. But what might this point come to other than a simple rearguard defence of the view that what student teachers require is a bit of practice with a lot of theory – the familiar academic diet of social and psychological theory of modern professional preparation? Again, however, while I do not wish to devalue the potential contribution of such theory to an educated view of teaching and learning, my point is still to reaffirm the crucial thesis of this work that the knowledge and understanding primarily presupposed to competence in the capacity sense is not theoretical knowledge (in the sense of, say, scientific knowledge), but *practical* knowledge. But it is of just as much importance for understanding the idea of professional competence, to grasp that this practically-grounded expertise should not be misconstrued as a matter of experientially *rather than* intellectually-grounded dispositions either.

Once more the key issue here turns upon the Aristotelian distinctions mentioned in the previous chapters. The distinction between theoretical and practical discourse is less (if at all) a distinction between the mental and the physical, intelligence and action – more a distinction between two rather different kinds of human concern: precisely, a distinction between understanding and explaining the world on the one hand and effecting rational changes and developments in it on the other.[15] In these terms, the rational discourse presupposed to the acquisition of professional educational competence in the capacity sense is fundamentally concerned with the discernment of principles, policies and practices appropriate to the proper conduct of that important dimension of the promotion of human flourishing commonly called education. To this end, of course – since the causal efficiency and effectiveness of our practical attempts to improve aspects of the human condition is unlikely to go well in the absence of some clear understanding of how things stand (sociologically or psychologically perhaps) in the world of human and other affairs – some grasp of theories and evidence will certainly be to the point. But any theoretical knowledge required for sound professional practice is, in a sense, *applied* rather than pure knowledge; it is ultimately required for better conceptualisation of the various ways in which pupil misbehaviour or learning difficulty might stand to be practically addressed or remedied.

But, by the same token, it is equally crucial not to construe any practical knowledge which teachers may require for effective conduct as simply a matter of straightforward *technical* application of the kind of academic theories of learning, motivation, organisation and management which have their source in such 'soft' human science as psychology and sociology. Again, the Aristotelian distinction of practical from theoretical reason is more a substantial distinction between the *aims* and *content* of diverse forms of human enquiry than a distinction between speculative or abstract reasoning, and instrumental or procedural reason; whereas for Aristotle, the goal of theoretical enquiry is distinguished by its concern for the discovery of *truth*, that of practical enquiry is marked more by its concern to secure the *good*. To this end, practical enquiry or deliberation – at any rate, that practical enquiry which Aristotle distinguishes from *techne* as *phronesis* or practical wisdom – has a primarily ethical-evaluative purpose; practical reason is grounded in moral or evaluative discourse, and practical enquiry is basically values-driven. In so far as this is so, the forms of practical understanding which inform the rational, principled and civilised conduct of education are also inevitably grounded in moral and evaluative enquiry.

We have previously noted that this point is of some significance in so far as certain recent educational speculations claiming Aristotelian inspiration have sought to locate professional educational knowledge in the idea of a 'practical (or moral) science'.[16] But the idea of a 'practical science' – which may indeed offer hostages to the fortunes of a misleadingly 'applied-science' technicist or instrumental craft-based view of education and teaching – is certainly foreign to Aristotle. Although Aristotle does distinguish within the idea of practical enquiry between two different forms of practical deliberation – the first (*techne*) concerned primarily with the promotion of technical success, the second (*phronesis*) concerned with evaluative choice and moral conduct – he leaves us in little doubt that the former has generally to be subordinated to the latter in any serious contexts of moral, social or political activity. Moreover, in the *Nicomachean Ethics* Aristotle gives an account of the difference between wisdom and mere cleverness – which is explained precisely in terms of the distinction between moral and instrumental deliberation; technical cleverness is simply knowing how to get what we want, whereas wisdom also entails wanting the right sorts of things in the light of mature reflection on the ends of human flourishing.[17]

Thus, wise or good practice in the sorts of contexts with which we are here concerned is that in which instrumental considerations are entirely secondary to moral considerations; any instrumental deliberation must be led by proper moral-evaluative reflection upon the moral ends of conduct, rather than (though this has its place) by scientific-theoretical research into the empirical processes of education. Furthermore, it is not difficult to see that educational policy and practice is deeply implicated in the kinds of discourse and enquiry in which this order of priority between the moral and the technical obtains. Since it is hardly possible to formulate any serious policies in education in the absence of rational moral reflection upon the nature of human flourishing, deciding what constitutes optimal educational provision for children in terms of their present or future development is an unavoidably moral-evaluative matter. Such reflection is also, moreover, an occasion for the development of *attitudes* of genuine moral commitment to these goals – and this important consideration reinforces yet further the point that professional competence in the capacity sense cannot be reduced to competency in any narrower technical-dispositional sense. It is a crucial component of professional competence to profess and exhibit such moral values as a respect for persons; but failures to show respect for children are seldom *primarily* (if at all) failures of technical skill.[18]

## The moral basis of educational practice

At all events, it seems more reasonable to construe the knowledge and understanding constitutive of both capacity and dispositional senses of professional competence, as a blend of practical enquiry and expertise (basically an amalgam of Aristotle's *phronesis* and *techne*), concerned with the diagnosis and pursuit of what is humanly worthwhile in this or that field of endeavour, than as a form of theoretical enquiry whose goal is truth. At the same time, what is essentially a practical mode of engagement needs also to be distinguished – by virtue of its multiform normative involvement – from mere *doing* (as opposed to thinking). Indeed, we have seen that although the practical expertise of professional competence has both technical and evaluative dimensions, the instrumental is invariably subordinated to the moral in contexts of mature professional judgement and deliberation. It is therefore arguable that the rational educational discourse into which educational professionals require to be initiated in the interests of achieving full professional competence is primarily *neither* a form of theoretical science (though aspects of such sciences may inform it), *nor* a kind of practical science (though technological and other considerations of causal efficacy are also proper educational goals), but a form of ethical or moral enquiry. Put another way, the knowledge which informs the professional expertise of the competent teacher is *neither* the 'knowing that' of empirical theory, *nor* the 'know how' of routine craft skills – however much it may draw upon the one and inform the other – but a form of moral sensibility grounded in an educated appreciation of the broader evaluative as well as the narrower technical dimensions of the educational project.

All the same, the source from which the professional competence of capacity springs cannot but involve thorough initiation into the diverse modes of rational discourse, the plurality of voices, in which the character and quality of educational goods has traditionally been discussed and evaluated. This is likely to include acquaintance with questions about what is of educational value in curriculum terms, what constitutes just and equal educational access, what counts as morally acceptable (and not just technically efficient) pedagogy – as well as some appreciation of those wider social and political issues concerning human well-being in which any talk of educationally improving people (often against their wishes) is invariably implicated. In short, the professional competence of capacity requires nurturing in the soil of those kinds of professional knowledge and understanding which have, by and large, long been pursued in institutions concerned with the education and training of teachers. But what of competence in that more basic dispositional or causal effectiveness sense, which seems to be the object of so much current public concern? Is there still not an unbridged gap between the professional reflection of capacity and the appropriate professional exercise of dispositionally defined skills, and is it not also the case that efficient practice may fail to follow from educated reflection in the absence of careful pre-specification of basic craft skills – as well as provision of systematic opportunities for their rehearsal in schools. Whatever may be required in the way of evaluative reflection on practice, someone might say, teachers still need to acquire the skills which get things done. Thus, to whatever extent we should allow some of the chatter *about* practice to continue in the colleges (or some attenuated version of them), we have still to attend to the serious business of competency training – promotion of causally effective skills and dispositions – in the schools.

If there is anything in what I have tried to argue so far, however, it should be apparent that this objection is deeply confused. For it has been basic to that argument that the technical and instrumental aspects of education – dimensions of causal effectiveness – acquire sense only in the context of wider moral and evaluative considerations, and cannot be coherently separated from them. While this means that all educational projects and endeavours are conceived in the light of *some* vision of human good or flourishing, it also follows that there is widespread dispute and disagreement about educational ends and goals in the teeth of rival conceptions of such flourishing. Such disagreement is also, moreover, susceptible of different forms and degrees. Thus, while there may in some cases be widespread uncertainty or dispute about the means to achieve a largely *agreed* end, there may, in other cases, be considerable disagreement about *both* ends *and* means. In that event, the question of what counts as an appropriate educational means to a worthy educational end will be a doubly disputed one.

Thus, the problem with attempting to pre-specify competences in dispositional terms and conceiving capacity competence as the sum of such dispositional competencies is not just (as it is often said) that this strategy is *reductive* or *fragmentary* of the complexities of professional initiation; it is rather that in so far as it is not possible to understand what would count as an instance of good or bad planning, organisation, presentation or class control apart from some wider normative perspective of the sort presupposed to capacity competence, it is barely *intelligible*. Although we do ordinarily acknowledge certain giddy limits to reasonable professional practice, there is nevertheless ample educational scope for wide (even contradictorily opposed) differences of approach to pedagogy, management and discipline – which, as we shall see, are not obviously decidable by exclusive appeal to what is correct in any value-neutral scientific-technical sense. In short, any case for the educational effectiveness of a particular set of professional competencies over another – unless the items in question are expressed in terms of such generality as to be less than useless for any particular prescriptive purposes – can hardly avoid presupposing some larger *contestable* vision of the overall rational direction of educational endeavour. Indeed, it would nowadays be widely regarded as an elementary mistake of philosophical psychology to try to make sense of particular human dispositions or actions as value-neutral causal processes regardless of the purposes, values and goals of which they are individually expressive;[19] it is therefore hardly unreasonable to suppose that what, among the range of different possibilities, count as defensible instances of good educational practice – of planning, organisation, discipline and the like – may be determined only by reference to this or that more general normative educational perspective. But, then, in the interests of informed critical comparison between rival evaluative possibilities, any adequate professional education will require acquaintance with the widest possible range of educational views in which such possibilities are displayed. This being so, however, it cannot be that capacity competence is understood as the sum or product of dispositional competencies; on the contrary, dispositional competencies cannot be understood apart from the knowledge base of evaluative possibilities which is presupposed to capacity competence.

## Diverse conceptions of the relationship of reason to practice

A predictable objection to my argument so far, of course, is that it still leaves something of a gap between theory and practice of precisely the kind that competency thinking was designed to close. It may still be said that any 'top-down' approach to thinking about professionalism which proceeds from a basis of educational reflection to appropriate educational practice creates an unbridgeable divide which is avoided by the more 'bottom-up' approach from practical competency training to professional reflection. Indeed, it has been expressly claimed that the knowledge required for general competence *is* in principle available via precise specification of craft skills in some more particular dispositional sense.[20] The argument put forward in this chapter suggests that any such attempt to construct capacity from disposition must anyway be incoherent – but I also believe that it is just such a perspective which fuels the vexed educational theory–practice problem. The trouble is that once dispositional competencies are detached from the normative contexts which serve to give them sense, it becomes difficult to see how they might become re-attached. It is this problem which leads to those invariably artificial strategies designed precisely to reintroduce the contexts of understanding needed to give sense or content to dispositional competencies – including the fabrication of *other* dispositions concerned with the mastery of professional knowledge. Thus, for example, competency models of professionalism which commence by specifying certain fundamental craft skills of planning, organisation and discipline will often proceed – when such skills appear mindless, routine or uncreative – to specify further 'skills' of critical evaluation, interpretation and contextual appreciation.

However, just as we earlier noted that a teacher's failure to respect children is normally a failure of moral attitude or value, more than a failure of skill or technique, so it is not so much a failure of *skill* if a teacher cannot locate his or her teaching in a wider context of educational considerations, but a failure of *understanding*. Contextualisation is not a further skill which helps us to secure other practical ends or goals, it is that which assists us to *explain* or make sense of our educational practice. Once free of the idea that general professional competence is simply the sum of particular abilities, that capacity is purely a set of dispositions, we are in a position to see the error of certain sorts of questions which often arise in relation to competency models of teacher training:

questions, for example, about which competencies the school has the responsibility to promote and which are the responsibility of the academy. In fact, to the extent that school and academy *both* contribute to the promotion of the professional competence of capacity – by providing opportunities for rational initiation into modes of educational discourse *and* for the practice of those dispositions which such discourse reveals to be worthy of our best efforts – any college–school division of professional education and training is better construed in terms of common concern with rather different aspects of the *same* task, than in terms of separate concern with *different* tasks. From this viewpoint, it is difficult to comprehend what is so problematic about the idea that a lecture on educational history or sociology, and a given opportunity for a student to practise group work in the classroom, may *equally* contribute to and reinforce a trainee teacher's professional competence of capacity. (Though, of course, there are and always will be perennial questions about whether we have got matters of professional curriculum balance and course coherence precisely right.)

However, any 'bottom-up' model of professionalism which attempts to define capacity competence in terms of dispositional competence *does* give rise to a theory–practice problem, precisely in leaving it less than clear what relevance the various forms of professional educational discourse studied in the academy have to the development of the occupational skills of the teacher. Moreover, I suspect that some such mistake about the relationship of educational theory to practice, grounded in a confusion between different senses of competence, underlies many currently fashionable professional attempts – such as intern schemes and mentoring programmes – to achieve 'reconciliation' of theory and practice via 'partnership' between academy and school. Indeed, it might be argued that schemes with such intent (there are, of course, other reasons for seeking partnership) are vulnerable – like Plato's ill-starred theory of universals – to something like the 'third man' argument of Parmenides;[21] for having, like Plato, construed particulars as separate from the forms in which they partake, the problem now arises of grasping a further relation by which the forms can be linked to the instances. In a not dissimilar way, models of teacher training disposed to the identification of professional competence with the acquisition of a range of hands-on occupational skills of school practice seem to run into a similar problem of explaining how the discourse of the educational academy relates to the particularities of educational engagement which it is the precise business of such discourse to illuminate or explain. For those who are disinclined to sever the Gordian knot of this problem via anti-theoretical denial that academic discourse about professional practice has *any* relevance to actual professional practice, the invention of further agencies (for example, 'mentors') who might serve to link the impotent academic chat to the 'real' work of the field may seem to be the only alternative. What does not seem to be recognised is that any such manoeuvre only shifts the ground or location of the 'theory–practice problem' – without resolving it. But, of course, in so far as the problem appears to rest on a conceptual mistake, it is difficult to see how any practical strategy could resolve it.

Certainly, it would be foolish to deny that knowledge-based conceptions of professional education and training generate *any* problems about how academic professional understanding might find expression – as dispositional competences – in satisfactory practice. All the same, if the present argument is on the right lines, it would appear that these problems are not helpfully characterised as problems about the relationship of 'theory' to practice; they are simply the problems which arise in any profession, trade or craft with respect to how we might teach trainees to utilise or exploit professional wisdom and insight to best effect in actual practical contexts. From this perspective, there is perennial need for teacher trainers to address – as they have always addressed – serious questions about the proper balance of academic studies and opportunities for practical experience; to this end, recent moves towards closer co-operation between college tutors and school supervisors in professional preparation are not to be belittled and, instead, should be greatly welcomed.[22] What should be resisted, however, are more radical attempts to homogenise the roles of all involved in teacher education and training. It is arguable, for example, that the move – in some respects constructive – away from the academic-based teaching courses of the 1960s and 1970s has in some places already gone too far in the direction of nuts-and-bolts conceptions of professional training, focused primarily if not exclusively upon quasi-technicist initiation into craft skills. It has been the main aim of this chapter to show that any such conception of educational professionalism is seriously and dangerously confused. In this connection, moreover, it is only sane and sensible to observe a certain proper traditional division of labour between college tutors and school-based trainers with respect to professional preparation; recognising that as well as receiving proper help and guidance from seasoned practitioners in schools, prospective teachers also require to be exposed to academically rigorous, informed and up-to-date tuition from scholars who are at the leading edge of serious enquiry into conceptual and empirical problems about education. In short, there is clearly room for specialism in professional education and it is unwise to require exactly the same character of professional support from all who are involved in it.

It is worth some re-emphasis, by way of conclusion, that although there may indeed be very real problems about how to design courses in which these different aspects of professionalism come together most effectively, these are not problems about the relationship of theory to practice in the sense of understanding the relevance of professional discourse to professional practice (for what could be clearer than that?). With regard to this, it is also a mistake (the sign, Aristotle would have said, of a bad education) to ask of an academic lecture on the history, sociology or philosophy of education what might be its immediate practical utility for the classroom. It is a mistake precisely because any understanding to be derived from knowledge of an educational discipline cannot and should not be expected to inform or contribute to the professional competence of capacity in the same way that guided experience and opportunities for practice contribute to dispositional competence. Indeed, it is precisely such confusion between different senses of professional competence which leads to reductive attempts to construe educational professionalism exclusively in terms of simple craft skills, and/or to devise quasi-behavioural schedules or checklists for the promotion of such skills in the course of professional training. Indeed, although the dispositional competencies of skill or technique should no doubt be given their proper place in the education and training of teachers, professional competence does not even begin to be exhausted by them, and – as it is a large concern of this work to show – defects of craft skill or technique are by no means the most significant of professional educational shortcomings.

# Part III

# PROFESSIONAL VALUES AND ETHICAL OBJECTIVITY

# 7

# PROFESSIONAL VALUES AND THE OBJECTIVITY OF VALUE

## Subjectivist views of value judgement

In the previous chapters we have sought to show that evaluative deliberation lies at the heart of professional expertise; while it should certainly be acknowledged that teachers need technical skills of communication, management and organisation for effective classroom practice, such skills are meaningful only within larger contexts of professional judgement in which evaluative considerations are paramount. First, as already indicated, it is not just difficult but *impossible* to identify or characterise conduct as expressive of a professional skill of, say, discipline without reference to normative considerations – for what could count as punishment on one conception might not so count on another; but second, by the same token, it is hardly possible to determine on some neutral grounds of technical effectiveness whether a given mode of conduct – for example, corporal punishment – counts as educationally appropriate discipline, for there are no such neutral grounds. Appeal to facts or evidence alone will not tell us which of a range of rival or competing educational strategies or policies is correct, and, since education is a contested concept, we have to acknowledge that there are seriously competing conceptions of education and teaching. On the face of it, this is a very serious difficulty; perhaps *the* most serious conceptual difficulty facing contemporary educational policy-makers. It is, indeed, just a special case of a general problem about value and public policy with which the best post-war minds of moral and social theory have grappled; for if no appeal to hard objective fact is available to help us decide between two alternative – even contradictorily opposed – evaluative perspectives, must it not be the case that our educational judgements

111

are purely *subjective* and that there can be no rational gainsaying of any proposed concept of education? Despite the awesome difficulties of this problem, we nevertheless need to consider in this chapter what might be said by way of countering any such disastrously sceptical conclusion.

First, it should be clear from the previous chapters, and would nowadays I think be generally agreed, that the received empiricist distinction between facts and values is quite untenable. It was because empiricists from Hume to the logical positivists[1] recognised only two kinds of meaningful statements, those expressing logical truisms or rules of usage and those reporting empirical fact, that they denied any rational basis or validity to evaluative judgements – thereby consigning value judgements of moral, aesthetic, religious, political and other kinds to the realms of personal taste or inclination. On this view, to judge that physical exercise is good or smoking bad for health could only be to express a personal predilection, with which others – in the nature of personal evaluation – would be free to disagree. Value judgements, in short, were to be regarded as little more than personal tastes and 'I think that X is good' would be just another way of saying 'I like X'. A familiar objection to this line of argument,[2] however, is that these statements do not appear to mean the same thing – since, for one thing, judgements of goodness appeal to objective grounds in a way that liking does not: hence, it hardly cuts much evaluative ice to justify smoking as such in terms of one's personal liking for it. Indeed, with regard to this very case, though we can hardly deny that people do still disagree about the effects of smoking, debates over the pros and cons of smoking are commonly held to have serious life or death implications to which right reason and sound evidence are all too relevant. Notwithstanding this, however, it is a familiar feature of modern moral philosophy that some of the bitterest attacks on empiricist emotivist construals of value judgement have come from those who wish, in the name of a particular conception of the autonomy of moral judgement, to draw their own distinction between facts and values.[3] There have been those, in short, who would agree that there is hard evidential basis for some value judgements – that, for example, smoking is bad for one – but who are also inclined to deny that any empirical evidence could be relevant to a person's sincere moral commitment to the sanctity of marriage or the right to choose abortion. Thus, it has been held by many post-emotivist, moral non-cognitivists, that although there may be genuine reason in the realm of moral judgement, it is not a form of reason which holds out much hope of evidence-based adjudication in the event of moral disagreement.

## The historicist turn

What seems to have gained ascendancy of late, however, is a conception of evaluation which precisely rejects the assumption – common to both emotivists and prescriptivists – that there is any genuine distinction to be observed between factual and evaluative discourse. Indeed, the view that there are no objective 'value-free' facts seems to have followed in the wake of a more general neo-Hegelian and/or pragmatist thesis – one which very much lies at the heart of so-called 'postmodern' perspectives – about the essential *interplay* of theory and observation or 'evidence'. For present purposes I must be all too brief with a very complex philosophical doctrine which has, to my mind, had profoundly debilitating consequences for recent educational philosophising. Indeed, it seems to me that fairly widespread acceptance among educational and other philosophers[4] of half-baked notions about the impossibility of theory-free observation or value-free fact – ideas which have often been held to preclude any possibility of neutral rational adjudication between socially or culturally constructed conceptions of education (or whatever) – is cause for great current educational philosophical concern. Moreover, since, like most other influential philosophical theses, the general idea of the inextricability of theory and observation, value and fact, appears to be a fairly rich stew of important insight and conceptual error, my use of the term 'half-baked' is more descriptive than abusive. It may be much to the present purpose, then, to try to salvage some of what is true from what is less so about this idea.

Generally, the notion of the theory dependence of observation is a philosophical descendant, via German Idealism and North American pragmatism, of Kant's crucial point against his empiricist contemporaries that there can be no such thing as *unconceptualised* experience – on the grounds, in Kant's own words, that 'intuitions without concepts are blind'.[5] This idea is nothing less than fatal to any unreconstructed empiricist attempt to found knowledge on brute data of experience – unconceptualised phenomenological 'givens', at once basic to but also uncoloured by the received categories of human thought. Briefly, Kant attacks the questionable empiricist assimilation of the distinction between objectivity and subjectivity to that between 'things in themselves' and the appearances of things, an assimilation which, amongst other things, inevitably leads to scepticism concerning knowledge of external reality. On the empiricist view, since we can have only ostensibly 'psychological' acquaintance with the appearances of things, there is an important sense in which knowledge cannot be objective. Kant's own distinction between objectivity and subjectivity, however, cuts across the distinction between 'things in themselves' and their appearances. He argues that although (theoretical) knowledge is indeed limited to our experience of things – as empiricists maintain – the possibility of conceptualising experience via rational categories of object and subject, cause and effect, and so on, is nevertheless presupposed to the very idea of experiential *knowledge*; in short, if experience of reality was entirely a matter of subjective impressions in the way some empiricists seemed to suppose, we could have no *knowledge* of it. More strongly, indeed, Kant shows that the empiricist case cannot even be stated without covert reliance upon the very distinction between the objective and the subjective to which empiricists are not, on their own premises, entitled. All the same, for metaphysical reasons, Kant is unable to abandon the idea that there are 'noumena' or things in themselves – which cannot be *known* 'in themselves' – that is, other than through our experiences of them: these are after all the things to which we refer whenever our statements about the world are true. However, the subsequent abandonment of the metaphysical 'thing in itself' by Kant's German Idealist successors[6] precipitates the collapse of Kantian conceptualism into a kind of *collectivist* subjectivism which licenses the relativisation of human knowledge to particular socio-culturally constructed value perspectives. In short, this opens the possibility of more or less complete assimilation – via a bizarre inversion of empiricist priorities – of fact to value. This does not necessarily, of course, lead to any *relativist* rejection of the notion of objective truth as such; there remains, to be sure, a familiar Idealist conception of *absolute* truth as a kind of ultimate (God's eye) synthesis of the theses and antitheses of rival ideologies. But it does give rise to a deeply ambivalent perspectivalism, which is, and has been, susceptible of radically relativist interpretation in 'post-empiricist' epistemology.

Moreover, any such Idealist notion of truth must be more a matter of theoretical or conceptual *coherence* than of empiricist correspondence to fact, since, of course, there are no objective 'facts' (in the required sense) to which our perspectives or theories might correspond – and a coherentism very much along these lines has exercised considerable influence in modern pragmatist philosophy of science. Hence, in his own classic rejection of the empiricist distinction of truths of experience from truths of logic – and, by implication, observation from theory – the high priest of modern pragmatism, W.V.O. Quine, famously observes that 'theories face the test of experience not singly, but as a body'.[7] Like post-Kantian Idealists, then, Quine and other modern pragmatists reject the classical empiricist notion that there are any brute unconceptualised data upon which scientific theory construction might go to work, and they subscribe to a general (now widely conceded) *fallibilism* concerning scientific and other human knowledge, which insists that it is a mistake to think of knowledge as fixed, final or immune to critique or overturn. From this viewpoint, the most up-to-date developments of any given branch of human knowledge at any given time can represent no more than an incomplete, partial and inadequate understanding of things which fresh discoveries are liable to overthrow; in one famous version of this view,[8] one should regard classical empiricists as having been wholly mistaken in exalting verifiability as a criterion of genuine knowledge, in so far as it is fundamental to knowledge claims counting as scientific that they are in principle refutable. Do not views such as these show conclusively that there can be no distinction between evidence and theory, or fact and value?

There can be little doubt of the influence of pragmatist as well as Idealist ideas on postmodernism, or that the arguments of Quine and other modern pragmatists have frequently been invoked in support of more radical and relativist forms of postmodern epistemological scepticism. But aside from the consideration that Idealist and pragmatist views clearly undermine the classical empiricist conception of human knowledge as a matter of value-free theory construction on the basis of brute experiential data, it is very doubtful whether they support the more sceptical postmodern conclusions which seem sometimes to have been drawn from them. To be sure, while pragmatist critiques of the analytic-synthetic distinction are not entirely at odds with the spirit of Kant's account of the crucial interplay of the sensory and conceptual in empirical evidence, pragmatist questioning of the very distinction to which Kant appeals in explaining that interplay does seem distinctly more problematic. But Quine does also speak (again famously) of theory as 'underdetermined' by *evidence* – of the consistency, that is, of any given set of observations with any number of theories – a claim which is hardly at one with denial of *any* distinction between theory and evidence or observation.[9] In the long run, however, it is probably wiser to take the strictures on traditional empiricism of Quine and others as addressed to fairly rarefied theoretical issues, and as having few direct implications for more workaday distinctions between theory and evidence. From this viewpoint, there would seem to be little in mainstream pragmatism which should incline us to hold postmodernly that when we speak of there being three polar bears in Edinburgh zoo, of these bears being mammals, and of their having come into the world by way of certain biologically explicable reproductive processes, these are just socially constructed fictions or narratives which do not depend for their truth or falsity upon how things *actually* are in world.

## Facts and values: evidence and theory

But, in any case, there would appear to be several connected confusions in any postmodern denial of the distinction between evidence and theory – and, as a special case of this, between fact and value – which follow from too easy movement from the Kantian truism that there can be no unconceptualised experience to neo-Idealist or post-structuralist[10] conceptions of knowledge as socially constructed cultural perspectives or 'narratives' with no objective or cross-perspectival evidential bases. Indeed, it is arguable that widespread blurring of a crucial distinction between *different* senses in which we claim knowledge is entirely due to a mistaken reading of the Kantian truism. To begin with, ordinary discourse of human knowledge recognises a difference between *explanation* and *description*: on the one hand, talk of knowledge of quantum physics or Darwinian evolution primarily concerns theories or explanations of this or that realm of experience which stand to be overturned or falsified by better *understanding*; on the other hand, talk of knowing that there are three polar bears in Edinburgh zoo expresses a claim which stands to be true in so far as there are just three bears in the zoo which are polar. Postmodern scepticism often seems to assimilate the second to the first of these senses or levels of knowledge. Why? Because the Kantian truism that there is no unconceptualised experience – or, by way of the usual elaboration of this truism, the claim that we describe or classify experience in accordance with our interests and preferences (so that there might be other preference-related ways of classifying experience) – is taken to mean that received classifications are really arbitrary constructs or hypotheses rather than descriptions of how things are. But the Kantian truism entails no such consequence. First, it hardly follows that because there are different interest-related ways of describing experience that there is no objective reality to which these different descriptions purport to refer; the fact that Inuit have more words in their language for 'snow' and can make more judgements about snow than those from other cultures does not reduce facts to values or observations to theories, it merely shows that more (survival-related) facts or truths are available to Inuit observation (and presumably, with practice, ours too). Second, it just as certainly doesn't warrant substituting socio-cultural consensus for objective evidence as a criterion of the truth of our descriptions of the world; an as yet undiscovered Amazonian tribe who described an aeroplane as a large bird, or regarded a lump of wood as an intelligent being to which young virgins should be sacrificed, would be simply and demonstrably *wrong* in their descriptions (and consequently their explanations) of these things – primarily because the world is simply *not* as they take it to be.

None of this, incidentally, is at odds with modern epistemological *fallibilism*; elimination of false Amazonian scientific or theological views does not imply that even the pick of our current scientific theories is a fixed and final product. But it does reveal something of the topsy-turvy world of postmodern reflection. Notice, for example, the complete nonsense that postmodern assimilation of evidence to theory or fact to value makes of any understanding of *evaluation*. In arguing for reduction of description to evaluation in human understanding postmodernists or other relativists will advert to the way in which different preference-related interests are exhibited in different grammars or vocabularies; the complete relativity or incommensurability of human conceptual schemes is explained by the diversity of interests actually apparent in the different languages of humankind. But far from eroding any common-sense distinction between fact and value, any such explanation of conceptual difference actually presupposes it; for how could one possibly explain local differences of interest (such as that of the Inuit in snow) other than by reference to the different circumstances in which people find themselves which occasion those interests – and this is indeed the way that postmodern anthropology routinely goes. As naturalist critics of prescriptivism argued many years ago,[11] whatever is good is not so because I am disposed to commend it – on the contrary, I am disposed to commend it because it is good; going to the dentist in the event of tooth decay is not to be considered good because it expresses an interest of mine – there is clearly a real enough sense of 'interest' here in which it may do no such thing – it is good because there are painful facts about tooth decay which would give any sentient human a *reason* for seeking treatment.

Notwithstanding the important contributions of neo-Hegelians, pragmatists and other non-realists to our understanding of the errors of classical empiricism, then, it is reasonable to suppose that our ordinary intuitions about the nature of theories, values, facts and observations are in good philosophical order: that pre-theoretical observations are what our theories seek to explain, and that facts (including observations and interests) are what our moral and other values are indeed based upon. What critics of empiricism mostly seem concerned to defend is the insight of Kant's first *Critique* that there is no such thing as *concept-free experience*; this is *not*, however, the same as the ideas that there are no *theory-free observations* or *value-free facts*. Moreover, despite that the mistaken conflation of these distinctions leads inexorably to the pernicious moral constructivism, idealism and relativism which so deeply infect postmodern thought, there is no incompatibility between the impossibility of *concept-free experience* and the possibility of more or less correct description of the world. Thus, in terms of ready-to-hand conceptual resources, it can be in Aristotle's basic sense of truth (where 'to say of what is that it is not, or of what is not that it is, is false; whereas to say of what is that it is, or of what is not that it is not, is true'[12]) quite *uncontroversially* true that there are three polar bears in Edinburgh zoo, they are mammals and they have come into being via certain biologically explicable reproductive processes. Moreover, once the postmodern gulf between thought and the world is bridged via the common-sense idea that our concepts directly identify and describe *real* features of an external world – rather than socio-culturally constructed fictions – the way is clear to a more apt view of the relationship of facts to values. In brief, it becomes clear given the way the world is why human beings have largely the values they do – why courage is valued in a hazardous world, why co-operation is prized where projects are beyond the skill and strength of single individuals, why honesty is needed in the interests of social co-operation, and so on.

But why the present necessity, impatient readers might ask, for this apparent detour around the philosophical complexities of the objectivity or otherwise of truth and value; what could be the possible implications of this issue for questions of teacher professionalism? Clearly, it matters in the case of education and teaching for at least two substantial reasons. First, any radical epistemological scepticism about the possibility of accessing truth through reason threatens to undermine the intelligibility of education, ordinarily understood as a matter of liberating minds from ignorance and irrationality; if there is really no such thing as objective truth to be had, even in principle, then education – understood as anything more than equipping people with useful practical skills through hands-on apprenticeship – is simply sophistry and delusion. Indeed, radical calls for the de-professionalisation of teaching often seem to be inspired by some such (probably neo-Idealist) epistemological scepticism, according to which 'bourgeois education' is really just a matter – via the promotion of 'knowledge' of no real objective value – of the exploitation of one class by another.[13] But such considerations concerning the content of education have also more *formal* implications for any understanding of teaching as a professional activity. To conceive education only in terms of diverse practices of social or vocational initiation, developed in response to local need, is to offer little or no objective rational basis for regarding teaching as a matter of principled obedience to more general *professional* imperatives. Radical epistemological scepticism of postmodern and other kinds undermines not just the content of teaching, but – when all is regarded as a matter of contingency and particularity – any notions of professional obligation with respect to universal educational entitlement. As we saw earlier, however, it is significantly, perhaps primarily, because we can make sense of universal *rights* (however particularly interpreted in practice) to freedom from injustice, disease and ignorance, that we can also make sense of professional legal, medical and pedagogical *duties* or imperatives with respect to universal promotion of law, health and education.

We also need to be reasonably clear about the relationship of value objectivity to universality; it is not, for example, that certain values – professional values – have to be *universal* in order to be *objective*, but that there has to be value objectivity if we are to regard some moral or professional values as universal. For example, we may reasonably suppose that there are objective grounds – based, that is, on considerations other than personal taste or caprice – for finding heart surgery humanly valuable; it is on this basis that we might proceed to argue that it is a general duty of medical practice to provide such surgery where and whenever required as a matter of professional principle. The point is that there could be no universal duty to promote the good celebrated in a given human value unless that value expressed something more than a subjective preference. However, the idea of professional duty does not automatically follow – without further argument – from the objective worth of some item or activity; it does not follow from the apparent objective human convenience of private transport, that the car industry has a duty to provide every citizen with their choice of automobile as a matter of right. What is needed to show that some, but not all, objective values deserve general promotion via professional provision is a case to the effect that the values in question embody some general human good which it would be *unjust* to extend to *some* and *deny* to others. I think it would be widely agreed that there is at least a *prima facie* case for such professional provision in the realms of medicine and law which purport to answer universal human needs for health and justice, the lack of which is liable to imperil human life in a way that auto-deficit would not.

What, however, of the possibility of grounding the professionality of teachers in universal educational values? At first sight, as previously observed, it would appear that education performs well on this score; one might reasonably suppose there to be as much of a universal need for freedom from ignorance as for freedom from disease or injustice. However, to the extent that it is less easy to identify a case of general educational deficit which some unitary conception of education might be supposed to make good, the issue is not quite as clear-cut as it might first appear. For if, in the medical example, every child needs freedom from illness and disease, what could there be of a comparable order in the educational case that *every* child needs? It might be thought that this question rests on simple logical confusion; for is the point not just that *particular* young people have individual needs and should therefore not all be treated the same? And have we not already conceded that not all objective values are universal, and that even universal values are liable to particular instantiation? Hence, to hold that all have a right to health is not to embrace the absurdity that all should receive the *same* medical treatment – for any sane medical treatment will obviously be tailored to each according to his or her personal needs. Can we not, then, say the same of education? The difficulty is, however, that any duty to provide medical care – whatever care is required in the particular case – is owed to *everyone* by virtue of a common human condition, irrespective of nationality, culture and creed; by contrast, it is not clear that anything is *educationally* owed – irrespective of nationality, culture and creed – to everyone by virtue of a common humanity. To see this we need to revisit the issue of the relativity or otherwise of values, via closer attention to the different *grounds* of human value.

## Local and universal value

Previous discussions have clearly raised serious problems for any subjectivist conception of values *tout court*. Indeed, I am inclined to regard *any* idea of the *subjectivity* of values as little more than a contradiction in terms, since, for a preference to count as a value at all, it would seem necessary for it to be based on reasons or considerations which go beyond the realm of personal predilection. In view of this, I have elsewhere characterised a value as a rational or *principled preference* which one would normally give *reasons* or grounds for entertaining; since I have no reason for preferring strawberries to raspberries, it would be odd to number such a preference among my values, as distinct from, say, my tastes. Indeed, I suspect that the main source of error on this issue is confusion of *subjectivity* with the rather different notion of the *personal*. But I can clearly have reasons for valuing things which are at once both personal *and* objective. I may, for example, treasure a particular interest or item of property for reasons of personal association which are not shared by others; but it would be appropriate to speak of my *valuing* such objects, or to include personal regard for them among my values – as it would not be so in the case of my liking for strawberries.

But even if we concede that there is something a touch oxymoronic about talk of subjective values, it should also be evident by now that there can be *different* reasons for holding, or different levels at which we can hold, values of one or another sort. Indeed, one may subscribe individually or personally to a value which one would not require anyone else to share; one may subscribe as a group member to values which one is only entitled to expect other members of that group to share; or one may endorse a value which one would want to be shared by every other human individual – irrespective of partisan affiliations. Moreover, it should also be apparent that although personal, communal and universal reasons for holding a given value are by no means mutually *exclusive*, they need not go together. Thus, a person might embrace a particular religious faith for purely personal reasons; he or she approves of the ethical values of that faith, gains considerable aesthetic satisfaction from attending services, derives much spiritual solace from its sacraments or devotions, and so on. Nevertheless, any benefits thereby derived are regarded as entirely personal, and there is no expectation that anyone else, even co-religionists, should value the faith for the same reasons that the private devotee does. It may even be held, perhaps under the influence of phenomenological or existentialist theology,[14] that no one *could* share anyone else's precise experience of religious faith.

On the other hand, however, it is possible – perhaps not uncommon – for people to follow a particular faith on largely communitarian grounds, and to accept the rules of religious engagement as one might largely accept the rules of club membership. Certainly the ritual practices of some traditional religions would appear to be observed by their followers in some such way; it is likely, for example, that at least *some* contemporary Jews observe Judaistic practices more in the spirit of cultural affiliation and loyalty than belief in the God of the Old Testament – and the same may be true of many Catholic, Protestant and other Christians living in the largely secular conditions of such post-colonial and immigrant societies as the United States. Since a sense of individual identity is for many people associated with cultural affiliation, it may be the only recourse for individual inhabitants of societies lacking common cultural traditions to seek the kind of association afforded through loyalty to ancestral religious traditions, even if one is no longer persuaded of the literal truth of the associated religious doctrines. At this level, of course, it is open for such socio-cultural 'believers' to criticise other club members for any lapses into religiously heterodox views – but no real question need yet arise of criticising non-believers for their non-adherence to the faith. But now, of course, any such faith of cultural affiliation may be contrasted with that of those who believe that their religion is actually *true*: those who hold that it is proper to regard their faith as applicable in principle to all human agents irrespective of their personal predilections, particular social circumstances or current cultural affiliations.

## The spectre of relativism

This, however, may well enough serve to show how personal, sociocultural and unconditional reasons for subscribing to a particular value may come apart – with potentially problematic consequences for theorising the professional basis of educational practice. Indeed, it is primarily the possibility of subscribing to a given value *exclusively* on socio-cultural grounds which gives purchase to the idea of moral relativism. For reasons already indicated, it is extremely implausible to hold that human values are *entirely* relative to particular cultural circumstances. Moreover, we can make sense of the idea of human rights only in so far as there are human needs and interests which cut across differences of cultural perspective or affiliation. In this connection, indeed, it is rare for regimes accused of human rights abuses to defend the murder, torture, enslavement, starvation or unjust imprisonment or execution of their subjects on the grounds that they subscribe to an alternative set of moral commitments to slavery and torture; it is more common for them to deny that such abuses are taking place, or that what they are doing actually counts as torture or murder. Clearly, again, any talk of general medical or legal obligations to promote physical well-being and basic liberty derives much of its sense from the idea that there are universal human rights to these conditions of human flourishing. The best case for moral relativism, however, arises in relation to practices which we might find abhorrent from our point of view as Christians, liberal democrats or whatever, but which other socio-cultural constituencies might regard as constitutive of their human identity. It is well known, for example, that some religious cultures – home-grown as well as exotic – endorse views of the proper place of women in the divine order of things, which secular liberal feminists regard as both unjust and offensive. Moreover, even in such an ostensibly civilised and enlightened liberal polity as the United States, many democratically agreed state laws sanction the death penalty as just punishment for murder or other serious crimes of violence – a practice which is liable to be regarded as barbaric by other states or societies.

Even in such cases, of course, one need not despair of rational ethical arbitration of these opposed perspectives. It is likely, for example, that many culturally enshrined gender inequalities are more the hand of man than God, and are therefore objectionable on broadly the same moral (and, more than likely, theological) grounds which should lead us to reject torture and slavery. I also believe it possible to argue rationally that the death penalty (or, relatedly, corporal punishment in schools) is quite incompatible with any notion of civilised polity. All the same, it seems hard to deny that cultural differences do sometimes reflect morally significant contrasts between quite diverse, in some cases contradictorily opposed, conceptions of human flourishing. In this connection, to whatever extent sincere, civilised and decent Catholics, Jews, Marxists, Muslims, secular humanists, and so on, may actually agree in rejecting slavery, race hatred and political oppression in the name of social justice, it is also clear that they often differ considerably with respect to their reasons for finding such moral evils universally intolerable – precisely in the light of rival conceptions of human flourishing. Moreover, one of the principal ways in which rival conceptions of flourishing are liable to show up is in different views of human growth and human development, specifically in different conceptions of freedom and discipline in the education of young people. From this point of view, one can hardly fail to notice that general public, political and professional aspirations to common universal educational provision have ever been compromised by calls for alternative forms of schooling, respecting different and diverse conceptions of human growth and fulfilment. Not only have such different British religious constituencies as Catholics and Protestants, Jews and (more recently) Muslims, sought separate educational provision, but the independent education sector has long been host to progressive educational experiments – often at serious odds with the received values of conventional state schooling.

In short, the issue of cultural diversity must affect questions of education and the professionality of teaching, in so far as educational provision is liable to be compromised by such diversity in a way that medicine or law are not; whereas nationality, culture or creed are arguably of little or no concern to a doctor seeking to cure a child of a particular ailment, such considerations may be relevant to educational provision. At any rate, one's moral sympathies may in this respect lie more easily with a doctor who overrode a parental decision to deny a child a blood transfusion on religious grounds, than with a school which refused to allow some of its pupils to wear turbans or trousers. Indeed, what could be more striking than that education has often been defined – albeit in diverse senses – as 'the transmission of culture'. In this connection, irrespective of whether 'culture' is construed *descriptively* as all the customs and practices which constitute a given form of life, or *evaluatively* as the highest achievements of human culture – it is arguable that a non-contingent connection between education and culture raises very real difficulties for any attempt to ground education and teaching in professional obligation with regard to universally specifiable human need.

The idea of education as culture transmissive – in either the descriptive or evaluative senses of this label – is associated with what we might broadly term educational *traditionalism*. The descriptive interpretation is associated with those kinds of consensual and structural functionalist sociology which cast education in an essentially socially reproductive role.[15] On such views, it is the task of teachers in schools to induct each new generation into the knowledge, values and beliefs of previous generations. Whilst this is an essentially conservative view of the role of education, it is also, as we have already seen, susceptible of relativist and radical interpretations. First, if it can be shown – as sociology and anthropology have from the start apparently sought to show – that human societies and cultures embrace markedly different (if not actually mutually contradictory) beliefs and values, then the process of culture transmission is liable to be substantially, if not formally, different in different human localities. In that case, since what is educational sauce for the goose is not necessarily so for the gander, we seem stuck with one kind of relativism. But second, without seriously questioning the common assumption that it is the main business of education to equip individuals for effective functioning in their actual social and economic circumstances, one may require that educational provision should continually adapt to changing economic circumstances and developing technologies. To this extent, although radicals are invariably critical of the conservatism of much traditional and conventional education, their complaints are mainly directed at the outmoded curricula that they take to be characteristic of traditional education and against the hegemonic exploitation which they take to be an inevitable concomitant of such curricula. But, notwithstanding this, radical conceptions of education as essentially concerned with assisting effective functioning in the interests of survival are not at all inconsistent with a horses for courses educational relativism – which is also, as previously seen, uncongenial and unsympathetic to notions of educational professionalism.

A more philosophical version of the view that education is essentially a matter of cultural initiation is mainly associated with such nineteenth-century founding fathers of liberal education as Newman and Arnold; it was Arnold who gave us the 'high church' definition of education as the transmission of 'culture' understood precisely as 'the best that has been known and said in the world'.[16] Moreover, despite its unashamedly normative character, this evaluative conception of culture was clearly intended to ground a universal non-relativistic notion of education as a matter of initiation into forms of *objectively* valuable knowledge, understanding and appreciation. The basic idea of this version of educational traditionalism is that the growth of human culture is measurable by reference to discernible progress in a range of fields of civilised enquiry and endeavour. The culture with which it is the task of education to acquaint at least those individuals capable of benefiting from it is the very flower of human philosophical, artistic, scientific, technological, moral and spiritual achievement. This would for the most part mean – since human achievement seems to have been for the nineteenth-century fathers of liberal education mainly, if not exclusively, European, bourgeois, male, Caucasian achievement – acquainting young people with the philosophy of Plato, Aristotle and Kant, the science of Newton and Galileo, the painting of Rembrandt and da Vinci, the drama of Aeschylus and Shakespeare, the poetry of Milton and Keats, the religion and morals of the Old and New Testaments, and so forth.

At this point, it is important to recognise that the nineteenth-century liberal traditionalists did not think of acquaintance with culture so conceived as an initiation into a final and finished product; on the contrary, one purpose of such initiation was to provide the point of departure for able individuals to develop living traditions of philosophical, scientific, artistic, moral and spiritual traditions yet further. It is possible that this point emerges a little more clearly in the liberal traditionalism of post-war analytical philosophers of education who – able to draw on modern structuralist and use-theoretical accounts of enquiry and understanding – placed the educational emphasis more on the mastery of different sorts of rational 'grammar'.[17] For the new liberal educationalists, what mattered educationally was less acquaintance with a particular culturally significant *content*, and more the process of initiation into those ways of making sense of the world allegedly enshrined in logically distinct forms or modes of rationality. In one famous version of such a story, these forms – the scientific, the mathematical and logical, the interpersonal, the artistic and aesthetic, the moral, the religious and the philosophical (or some variant of these) – were alleged to number seven or eight.[18] Moreover, the emphasis on cultivation of *modes of rationality*, rather than specific socio-cultural achievements, seems to have been at least partly intended to forestall complaints to the effect that liberal traditionalism was tantamount to rationalisation of a particular ideological agenda. It could be argued that it was perfectly acceptable educationally for a different history or set of moral virtues to be taught in some other socio-cultural context – just so long as that history or morality conformed to the basic universal grammar of historical or moral understanding.

All the same, complaints along these lines could not be held off for long. Indeed, radicals and Marxists claimed from the outset that curricula of forms of knowledge were little more than expressions or instruments of class oppression and domination; in particular, they deplored that traditionalist exaltation of the academic over the practical and vocational which all too often seemed to be a hallmark of such curricula. Moreover, yet more damaging theoretical influences were already at work in those pragmatist ideas which, through their influence on official British primary education policy-making in the mid-1960s,[19] seriously questioned the purported logic of traditional academic distinctions between kinds of rational enquiry. However, as the attentions of new generations of post-war educational philosophers have strayed beyond the analytical tradition to take on board ideas from post-structuralism, pragmatism, critical theory, and so on (and as analytical philosophy has itself felt the impact of such influences), the very assumption that there might be *universal* canons of rationality which might serve to ground some monolithic conception of educational professionalism has seemed increasingly open to question. Hence, as already noted, it seems nowadays more or less taken for granted in some influential educational philosophical quarters – moving well beyond the fallibilism which says that universal or absolute truths are unavailable to humans in their epistemically fallen state to a denial that there might be any universal or absolute truths to be known – that there is little more to be humanly had in the way of knowledge than rival cultural myths or narratives.

## The communitarian threat to educational professionalism

It is arguable, once again, that much thinking of this kind rests on a number of fairly simple philosophical confusions. At the same time, it is also clear that some of it is little more than a garbled version of a position, the new communitarian critique of liberalism, which is worth closer examination in this context, especially since one of its leading spokesman, Alasdair MacIntyre, has explicitly explored the educational implications of communitarian ideas in a number of significant essays.[20] Thus, among other things, new communitarians reject what they take to be ahistorical liberal conceptions of human knowledge – the proverbial 'view from nowhere' – in favour of an epistemology of cultural inheritance indexed to local practices of identity constitutive (moral and other) kinds. Communitarians, then, regard the 'thin' procedural principles of liberal morality as incapable of doing justice to the rich complexities of human evaluative life, and as serving only to obscure the depth and diversity of moral commitments. With particular respect to education, MacIntyre has argued: first, that the social and cultural circumstances of modernity *generally* preclude the possibility of a common education – or 'educated public' – of the kind envisaged by post-war analytical educational philosophers;[21] and second, that since there can be no 'shared public morality of commonplace usage' there cannot *in particular* be any common moral education of the kind envisioned by post-war liberal educationalists and moral structuralists.[22] On the surface, these conclusions may seem to have devastatingly relativist consequences for education, as well as for teacher professionalism. But since they also seem susceptible of diverse interpretations, it is also worth asking whether (or in what sense) MacIntyre is any kind of relativist.

Certainly, if MacIntyre's thesis should turn out to be a version of the previously noted postmodern epistemological scepticism about the very possibility of truth, then I think that it should be dismissed as unworthy of further serious attention. Although such scepticism fatally undermines any concept of education whatsoever, it is also deeply incoherent; for, as already argued, it is hardly possible to make any sense of human evaluation at all, even of alternative or rival evaluations, other than via reference to the basic conditions of human weal and woe to which such evaluation needs to be conceived as a response. However, MacIntyre's own repeated defence of truth gives us sufficient reason to suppose that he would reject any such radical epistemological scepticism. Moreover, although MacIntyre's idea of truth seems to be a basically neo-Hegelian notion of synthesis of the theses and antitheses of rival traditions – an idea dangerously liable to collapse into the conceptual idealism of social construction – it is nevertheless ostensibly consistent with the idea that the pursuit of truth is a primary educational goal. In that case, the point behind emphasis on rival traditions would be that any such pursuit of truth cannot but start from the kinds of substantial epistemic and/or evaluative commitments which utterly preclude any liberal aspirations to context-free value-neutrality. Be that as it may, the idea that some teachers will be Roman Catholic and others will be secular-liberal seems no more preclusive of a common conception of educational professionalism than the notion that some doctors are Muslims and others secular humanists precludes a general account of medical professionalism.

Still, previous discussions of objectivity and value are suggestive of another way of interpreting the rival traditions thesis which does appear to have problematically relativist implications for education and teacher professionalism. On this view, it would not be necessary to deny the possibility of objective truth as such, and education might still be conceived as, at least in part, a matter of assisting people to acquire correct information or master useful skills. However, what would give point and poignancy to talk of rival traditions of education would be: first, the idea that there could be no *common* framework of values and virtues – worth calling *education* – within which such information and skills might be communicated or transmitted; second, the thought that the only sense we could make of a specifically *educational* framework of values and virtues would be one which enshrined particular ideals of human formation which were matters of local preference in the previously noted sense of 'club membership'. Thus, without in the least denying objective truth, one might hold that *education* is less a matter of information and skill transmission, more a matter of initiation into a particular lifestyle embodying particular virtues, values and developmental norms, and that this must therefore place education beyond the reach of universal professional prescription. For example, it is clear that widely different notions of freedom and discipline – indeed of what it is to learn as such – are enshrined in liberal and religiously-grounded concepts of education. Moreover, in so far as this is so, it is not unknown for *non-believers* to send their children to religious schools entirely for the character formation such schools are thought to provide. Of course, people do argue endlessly about the way children should be brought up: you accuse me of being too permissive, I accuse you of being too strict. But if child rearing is just a matter of free choice among alternative *lifestyles*, and if there are no *objective* grounds upon which we might decide questions of correct upbringing, then any talk of professional educational expertise becomes seriously problematic. The problem is now not just that there are rival professional conceptions of education which call for rational evaluation, but that there are incommensurable concepts of education which preclude the very possibility, even in principle, of any such rational professional evaluation. In the next chapter, we shall further consider this question in relation to one of the most vexed of past and present educational controversies.

# 8

# RIVAL CONCEPTIONS OF EDUCATION

## Universality and professionalism

It is of some importance to appreciate the precise implications for educational professionalism of the issue about educational values raised at the close of the previous chapter. As already argued, empiricist and post-empiricist philosophers certainly seem to have been mistaken in holding (respectively) that values *per se* are either subjective attitudes or expressions of local cultural affiliation. Indeed, in so far as values may plausibly be distinguished from mere likings or tastes by their relationship to reasons or grounds, we have suggested that there is a case for regarding any exclusively subjectivist account of values as little more than a contradiction in terms. On the other hand, however, uncritical conservative protests against the 'dragons' of subjectivism and relativism[1] may err just as much in supposing that *all* morally implicated values are such as to require universal application. But although the view that values have to be universal in order to merit the status of values has probably been reinforced by some modern philosophical routing of at least moral objectivity through universality, it is not obvious that such universality is a necessary feature of evaluation – and it has been a timely lesson of new communitarians, virtue-theorists, feminists and other philosophers to question any such assumption. It is not just that there seem to be morally significant qualities and responses which are not readily expressible in the deontic language of universal right and duty, but also that even where it may be appropriate to talk of duty and obligation it need not be required to speak of such dues as *universal*. Clearly, for example, it may be incumbent upon me as a member of a particular cultural community, family, religious congregation, club or professional association to return those duties back as are right fit to other members, but there may be no universal moral requirement to extend those duties to non-members. Just as importantly, there need be no universal moral requirement on non-members to join that club or acknowledge the duties enjoined by membership of it.

From this viewpoint, it is arguable that the key issue for professional ethics with respect to the logical status of values and evaluation is not that of the *subjectivity* or otherwise of value, it is rather that of whether such values are, irrespective of objectivity, relevant or applicable across the board of professional conduct and endeavour. In short, what requires closer present attention is the question of what count as reasons for values, and the issue of the relevance or otherwise of such reasons to professional reflection and judgement. Developing a key distinction implicit in much that has already been said (and *pace* postmodern scepticism), my reasons for believing that the earth is not flat, or that cobras are venomous, are clearly tied to *evidence*, which is not only independent of me, but need not in the least engage my personal concerns or interests – however much it may be of benefit to human agents to know such facts in some circumstances. Moreover, it is typical of the beliefs upon which knowledge is built to be of this evidence-based kind. But, of course, since values are not just judgements to the effect that something is thus and so, but expressions of *attitude* or commitment towards whatever is judged to be so, they are liable to vary in the scope of their application. In this respect, *some* values – and it is of some importance to observe that moral values may feature among these – may be considered to have relevance for *any* human agent; thus, I may be expected simply by virtue of being human to value life, liberty and the absence of pain, and to deplore murder, slavery and torture.

It might here be objected that people have often valued life, liberty and the absence of pain for themselves at the cost of the murder, enslavement and torture of others. But it is by now a commonplace of moral theory that – especially if a moral value makes real sense only as a rational or principled preference – there is something morally problematic about any human failure to recognise as evils for other humans what one would be quick to acknowledge as such in one's own all too human case.[2] We should also dispose here of the common red herring that since we may utilitarianly regard the slaying of an Adolf Hitler or Charles Manson as having salutary moral consequences, we cannot in that case *really* believe that murder is wrong – for there is clearly not the least contradiction in appreciating the fringe benefits of a particular murder and deploring murder as a general human evil. Thus, there is no difficulty at all in supposing that there are what we may refer to as *agent-neutral* moral and other reasons for valuing certain practices or courses of action, reasons which apply *universally* to all agents – or, at any rate, to all agents in so far as they are human. However, we may contrast these with reasons for valuing which are only *agent-relative*. A striking example of such an agent-relative value might be the sportsperson's aspiration – which might entirely dominate his or her life – to win an Olympic medal. It is not just, after all, that there is no requirement on anyone who is not an athlete or sports fan to value such a medal – as one might expect anyone by virtue of being human to value health or freedom from pain – but also that realising the goal, actually winning the medal, is something that an athlete can *only* coherently wish for him or herself. Winning a medal is the sort of aim that has been called a 'positional good';[3] it is something which I can achieve only if you do not.

## Reason and value

From the examples given, it should be clear that the difference between agent-neutral and agent-relative reasons is not that the former are *objective* and the latter *subjective*; since the sporting aspiration makes just as much sense as a human goal of development and flourishing as any general desire for health and prosperity, both are entirely objective. It is rather that they are *different* sorts of reasons – and that however much I may recognise other people's goals of development and flourishing as valid for them, I am not thereby required to accept them as relevant to me. Indeed, in respect of familiar facts of individual difference, this point could hardly be more evident: if I am tone deaf or physically short and stout, then the lives and goals of a (successful) musician or ballet dancer are unlikely to be realistic aspirations for me. Clearly also, 'natural' temperament, personality and disposition will influence the kind of life I find fulfilling – whether it is solitary, scholarly and ascetic, or social, sporting and aesthetic. Thus, despite what human beings have in common as a species, they differ widely as individuals – and, although the goals and aspirations of other people may make perfectly good objective sense to me (I may well, to be sure, applaud the talents of an Oscar Peterson or Anna Pavlova), they will all too often be goals which I could not reasonably share and may well not even wish to share. Indeed, in reflecting upon the nature of human development and education, it is of the utmost importance not to fall into the trap, as I suspect that at least some common compulsory thinking about the school curriculum may have fallen,[4] of supposing that if something can be shown to be an *objective* human developmental good, it is thereby a good (or a realistic goal) for *anyone*.

However, since socio-cultural as well as individual factors are also generally agreed to be determinants of human growth and identity, it seems reasonable to suppose that notions of human learning and development cannot be other than *normative*: that, in short, there cannot be any notion of human formation which does not embody some specific conception of human flourishing – which may also be entirely at odds with other conceptions. Hence, in relation to the sorts of example paraded in rival traditions' accounts of education, I may prefer to rear my child as a Catholic, Muslim or secular-liberal, either because I believe that my preferred life is right for everyone, or because I believe that such a life is right for me or people like us. Either way, however, I am not bound to insist that any who are not Catholics, Muslims or liberals should so rear their children. As a liberal, of course, I will be above all committed to a policy of live and let live; so, although I may deplore the whiff of indoctrination I seem to get from religious education, I could hardly consistently deny someone else's right (leaving aside sensitive but legitimate questions about whether even liberal parents are entitled to shape the beliefs of their children) to transmit their cultural and spiritual heritage to their own offspring. However, even as (for example) a Catholic, it is by no means inconsistent of me to believe that Catholicism is the one true faith and to wish that the whole world might be converted, yet accept the fact that Protestants, Hindus and Muslims will for their part desire, and should therefore be accorded, the same right as myself to rear their own children in their own faiths and values. This would *not*, of course, be *relativism*, since I believe in this case that the non-Catholic is objectively *wrong*, and I am right. That said, however, being a Catholic or Muslim *is* clearly consistent with the kind of socio-cultural relativism of club membership mentioned in the last chapter – which is *also* nevertheless a kind of (albeit weaker) value objectivism.

On this view, in so far as a faith is a cultural heritage – a vital identity constitutive link between past and present which significantly reflects and celebrates the trials and triumphs experienced by this or that human group in the course of its socio-spiritual-economic development – someone might hold that Catholicism is absolutely right for me, but Islam absolutely right for them. Whereas ancient farmers and gardeners worshipped female divinities of earth and fertility, hunters and herdsmen had male gods of sky and warrior prowess; where males were dominant but in short supply, polygamy made sense – but where the female was revered and less available, polyandry has appeared a better option. In rather less exotic versions, however, such weak relativism – exhibited in the idea that specific spiritual values or cultural characters have emerged in particular places under the influence of unique socio-economic pressures – is entirely intelligible; it is, indeed, a potent source of many contemporary demands for equal cultural recognition.[5] Moreover, although such modest relativism is likely to entail a degree of genuine moral incommensurabilty – there may simply be no rational resolution of disagreements between meat-eaters and vegetarians, or between those who accept homosexuality and those who consider it sinful – it is not in the least inconsistent with the idea that there are *universal* human rights to freedom, respect and well-being which are owed to all people in virtue of a common human condition. But as new communitarians are not slow to point out, such considerations do appear, in so far as education seems inextricably implicated in questions of culture transmission and identity formation, to raise problems for any idea of a *common* education. For how, such communitarians argue, can one conceive of a common *education* – considered as an initiation into substantial virtues and values – which might be applicable across the diverse cultural constituencies of Catholicism, Protestantism, Islam, secular-liberalism, and so on?[6]

Again, however, we need to keep the nature of the issue before us in clear focus. The threat to common education – and thereby to any concept of educational professionalism entailing genuine rational interrogation, in the interests of an objectively defensible conception of human development, of processes of learning, instruction and discipline – is not in itself caused by the recognition of different cultural constituencies. It is engendered rather by the communitarian claim that the values of diverse cultural constituencies are no more than values of club membership, and that there cannot therefore be, even in principle, any *agent-neutral* reasons for requiring general subscription to this club rather than that. Of course, if it makes sense for me to argue as a Catholic teacher in a Catholic school that the Roman faith is *true*, and that Catholic pedagogy enshrines a correct view of human development, there would be no reason in principle why Catholic teachers should not be conceived along with teachers of other religious or cultural affiliations as participants in a common professional dialogue about the proper character of human pedagogy. The trouble is that this is nowadays a very unfashionable notion – probably mainly due to the influence of certain modern trends of existential or fideist theology which characterise religious belief as less an intellectual or rational response to experience, and more as a leap of (arguably irrational) faith.[7] On this view, since there is no rational basis to the often exotic metaphysical and ontological commitments of traditional or New Age religions, there cannot therefore be – despite the sincere personal commitment of their followers – any way in which they might be proved *true* or *false*.

Of course if one persists (as I do) in the unfashionable view that religious narratives may be potential sources of genuine human understanding and insight (which may even claim a certain priority over other sources of understanding – though there is also, I believe, a corresponding requirement on reasonable faith to be consistent with the best that has been thought and said in other rational spheres), then a way is opened to rational debate about the truth or falsity of one or another religious faith, and of any conception of human flourishing and development it may entail. In that case, although one may be persuaded by the communitarian view of value formation that there is a need for different kinds of schools to transmit the values of different cultural constituencies,[8] there need be no reason why Catholic, Muslim and secular-humanist teachers should not be regarded as partners in a common professional debate. Indeed, since I personally do *not* hold that differences of culture and religion necessarily preclude common professional debate between teachers of different cultural (in this sense) affiliation, it may now be more instructive to remove the issue of the relativity or otherwise of professional debate about learning and development to less metaphysically muddied ground. Is it possible, then, for there to be genuine relativity or incommensurability between conceptions of learning and development which are grounded less in cultural allegiance, and more in simple differences of lifestyle preference? While this would not entail any problematic 'club membership' notion of cultural relativity, it might nevertheless force recognition of inherently *agent-relative* educational reasons.

## Educational traditionalism and progressivism

In this connection, I suspect that the well-trodden ideological conflict between educational traditionalists and educational progressives, knowledge-centred and child-centred educational theories, offers the best case for any such incommensurability of educational conception. Indeed, this is an issue to which I have repeatedly returned over the years, precisely because it seems to have extremely complex – not to say potentially embarrassing – implications for teacher professionalism.[9] There can be small doubt that the traditional–progressive issue has long been the focus of deep public, political and professional educational concern. Moreover, despite occasional claims that the issue is more apparent than real and/or doubts about its contemporary relevance, it seems to be no nearer to final resolution than it has ever been. Indeed, each new outbreak of the issue in various debates about learning or discipline seems to produce more heat than light – not to mention the sort of bunker mentality in which no rational negotiation between alternative child-rearing preferences appears possible.[10] The implications of such deadlock for teacher professionalism, however, could hardly be clearer. To begin with, differences between so-called educational traditionalists and progressives concern issues of human development and well-being which lie at the very heart of professional educational endeavour. In this respect, it is clear that the separate protagonists of debates over the respective merits of traditionalism or progressivism do seem to agree that this is a question which needs resolving in the interests of child development *as such*; it is not that they believe, as one might hold in relation to Catholic education, that although a given education is suitable for this child (in virtue, say, of its cultural heritage) it is not in the same way suitable for that. In that case, however, it surely ought to be possible to discover something in the nature of *agent-neutral* grounds for supposing that one sort of education – a child-centred *or* a teacher-centred one – is appropriate for *all* children. But this is just what educational enquiry and research, for reasons we shall shortly proceed to examine, has arguably failed to discover in support of either of these alleged educational alternatives.

First, however, how should we understand any distinction between educational traditionalism and progressivism? Any straight answer to this question is somewhat impeded by the variety of uses which have down the years been given to such terms as 'traditional', 'progressive', 'child-centred', 'teacher-centred', 'radical', and so on, in contexts of educational discourse and debate. Popular wisdom offers identikit pictures of educational traditionalism and progressivism as variously structured configurations of more or less coherent educational trends and proclivities, which are, all the same, doubtfully faithful to any actual historical educational initiatives or proposals. Such pictures are often, to be sure, little better than the wildest caricatures of undergraduate student teacher essays. Basically, then, traditionalism is painted as an uncompromisingly authoritarian mode of subject-centred education and teaching. Traditionalist teachers are held to be interested only in the most basic skills of literacy, numeracy and vocation, and in the inculcation of rules of moral and social conduct which are to be slavishly obeyed by young people, and disobeyed on pain of the direst punishments. Traditionalist teaching is alleged to be exclusively a matter of direct instruction orchestrated by teachers who, like orchestral conductors, direct all pedagogical activity to classes ranged in forward-facing rows of fixed wood and cast-iron desks (with troublemakers at the front). All traditionalist classrooms are self-contained, and no pupil may leave the room or his or her place without explicit permission. Traditionalist teachers also teach to precisely specified attainment targets in accordance with rigid schedules of behavioural reinforcement, and the main object of education is mindless drilling in facts and rote mental operations for purposes of examination and certification. All this is held in place with the most ruthless and relentless discipline; pupils should not speak unless required to do so, and mutiny is discouraged by a strictly enforced system of discipline ranging from (formerly) physical punishment to detention, lines and loss of privileges.

Educational progressivism, on the other hand, is often held to be child-centred to the extent of reckless and irresponsible abandonment of any and all adult authority. In deploring the regimentation and indoctrination of traditional approaches to education, progressives swing to the other extreme of absolutely respecting the child's liberty to grow and develop as 'nature' intended. Progressives believe in spontaneity and creativity which they also hold to be stunted by external imposition on a basically altruistic and beneficent human nature of social rules and discipline. Consequently, progressives are less interested in those aspects of the school curriculum which involve conformity to established usage – for example, standard rules of grammar, spelling and punctuation – and are more interested in those areas of creative linguistic, musical, plastic or other expression which serve, so it is alleged, to promote qualities of artistic and moral imagination. Progressive classrooms are therefore places where children are not forced to do anything they do not want to do, and where they are free to play and socialise with others as they please. Progressive pedagogy is therefore a matter of free discovery and experiment, of 'process' rather than 'product', where teachers, like angels, should greatly fear to tread. Progressive teachers do not, moreover, believe in punishing children for deviation from norms of conduct, precisely because there are no such norms; any attempt to lay down laws would be an illiberal and intolerant violation of children's rights to express and define themselves as free authors of their own personal fulfilment. Indeed, since progressive teachers have no more rights than those they teach, they have no business setting themselves up as authorities in anything; they are therefore more likely to seek peer equality with their pupils than to try to assert themselves over them.

It should hardly need saying that few parents would wish to have their children educated under either of these extreme dispensations, and there are two principal grounds upon which one might dismiss these caricatures – if not the entire traditional–progressive issue – as irrelevant to any professional debate about the nature of educational development and learning. The first point is what we might term the 'common-sense' view that, since these caricatures clearly identify two unacceptable extremes, the educational 'answer' must lie in some position of rational or logical compromise between them; in short, one may suppose that the answer cannot but lie, as student teachers are wont to say, 'in the middle', and there have certainly been, as we shall see, several theoretical attempts to show how just such a middle way might look. The second point, however, is that it seems extremely difficult to discover even proximate instances of such caricatures in the actual history of educational thought and practice. Indeed, a major difficulty here is that close scrutiny of the evolution of educational traditionalism and progressivism quickly shows that such terms have been used to label a wide variety of disparate educational perspectives which mostly resist assimilation to such caricatures. Moreover, as I have argued before,[11] because of the complex 'family resemblance' character of concepts of traditionalism and progressivism, a position which looks like progressivism on this version of the distinction may look more like a form of traditionalism on that. But this gives rise to the further difficulty that far from being consistent or mutually reinforcing, these two critiques of the caricatures actually *contradict* each other. It is precisely the claim that there have been different, not necessarily consistent, manifestations of traditionalism and progressivism in the history of educational thought and practice which undermines any 'common-sense' idea that the *right* educational answer must lie somewhere in the middle.

## Values and methods

One trouble with the caricatures is that they encourage an oversimplified picture of the issues involved in the traditional–progressive debate. Thus, for example, the account of traditionalists as teacher- or subject-centred and progressives as child-centred has given rise, in one very famous attempt to resolve the dichotomy,[12] to the idea that the two views are simply at cross purposes: that whereas traditionalism is an educational doctrine about aims and content, progressivism has been generally more concerned with issues about pedagogy and development. But this view is rather belied by the fact that progressives have often been extremely interested in aims and content, and traditionalists – especially since the advent of modern, purportedly psychologically-grounded, sciences of pedagogy (though such interest arguably goes back to Plato) – have been enormously exercised by questions of method. Yet more tellingly, however, perhaps the most renowned progressive educationalist of this century, A.S. Neill, appears to have had little or no interest whatsoever in questions of educational method, and his progressive school Summerhill was actually criticised by the Inspectorate of the day for its deployment of highly conventional formal and didactic teaching techniques.[13] The alleged progressive interest in method probably has its source in Rousseau's emphasis on something like discovery and enquiry in *Emile*, to later elaboration by such educational thinkers as Froebel and Montessori of a Rousseauian child developmental conception of learning, to Piaget's modern 'scientific' reformulation of this conception, and to Dewey's own development of a pedagogy of enquiry and experiment in the service of pragmatist epistemology.[14] All the same, there is no special reason to regard Piaget or any of his followers as educational progressives, the idea that there is some kind of developmental basis to cognitive growth is now more or less plain fare in primary education, Dewey explicitly repudiated the label of 'progressive', and no right-minded approach to education could nowadays reasonably deny the pedagogical value of discovery, enquiry and experiment.

Such points also clearly tell against widespread popular, political and professional construal of the difference between traditionalism and progressivism as a difference of educational methodology; on this view, traditionalists are held to be wedded to an exclusive diet of direct formal instruction which precludes any active pupil participation, and progressives are supposed to repudiate any explicit instruction in favour of doctrinaire commitment to a non-interventionist pedagogy of pure discovery and free self-expression. But again, apart from the fact that no sane teacher could possibly operate in either of these extreme fashions (and, as a rule, teachers are far from pedagogically demented), we have seen that this dichotomy does not well depict the actual pattern of historical development of traditionalist and progressive thought and practice. It has, however, encouraged a number of rather superficial modern attempts to address this particular issue. On the one hand, we encounter a famous modern attempt to decide the issue between traditionalism and progressivism by resort to experimental method;[15] on the other, we have a recent political-professional suggestion to the effect that the issue might be resolved via the adoption by primary teachers of a mixed economy of teaching techniques, combining instruction with enquiry.[16] But any notion that the issue between traditionalism and progressivism might be resolved by some more inclusive pedagogical strategy misses the point in exactly the same way as the ill-conceived attempt to decide the issue by empirical method. The trouble is that both perspectives assume, what we have serious reason to doubt, that there *are* empirically discernible teaching strategies – somehow neutral between different normative conceptions of human development and flourishing – appropriate to the promotion of decontextualised processes of human learning. In the next chapter, we shall give further reasons for doubting that this is so, but the difficulties which any such doubts must raise for any attempt to test empirically between traditionalism and progressivism should already be clear. Briefly, of course, they are those of identifying some common educational standard by which we might judge one approach to be better than another. To take a crude example, traditionalists might claim that progressive methods fail to secure traditional academic goals of getting children through exams; the difficulty, of course, is that child-centred educationalists are notoriously prone to reject what they take to be the sacrifice of other important goals of psychological well-being in pursuit of such arguably non-educational aims.

Indeed, we have already suggested that matters may be even more complicated than this example suggests, since there are clear dangers in speaking *generally* about what traditionalists or progressives *as such* actually believe. But is this to claim that no broad differences of educational perspective are discernible in the common opposition of traditionalism to progressivism? In the event, I believe that there is a very general difference which it may be useful to try to spell out a little more precisely for present purposes. It seems fair to characterise traditionalism as a social reproduction and/or culture transmission conception of education. It seems broadly definitive of traditionalism to hold that human development is a matter of progress from pre-civilised savagery and barbarism to the sweetness and light of civil society. A key element in this progress is development of that wisdom which alone enables release from Plato's cave of darkness and superstition into the bright sunlight of rational understanding. The traditionalist, one might say, is a believer in original sin, and the name of this sin is *ignorance*. The antidote to such ignorance is the knowledge and understanding, that 'best that has been thought and said' which is embodied in civilised human culture. Since the knowledge and values of received culture enshrine the highest of which humankind has here and there been so far capable, it is the responsibility of educationalists to ensure that successive generations are properly initiated into the epistemic inheritance of their society and culture. In default of such initiation human nature is prey to its lowest promptings and man is no more than a savage or barbarian. The central idea here is well expressed by R.S. Peters, a prominent modern traditionalist, who speaks tellingly of the young child as 'the barbarian at the gates of civilisation'.[17] Hence, a key idea in traditionalist conceptions of human development is that of *discipline*, particularly of the 'lower' impulses and inclinations of human nature. Without submission to intellectual discipline and the civilised order it entrains, there can be no worthwhile human association, personal emancipation or creative imagination.

All the same, Rousseau – the founding father of educational progressivism – utterly repudiated this traditionalist picture of education as concerned to curb natural human impulses in the interests of civil order. Whereas traditionalists held that human nature is basically flawed and salvation lies only in disciplined socialisation, he argued – in the context of anthropological, sociological and psychological investigations of great originality and frequent insight – that humans are inherently social, that this inclines them to be more *sociable* and co-operative than otherwise, and that the impoverished moral condition of men observed by writers of a more conservative temper was *product* of rather than occasion for their transfer from the natural to the civil state.[18] In particular, he held that the diseased *amour propre* at the root of human moral malaise was due rather to the social stratification and status differentiation of life in civil polity. It was on this basis that he developed a prophylactic conception of education which stands in some contrast to the traditional view. Whereas it is the role of traditional education and schooling to discipline unruly and anti-social human tendencies via the socialisation of young people into received mores and values, it is the aim of Rousseau's education to protect the nascent reasoning powers of the young from the potentially corrosive effects of social bias and prejudice; progressive sins are not so much original as *acquired* – and their names are *prejudice* and *intolerance*. Thus, Rousseau was particularly concerned to ensure growth in the child of an uncontaminated *moral* sense grounded in the nature of reason alone, and, indeed, this absolutist conception of moral reason is, arguably via Kant's ethics,[19] Rousseau's greatest philosophical legacy. All this, however, brings together two concerns which to some extent come apart in later progressive traditions. The first is a moral concern focused upon the role of education in the reconciliation of the natural and the social: here, whereas traditionalists hold flawed human nature to be redeemable only by engagement in social life, progressives regard innocent human nature as prone to social corruption. The second is an epistemological concern with what in the nature of learning might best conduce to the development of uncorrupted reason.

## Dim prospects for resolving the dualism

However, what should be clear from the nature of this educational controversy is: first, that it concerns different evaluative conceptions of human nature, civil society and of the role of education in reconciling natural with social needs and interests; second, that the debate seems to be defined by contradictorily opposed points of view. One likely response to more popular caricatures of this disagreement, of course, is that it seems extreme and that the traditionalist conception of freedom as exclusively a matter of rule observance is no more plausible than the progressive conception of freedom without rules; this rough ground has already been well trodden in the extensive literature on personal autonomy. But it would appear that much argument of this kind has been directed against straw men anyway, for it is frankly difficult to find any views in the serious literature of traditionalism and progressivism which maintain that human freedom is either *entirely* rule governed or utterly *anarchic*. On the one hand, then, most modern traditionalists (conservative as well as liberal) seem to have held that although the various mind-forming rational disciplines are crucial to living enquiry, any creative further enquiry is significantly liable to transcend established rational categories. On the other hand, even such an extreme educational libertarian as A.S. Neill does not reject the importance of rules and discipline for moral autonomy; it is rather that, like Rousseau, he believes that the discipline should be self-imposed and rules self-generated. But this may appear to bring the views of traditionalists and progressives much closer, and might at any rate suggest the possibility of resolving, at least in principle, disagreements between educational authoritarians and libertarians in favour of one correct conception of the proper place of rules and discipline in the development of human rational autonomy.

There are good reasons, however, for regarding any such optimism as quite misplaced. Once we dismiss the various misconceptions of autonomy grounded in the various caricatures of traditionalism and progressivism, it becomes clear that there is *no* common general conception of the development of rational self-determination, creative expression or whatever, of a kind that would license neutral scientific decision between the claims of discipline and liberty, head or heart, orientated educationalists. As far as rational self-determination goes, it has been argued by modern communitarians that ideas of both reason and self-determination are much more culturally specific and contested than liberal rationalist philosophies had once inclined to dream of, and it seems difficult to deny that what counts as creativity is liable to vary considerably according to one's cultural or personal aesthetic. Music considered by some to be the summit of artistic achievement because of its rationally architectonic nature is liable to be less highly regarded by others because it is too clinical and insufficiently emotionally charged. To be sure, since human development is profoundly implicated in questions of human flourishing, it is as much of a moral as an aesthetic matter; and, to the extent this is so, there can certainly be better *or* worse ways of bringing up children. Indeed, as a parent, one might well come to regret quite seriously having not more strictly disciplined a child in so far as such lack of discipline may seem to have contributed significantly to his or her life of dissolution, self-destruction or crime. In circumstances where such dire consequences are not obviously traceable to discernible defects of upbringing, however, it can be very much harder to know how I should go about assisting *myself* – still less another – to live the *best* possible life. Sometimes, indeed, there may be no question of *morally* worse or better, only of different kinds of lives. I would have been in a real sense a *different* person for having lived like Socrates dissatisfied, rather than a suiform satisfied, but I need not necessarily have been a *morally* worse person.

With the wisdom of hindsight, of course, I can seriously question whether it was better for me to have undergone that disciplined upbringing which issued in a life of ruthless and punishing ambition, than to have been reared in a less driven climate of warm affection which would have yielded less achievement but more personal contentment and fuller relationships. But we should also beware of the temptation at this point to suppose that this is a false dichotomy which might be resolved in a compromise life of happy achievement. I do not, of course, deny that there are lives of happy achievement, but if such a life is one that seeks to square the often competing claims of full and flourishing relationships and public achievement, then it is at least arguable that this might be practically impossible without some diminution of the quality of the lives which it attempts to balance. In that case, the compromise life is not some *scientifically neutral* norm of flourishing, but simply a further *evaluative* alternative to other possible lives. Indeed, this is but a special case of a general point about practical conflict which fatally scuppers problem-solving accounts of morality and moral education, as well as, of course, further serving to underline the point that traditional–progressive disputes about the proper course of human development are more moral-evaluative than scientific-technical. Considerations of this kind serve to support the case that empirical theories of development are in and of themselves insufficient to ground professional educational prescriptions, for, on this view, there seem to be no agent-neutral reasons for preferring, say, a traditionalist to a progressive or child-centred approach. Moreover, it is such thought – the idea that there are no empirical facts of optimal human development which can arbitrate between rival evaluative conceptions of flourishing – which might seduce us into thinking that educational traditionalism and progressivism (or whatever) are simply different kinds of club membership between which people are free to choose according to personal or cultural taste.

## Brighter prospects?

In the event, however, I suspect that any such conclusion reflects a tangle of conceptual mistakes about the nature of ethical generality, the normative character of human development and the evidential basis of values, which educational philosophy might have done more over the years to sort out. The difficulty as encountered to date is that if it is not possible to decide empirically between rival evaluative conceptions of development, then they can express no more than subjective personal or culturally-relative preferences. But then, if divergent evaluative conceptions of human development express only non-rational personal or cultural tastes, it is difficult if not impossible to make sense of any rational professional discourse and debate about what is surely the *raison d'être* of professional deliberation and effort – the promotion of human development. But whereas it seems to be a virtue of an empirical law to ignore individual differences of detail in the interests of fully comprehensive explanatory cover, it is a defect of a moral principle, as Aristotle discerned with respect to Plato's theory of justice,[20] to give similar priority to the general over the particular. Thus, whereas it is a proper ideal of progress in scientific theoretical understanding to comprehend more and more diversity under ever simpler and more unifying general laws, it is a mark of progress in moral understanding to grow in appreciation of the variety of interpretation to which universal concepts of justice and virtue are prone in particular application. Where science aims rightly for economy of understanding, the route to virtue lies in ever deeper sensitivity to the situational complexity of human association. But this observation may well open up the possibility of understanding particular rival, perhaps even conflicting, pedagogical strategies for the promotion of human development as nevertheless expressive of more general educational goals.

It is of some interest in this connection that some of the more outlandish or infamous of modern strategies for the promotion of self-determination – those entailing abdication of adult authority in favour of total pupil freedom – were developed in the course of work with emotionally disturbed 'problem' children. Psychoanalytically-influenced educationalists such as Homer Lane and A.S. Neill maintained that such young people were unable to recognise the significance of authority in human affairs because of their psychological association of authority with hostile, coercive and abusive power, and that the only way to free them from such association was to relocate, via strategies of 'self-government', the source of authority in the child.[21] At the most general level of educational aspiration, however, Lane and Neill do not disagree with more conventional educationalists that it is a fundamental task of education to engender that state of rational and emotional empowerment commonly celebrated in the idea of autonomy, and denied in the process of indoctrination. At a more particular level of practical application, then, it is not inconceivable that educational strategies for the development of self-determination which work for emotionally secure children might not work for damaged children, and vice versa. In that case, on the face of it, we have merely different, albeit incompatible, practical strategies for achieving a common educational goal with respect to diverse educational *clienteles*. But, in so far as it is part of routine parental experience that the diverse needs, proclivities and interests of different children call for different disciplinary, motivational and developmental approaches, we would also expect it to be a significant dimension of good professional practice for a teacher to know his or her pupils as individuals and to shape their teaching – with due respect to more general considerations of justice as fairness – to the individual requirements of children.

Thus, though empirical evidence cannot be expected to adjudicate between different value perspectives, recognition of the diverse range of actual individual needs is clearly a significant aspect of professional educational development; for, though good teaching brooks no favourites, it is not necessarily the teacher who applies rules with procrustean impartiality who is most just and fair. As Aristotle observed, as much injustice may follow from treating unequals equally as from treating equals unequally.[22] What seems implicit in the normativity of such developmental notions as self-determination, then, is not merely that there may well be alternative individually variable, yet equally legitimate, notions of self-determination, but that there can also be diverse professional strategies for the promotion of any one conception of autonomy. At the same time, it would be foolish to insist that all value differences are reconcilable after this fashion, or to ignore the existence of very real value disagreements on the proper course of human development and flourishing. We can hardly deny that secular humanists do disagree with, say, Catholics, (some) progressives with (some) traditionalists, on the ultimate ends of human life, as well as in their interpretations of such aspects of human development as individual self-determination. Whether or not such disagreements are fatally damaging to professional debate about the role of education in human development, moreover, may turn ultimately upon the extent to which subscription to traditionalism or progressivism, or to a given religious faith, is fairly construable in terms of club membership. For if we take the view that there is no reason for our educational practices other than that this is the way we as progressives or Catholics do things, then we have closed ourselves off from anything worth calling professional accountability with respect to such important questions.

Since, as already noted, I am inclined to the unfashionable (though not thereby necessarily mistaken) view that there can be a serious and genuine metaphysical or theological dimension to professional questions – that, indeed, there are substantial metaphysical and other grounds upon which a religious conception of education might be defended against secular-liberalism or humanism – I do not see that this has to be the case with regard to religiously-grounded education. But I also leave open the possibility that there may be logical or other considerations which might force us to regard a given religious, traditional or progressive form of education as fundamentally *incoherent*, and as therefore unworthy of further serious professional consideration. It is, indeed, one of the tasks of educational philosophy to try to show this where it can be shown, and I believe that educational philosophy has more or less conclusively shown this to be the case of *some* forms of educational progressivism *and* traditionalism. Moreover, if certain diverse conceptions of human development may be ruled in as educationally acceptable on the grounds that they are, after all, consistent with a general goal of personal enablement – the promotion of self-determination, which is a *sine qua non* of educational endeavour – it may be reasonable to rule out other conceptions which are not thus consistent as educationally invalid. From this point of view, I think it would be hard to deny that certain forms of religious initiation *are* inadmissible as conceptions of *education,* in any sense of 'education' significantly separate from other aspects of human formation. In the next section, however, we need to take a closer look at the sort of overall conceptual framework of education in terms of which any coherent professional debate about aims and methods would need to proceed.

# Part IV

# ETHICS AND EDUCATION, MORALITY AND THE TEACHER

# 9

# EDUCATIONAL RIGHTS AND PROFESSIONAL WRONGS

## Grades of normative involvement in teaching

Teaching, like other professional activities, is a *normative* enterprise; it is apt for appraisal according to measures or standards of goodness or badness, efficiency or inefficiency. However, it may further the interests of clarity here to distinguish different dimensions of such normativity, and one way into this is to distinguish the *different* kinds of *reasons* which might be given for judging a teacher or a particular teaching style as good or bad, effective or ineffective. First, then, we might consider a particular teacher, or his or her teaching, to be bad on grounds of *incompetence*, in that predominantly technical sense of competence elsewhere considered in this work. Thus, teachers may be found wanting on the grounds that they have no authority over their classes, are poor communicators, or have inadequate knowledge of what they are required to teach. These failures may be largely, though by no means necessarily, matters of personality, ability and technique, with no significant implications for the moral character of the individuals concerned: it is more than likely that there are many perfectly charming and decent people who could not (in this sense) teach. But, of course, teachers could well be highly competent, even expert, in this first technical sense of teaching, but be thoroughly bad teachers because they represent a danger or hazard to children. Hence, a *second* perfectly straightforward sense in which a person may be judged to be a bad teacher is that in which he or she is violent towards, sexually abusive of, or neglectful of, the health and safety of children.

However, there is a less obvious *third* way in which we might want to question the practice of teaching, which – though it also relates to what we might regard as a failure to achieve the proper ends of education – is not a *technical* failure in the sense just considered. Indeed, it may well be that the trouble with some teachers is that they teach *so* well and with such a passion for shaping young minds in a particular direction that they fail to promote individual independence of mind or mature responsibility. This is where we might want to say that whereas the teaching is excellent, it is something less than *educational*: where we might want to speak of *indoctrination* rather than education. In some ways, this third pedagogical defect occupies a space between the first two. Like the bungler, and unlike the child abuser, a Jean Brodie type[1] need not harbour any overt intention of harming children or exploiting them for personal gratification; but, as with the child abuser more than the bungler (since most of us have survived technically inept teaching), failure to understand fully the implications for teaching of *education*, as distinct from other forms of personal influence, may be a source of actual lasting harm to young people. On a *fourth* dimension, however, a teacher who scores reasonably well on the first three grounds – that is someone who teaches knowledgeably and skilfully with utmost respect for the physical and psychological health, safety, integrity and autonomy of pupils – might yet be regarded (rightly or wrongly) as professionally derelict by virtue of setting children a bad moral *example*. This might be either because the person in question is thought to exhibit an objectionable lifestyle, for example, he is homosexual, or she smokes cannabis, or because he or she has evident character shortcomings, for example, she is sexually promiscuous, or he is a heavy drinker or gambler. What, for example, should we say of an otherwise 'professional' history teacher, entirely and effectively mindful of young people's educational and welfare needs, who has a string of convictions for driving under the influence of alcohol? Is such a teacher, we might ask, the kind of *person* who should be in charge of children?

The second, third and fourth of these normative dimensions of teaching are of rather more present concern than the first, precisely because they are all implicated in *moral* or *ethical* issues. By that same token, however, it is crucial to grasp that these considerations are quite inseparable from any substantial notion of effective teaching, at any rate any *professional* conception of effective teaching. It is important to appreciate in the case of teaching, as in other professional spheres, that moral and ethical shortcomings are not just regrettable *external* blemishes on what we might otherwise continue to regard as occupational virtues: to see that, in the face of certain kinds of moral and ethical failures, it may make little sense to speak of professional virtues at all. Hence, while there is at least a certain intelligible sense in which we might speak of someone who overcharges, cheats or sleeps with his customers as nevertheless an excellent builder or a first-rate window cleaner, there is something more dubious about regarding sharp practising doctors or teachers who bed their sixth-form pupils as exemplars of their respective professions. Although there has of late been much welcome interest in the development of trade ethics, it might be (albeit cynically) observed that at least some of this represents a response to producer recognition, under pressure from contemporary consumer organisations, that it makes commercial sense to promote a high public reputation for fair dealing: that, in short, commercial enterprises which are widely perceived to have the best interests of customers at heart are more likely to increase sales. In the cold light of logic, however – and bearing in mind that tradespeople and businessmen are often sincerely and *genuinely* concerned to give the best possible value for money – there would seem to be nothing in the actual nature of trade or commercial bargaining which would give rise to any *moral* demand for distributive or other justice. On the contrary, it would seem to be the very point of such bargaining to secure the best advantage for oneself, irrespective of others' weal or woe.[2] Moreover, since anyone who comes off badly from a particular episode of bargaining may be considered to have entered the contract voluntarily, and with a clear view to potential gains and losses, there would seem to be few grounds for complaint if any final outcome is not to their advantage.

## Professional rights and wrongs

It is arguably otherwise, however, with an enterprise such as medicine, in so far as a significant level of regard for others seems built into the very notion of medical practice. Someone might say, I suppose, that a doctor need not in principle differ from a tradesman in this respect. As a doctor, one may value health with other human beings, but care particularly for it only in one's own case. Hence, any skills of healing one has taken the trouble to acquire may have been so acquired, not for any especially altruistic reasons, but only for their commercial potential. I suspect, however, that any such argument shows some insensitivity to the complex network of conceptual associations in which our understanding of medical motivation is commonly implicated. For surely it is the misan-thropic rather than the altruistic or philanthropic doctor who is the *exception* rather than the rule; whereas it is not hard to imagine a successful snake oil salesman who did not in the least care whether his patients got well, so long as they paid him or her a handsome fee, it is harder to associate such unconcern with successful medical practice. Bad experiences with particular doctors apart, then, we may reasonably suppose that a real concern for the health and well-being of others is what generally motivates entry into the medical profession: to be that, indeed, which draws many individuals who might well be able to gain considerably greater financial reward elsewhere into this profession. From this viewpoint, the Hippocratic oath may itself be construed as an attempt to give formal recogni-tion to the intuition that medical practice does generally entail wider moral concern for and commitment to the health and welfare of others.

But where is the inconsistency in conceiving doctors as *both* concerned to heal their patients *and* to extort the highest possible fees? Is there not still some room for logical manoeuvre between the idea that medical practice involves a level of commitment to improving the health of others, and the injunction that doctors should not financially or otherwise exploit them? However, this apparent difficulty is vulnerable to both general and particular considerations. Generally, it would seem that once purchase has been given to moral or ethical considerations via the idea that medical practice presupposes a degree of larger concern for others, it seems harder for medical practitioners to feign deafness to other moral concerns. Thus, commitment to promoting human welfare with regard to health does not appear to sit easily with willingness to undermine welfare in other respects, by, for example, commercial or sexual exploitation. More particularly, however, it is likely that there will also be occasions when service and profit motives pull in markedly different directions: when, for example, a doctor might be tempted by kickbacks from a drug company to prescribe what is either inappropriate or surplus to his patients' medical need. It is for these and other reasons that it is not really feasible to try to hive off specific professional concerns with particular aspects of human flourishing, from larger moral concerns that they should not be otherwise exploited or harmed. All of this arguably serves to implicate a professional practice such as medicine in a range of ethical considerations, which external consumer pressure might well be needed to force some recognition of in other occupational spheres.

What can we now say, on the basis of the above observations about the normative dimensions of teaching, about the proper professional shape and direction of educational practice? Could such observations, for example, be used to ground general or universal educational prescriptions or prohibitions of the kind to which many codes of professional ethics aspire? We may start with what is perhaps a fairly clear-cut issue: the requirement that, even if we are unable as professionals to promote any clear benefit to our clients, we should at least refrain from doing them any discernible harm or injury. Whilst something here depends upon what *counts* as harm or injury – and there will be those who hasten to point out that these are socially and/or culturally contested concepts – one may also anticipate considerable public, professional and political agreement, even in multi-cultural contexts, that some kinds of harm in the context of schooling are quite enough to warrant condemnation to the point of teacher dismissal. Thus, although it would be a (relativist) mistake to believe that consensus is sufficient to show the moral propriety or otherwise of this or that individual conduct or social practice – since social consensus has sometimes sustained quite morally odious forms of behaviour – we may be fairly sure in relation to anything approaching the sexual abuse of small children, that wide cross-cultural revulsion for such behaviour is firmly grounded in evidence of the real psychological and physical harm it causes victims. Moreover, right-minded consensus with respect to the evils of child sexual abuse does greatly oil the wheels of democratic legislation in this sphere. Hence, in so far as it would be difficult not to hold that proper professional conduct, at any rate conduct performed in a professional role, should at the very least fall within the law, the case for regarding illegal conduct as unprofessional, and as therefore absolute grounds for dismissal, seems clear enough.

## Crime and punishment

With respect to non-sexual forms of physical and psychological abuse in the context of educational practice, on the other hand, the moral issues may appear much less clear. Indeed, in so far as discipline is an integral part of any teacher's role, punishment has been routinely considered an inevitable consequence of discipline, and educators past and present have included various forms of psychological humiliation and physical coercion among the most effective forms of punishment. Moreover, since corporal punishment is now outlawed in many developed liberal democracies, it is a cause for some professional concern to teachers often faced with restraining – even defending themselves against – violent and disruptive pupils, that they run a daily risk of legal as well as professional retribution for any use of what might be regarded as excessive physical force. All the same, although nations that have made corporal punishment illegal invariably aspire to ground such legislation in some general human right to freedom from violence, there would appear to be significant cross-cultural difference concerning what actually constitutes unacceptable violence in child discipline, and a belief that spoiling the child is the price to be paid for sparing the rod seems to be globally widespread. Thus, many oriental cultures – including some of those developing Pacific economies to which recent British 'back to basics' advocators have (ironically) recommended we should turn for educational inspiration[3] – encourage climates of strict deference of youth towards elders which seem to be at least partly held in place by regular physical chastisement.

However, to the extent that our main present interest in corporal punishment concerns the proper logical or ethical form of any enquiry into this question, it is probably worth reaffirming an earlier point about the importance of distinguishing the different levels of practical argument upon which this issue is liable to be debated. We should at least be clear that any question about the *morality* of corporal punishment could hardly be resolved by empirical study of the effects of corporal punishment or its absence on the orderly conduct of school business, for it clearly makes perfectly good sense to argue that no school order secured by such means can be worth the price which has to be paid for it. In wider social terms, indeed, we might similarly argue that even if capital punishment, civil vigilantism or lynch law were to make our streets safer places in which to walk, we *should* not (even though we desire safer streets) want any form of civil association which would countenance such barbarities. But again, even if we could show (what I suspect to be the case) that corporal punishment is not an especially effective means of maintaining order, that it can sometimes cause even more disruption and disorder than it serves to correct, it would not be unintelligible either for someone to argue for the retention of such retribution, so that justice (construed reciprocally) might be *seen* to be done. The crucial point is that the question of the legitimacy or otherwise of corporal punishment as a method of school discipline is a *moral* or *ethical* one which no amount of empirical educational research could be sufficient to resolve for us. The real debate is not between those who affirm and those who deny that it *works*, but between those who insist that it is consistent with what is just, right and/or good in human affairs, and those who maintain that it is not.

In brief, justifications for punishment appeal either to deterrence, retribution or reform.[4] The argument which appeals to the deterrent value of punishment, for reasons already given, is not obviously a *moral* argument as such. This may appear surprising to those who have been accustomed to regarding deterrence as a distinctly *utilitarian* perspective on punishment; but it is not obvious that utilitarianism *is* a moral position in the sense required to do substantial present work. Certainly, arguments from utility can be forms of moral *argumentation*, but as such they are liable to deployment from a diversity of substantial moral perspectives, and it should be clear that divergent moral priorities can lead to *different* utilitarian conclusions on any given issue (in, for example, arguments about abortion between Roman Catholics and secular humanists). Generally, then, in so far as there is no such thing as arguing utilitarianly in abstraction from some set of evaluative priorities – apart, that is, from some larger vision of human good or flourishing – it is hard to construe deterrence as an unqualified good *in itself*. More particularly, since it cuts little ice to speak abstractly of the value of securing order apart from some conception of human order to which the practice of corporal punishment as a deterrent is or is not supposed to be conducive, what is seen by some teachers as a good form of deterrence from anti-social behaviour, may be viewed by others as an evil in terms of the physical or psychological damage it causes to individuals and the morally corrosive effects it has on wider social ethos. In this connection, difficulties of a not dissimilar sort attach to the idea of reform or rehabilitation as an aim of corporal punishment: one man's moral improvement – through, no doubt, the purging of an ill will through suffering – is another man's degradation and dehumanisation. Moreover, there is the added difficulty in the case of reform arguments that if corporal punishment is actually a form of beneficial re-education, such rehabilitation is not, in conceptual terms, *punishment* in any *real* sense. If, like the medieval inquisitor, I am saving a person's soul by torturing him, I am not so much punishing him as doing him a service.

However, it seems that the man on death row who believes that it is only right that he should pay by death for his crime does invoke a specific *moral* argument for punishment – one to the effect that crime upsets the balance of justice, and only punishment in kind can restore that balance. Moreover, the idea of retributive justice – the notion that punishment, whether or not it deters or reforms, is actually demanded by justice – is deeply ingrained in Judaeo-Christian thought, where it finds diverse expression in the Mosaic notion of an eye for an eye, in the concept of original sin and in the idea of (the) atonement. Notoriously, however, in so far as the idea of retribution is tied to that of *reciprocity* – on the notion of *exact* restitution for an offence – it can be something of a problem to make the punishment fit the crime. Thus, whatever sense we may make of the idea of a life for a life, problems immediately arise over determining appropriate punishment for burglary or sexual assault. Even in the case of murder, it may seem unfair to grant a murderer who has put his victim to a lingering death by torture a relatively quick and easy way out by gas or lethal injection. There is also clearly some contradiction within the Judaeo-Christian tradition, or at least between Judaism and Christianity, in that while the tradition does emphasise retribution, it also gives a central place to *forgiveness*. From this point of view, most reflective Christians would find not merely repugnant but actually incoherent the idea of visiting exactly the same barbarities on criminals that they would otherwise want to regard as barbarous, especially if such punishment is also expected to uphold or exemplify civilised as opposed to barbaric association.

Hence, even if someone is inclined to insist that there should, in the name of *real* justice, be some kind of punitive response to a crime or misdemeanour, there are clearly problems about any construal of this which would justify the use of capital punishment for murder or corporal punishment for school misbehaviour or bullying. It seems a dubious way to proclaim the unacceptability of taking the lives of others or of their physical intimidation to make reciprocal taking of life or violence to others the cornerstones of our penal system. Moreover, apologists for capital or corporal punishment will not infrequently argue in rather less than consistent ways about the pros and cons of such practices. Just as convicts on death row argue that they now no longer wish to live in the knowledge of what they did to their victims, so teachers in schools will point out that many pupils in schools are themselves inclined to request physical punishment for any breaches of school discipline. It is argued, with a rather ironic twist of logic, that children actually *prefer* being caned or strapped to detention or having to write punishment lines or essays because it is over more quickly. The peculiarity of recommending something as a punishment on the grounds that pupils actually prefer it, however, should be fairly apparent, and it may well be something of a subterfuge for perfectly understandable considerations of teacher convenience. To already harassed and beleaguered professionals, detention and punishment exercises are, like the trouble and expense of detaining murderers for life in prison, extremely labour-intensive and time-consuming practices.

## Punishment and civilised association

All the same, such pragmatic and/or economic reasons seem hardly enough in any civilised society to justify practices such as the death penalty, especially in the face of what is clearly *the* most decisive moral argument against such punishment: that miscarriages of justice are liable to occur which cannot be undone once a life has been taken. Indeed, if our conception of civilised life and community is one of liberal-democratic polity, it is difficult to ignore the concomitant commitment of free democratic society to ideas of the open-endedness of thought and enquiry. But, then, to the extent that the idea of open enquiry assumes the possibility of epistemological *fallibilism* – the idea that our knowledge claims are constitutionally liable to rebuttal or disconfirmation – the thought that our evidence for a given conviction might be mistaken hardly sits comfortably with a form of punishment which allows victims no redress in such cases. Someone will say, of course, that this hardly applies in the case of corporal punishment which is highly unlikely to result in actual fatalities. But such punishment clearly can, especially if inexpertly administered, result in appreciable physical injury, and much the same liberal principles which seek to protect wrongly accused criminals from unjust execution may also be invoked to protect wrongly accused pupils from any *possibility* of bodily harm. Presumably, such liberal principles would permit the physical mishandling of persons in the interests of restraining them from harming others; but once offenders have been so restrained, there could be little warrant for the deliberate infliction of any further physical violence on them. Thus, although one should be far from unsympathetic to the enormous pressures that contemporary teachers are under, in at least some schools, from uncooperative, undisciplined and sometimes violent pupils, it seems hardly possible to reconcile any kind of officially sanctioned physical chastisement of children with the values and aspirations of civilised polity.

It may also be worth noting that although school discipline and order continue to be problems of paramount contemporary concern, to which it may well be that no entirely satisfactory solution has yet been found, it is very doubtful that corporal punishment ever constituted a satisfactory solution to these difficulties. The records of corporal punishment which schools were required by law to keep invariably showed that, retribution apart, beating and caning have seldom deterred. Indeed, far from constituting an effective disincentive to further transgression, punishment books were more likely to record the same depressing inventory of familiar bothersome pupils day after day, and most schools would have their share of pupils who actively sought occasions for caning as a means of maintaining their school standing as desperate (or attention-seeking) characters.[5] Hence, although it is likely that the general run of reasonably well-balanced pupils who might be deterred by physical punishment would equally be deterred by punishment exercises, it also seems likely that those pupils who could *not* be deterred by more humane punishments were seldom effectively deterred by corporal punishment either. Some radical and progressive educationalists, of course, have wished to deny that there is any conceptual connection between punishment and discipline and have renounced deployment by educational institutions of *any* – not just physical – coercion. However, though it certainly seems to be true that there can be discipline without punishment, in – for example, the form of 'self-discipline' – the idea that schools can operate without any system of sanctions or penalties for breaches of conduct is probably at least unrealistic or impractical. Indeed, it probably gains what plausibility it has from widespread and habitual confusion between *education* and *schooling*. Hence, whereas a good education is certainly concerned with encouraging children to submit voluntarily to the various academic and moral disciplines which conduce to self-improvement, schools – as social institutions in which education, amongst other things, takes place – are also about other things. These include training young people in the observance of those public rules and codes of conduct whose infringement beyond school *would* certainly attract sanction and penalty.

All the same, for reasons already given, it would appear that the *moral* case against regarding physical punishment as a legitimate instrument of school order is a strong, if not decisive, one. Thus, despite the fact that the debate about physical punishment is far from concluded in many contemporary educational contexts, there are strong grounds for regarding such chastisement, along with sexual abuse, as professionally beyond the pale, and therefore, perhaps for conceiving freedom from any kind of physical abuse or interference (barring proper restraint of the violent or unruly for their own good or the good of others) as a *universal* right of pupils in schools.

## Unprofessional personal relations

On the face of it, we may be inclined to regard corporal punishment and sexual abuse as equally educationally objectionable in virtue of certain common features. Both, for example, involve contact with pupils which seems to extend well beyond the professional to the personal, and both appear to be implicated in relations which are actually physically abusive, degrading or exploitative. However, it is now worth asking – particularly because this is, not least in the sphere of education and teaching, a contentious professional issue – whether a relationship between teacher and pupil or student which involved both intimate physical contact and/or some measure of exploitation should always be considered professionally unaccept-able.[6] Certainly, the grounds for regarding sexual liaison between teachers and children below the age of consent as professionally unacceptable are reasonably clear; since such conduct is illegal, and it is difficult to consider any conduct which falls out with the law as professional, any such teacher–pupil sexual encounter must count as unprofessional by that very token. But what of children or young people who are *above* the age of consent? What of affairs between teachers and sixth formers, university professors and undergradu-ates or postgraduates, not to mention adult education lecturers and their fully mature night-school students? Can we here apply any blanket (so to speak) professional prohibition? In view of this range of possibilities, one may well be tempted to suppose that there are markedly different cases here, to which some sort of sliding scale, rather than any general prohibition, should be applied. To that extent, we might well doubt whether the issue of *consent* is the pivotal one. Indeed, we may be inclined to regard the professor and postgraduate affair as nearer to that of the adult lecturer sleeping with the middle-aged widow or divorcee in his pottery class, and poles apart from the blatantly unprofessional cases of school teachers' sexual involvements with either fourth formers or sixth formers – despite the fact that the sixth former *can* give consent and may be only a few years younger, and not significantly less mature, than the postgraduate.

Whatever the attractions of the sliding scale, however, there would appear to be something unsatisfactory about trying to distinguish these cases in terms of the age, consent and maturity of the parties involved. To be sure, there may be reasons for supposing teacher involvement with willing sixth formers to be more excusable than any absolutely inexcusable sexual abuse by teachers of small children, but that is not to say that there is nothing professionally untoward about the former involvements. If that is so, however, it may also give us grounds for deploring similar involvements between professors and postgraduates, if not those of night-school pottery teachers with widows or divorcees. But in what might this professional reprehensibility consist? There are clear prohibitions on sexual liaison between professionals and clients in the case of other occupations. Perhaps the case which most readily springs to mind is the prohibition upon sexual liaison between psychiatrists or psychotherapists and their patients. Indeed, it is noteworthy here that any sexual prohibition would appear to be derivative of considerations concerning the intimate personal association with their patients into which psychiatrists are required to enter in order to be of significant therapeutic benefit to them. Interestingly, from the present perspective, this relationship would seem to involve elements of trust and reliance upon authority of a not dissimilar kind to those which typify relationships between teachers and pupils. Indeed, psychiatry itself, unlike the general run of medical practice with which it is more popularly associated, often seems – via its concern with liberating patients from their anxieties or neuroses through an understanding of their psychogenetic causes – to resemble education or training, more than clinical intervention. Still, it should be clear that the unprofessional behaviour of any psychotherapist's exploitation of his or her patients in pursuit of sexual favours turns crucially upon the peculiar vulnerability of psychiatric patients to the influence of any in whom they have placed their trust.

In this respect, however, the case of the abusing psychiatrist seems to be more like that of abusing primary teachers – who also shamefully prey on the weak and vulnerable in the knowledge of their own position of advantage – and not especially like that of teachers or professors who fraternise with willing sixth formers or undergraduates. Indeed, such older pupils may know very well what they are doing, and it might well be more apt in some such cases to regard pupils as predators or exploiters, and to count their erring teachers or professors among the vulnerable exploited. But this way of putting things, the suggestion that in cases of dubious client–professional relationship received conceptions of prey and preyed upon might be revised or reversed, may take us closer to the heart of the general problems with any such association. The Hippocratic idea that doctors should not, in prospect of sexual or financial favours, exploit their virtual powers of life and death over others, seems to suggest that the traffic of exploitation is all one way, and that only the client is liable to be the loser by any such association. This appearance is not entirely dispelled, moreover, even when we move away from the psychiatrist–patient model of professional dereliction, to focus upon a more general objection that might be raised against doctor–patient or lawyer–client involvements. For, in response to the point that it can be no one's business but theirs what two consenting adults, professional and client notwithstanding, get up to out of hours, it seems a fair objection that even if such conduct does not directly harm this particular client, it may none the less harm others by virtue of the special attention he or she is likely to receive from any professional with whom he or she is personally involved.

In consequence, then, it may be thought that the beloved patient is liable to get more of the erring doctor's bedside manner, that the involved lawyer or judge may be more lenient to his or her criminal paramour, and that professorial Lotharios may be more disposed to overlook the defects of their student lovers' assignments. But, of course, things could well go completely otherwise. In by no means inconceivable circumstances, if errant barristers, surgeons or professors are committed to professional standards in all other respects (perhaps they have non-exploitatively and helplessly fallen in love with their clients, patients or students) it could be that they are scrupulous to a fault about making sure that their clients get a fair trial, that they wait their turn for operations, or that 'favoured' students' essays are actually marked even *more* rigorously than those of their peers. In such circumstances, the involved client, patient or student could actually come off *worse* than the rest, precisely due to a professional's concern to ensure that those with whom they are personally compromised should *not* be seen by others to be unfairly benefiting. But why should not a particular professional simply get things *right* with respect to fair treatment –

in any professional dealings with their paramour – via detached application of the same set of rules which they apply to others, leaving their personal favours for private moments? What is there, for example, to prevent teachers or academics treating their pupil lovers with the same scrupulous fairness as others in the classroom? A crucial problem in relation to this, however, is that professional responses to the difficulties of clients, patients and students are not anyway well conceived in terms of scrupulously equal distribution of time, attention and resources. It is absurd to suppose that doctors deal with patients or professors with students with the aid of a stopwatch, and how much time and attention it is proper to devote to a client clearly depends crucially upon sensitive professional judgement of personal needs.

But, from this point of view, it is not easy at the best of times for professionals – particularly such professionals as teachers, nurses and social workers whose occupations require a degree of *proper* personal involvement with pupils, patients and clients – to be sure that they are not spending more time with a particular needy case because this client has more readily engaged their sympathies than another. There is, in short, something of a professional imperative in the case of the 'people' professions to diminish rather than increase any factors or circumstances which might lead to bias or favouritism, or, for that matter, to equally unfair 'compensatory' discrimination *against* a favourite. Indeed, since, given the range of individual client needs, there are no general distributive rules of professional attention, it must always be a problem for the compromised lawyer, teacher or doctor to know whether the extra attention he or she is giving in this instance is due to proper personal regard for the exceptional case or improper favouritism. Moreover, the trouble with much ethical reflection upon this question may well be that there is some tendency to conceive professional justice (and perhaps justice in general) as a matter of each person getting his or her due, as though what constitutes a client's due is something to be counted in terms of equal distribution of time, attention or resources. This leads to the equally misleading thought that if clients, patients or pupils do receive their 'fair' shares of professional time and attention, then professional justice can be said to have been done. Thus, if doctors or teachers could arrange things so that the patients or students with whom they are compromised are not either unfairly favoured or discriminated against (they are subject to the same rules as others and others are subject to the same rules as they) then there might be nothing wrong with professional–client fraternisation.

The difficulty with this line of thought is not just that what is generally owed by way of justice by professionals to their clients is particular or context-specific, but that what is due to the clients, patients and students of such 'people' professionals as social workers, nurses and teachers is a particular quality of *personal* response. Thus, the same quality of sympathetic response required in the case of the fearful patient or the diffident student may not be called for in the case of the stoical patient or confident student. But this is to say that what determines proper interpretation and just application of professional principles to particular circumstances are professional *dispositions*, *attitudes* and *sensibilities*, more than general rules of distribution. Indeed, in the spirit of contemporary virtue ethics,[7] it is arguable that what is really required for understanding what counts as proper dispensation of professional justice is some conception of the professionally *virtuous* individual, and of what such an individual would be liable to do in this or that circumstance: in particular, some understanding of those special qualities of personal concern for clients as individuals which serve to promote wise, rather than merely calculative, professional judgement. Given that 'people' professionals' judgements cannot but be shaped by personal engagements, it is clear that a given teacher, social worker or nurse can never be *sure* that they have *entirely* eliminated all elements of personal liking for some individuals and dislike of others. But, from this perspective, it is crucial to proper development of professional virtues and sensibilities – as well as to proper exercise of the practical wisdom presupposed to such virtues – to avoid, wherever possible, any situations which might serve to obstruct such development. In sum, since professionals have to make decisions about client welfare in which personal considerations and relationships are *already* implicated, the route to ensuring that any such decisions are as objective as possible cannot but lie in the development of sensibilities which are, among other things, as far as possible uncorrupted by extra-professional feelings and considerations.

From this viewpoint, professional *justice* is compromised wherever and whenever professional *character* is compromised. It is therefore beside the point to try to excuse a fraternising professional, such as a male teacher who has a sexual relation with a female student, on the grounds that she is above the age of legal consent, that he fell hopelessly in love, or that he was scrupulous in his attempts to guard against favouritism in a professional role (and it should be borne in mind that it must make things worse rather than better if he was scrupulous *to a fault* in his efforts to eliminate bias). It would also seem to follow that cases of sexual exploitation of clients by professionals – or abuse of vulnerable children by teachers and other carers – while deplorable and unforgivable (though fortunately in teaching not very common), do not well illustrate what is generally 'unprofessional' about sexual or other personal fraternisation between professionals and clients. The heart of the problem is that such liaisons incline to erode the very basis upon which any proper professional involvements with clients – involvements which may require to be at one and the same time personally involved yet *also* objective and detached – requires to be built. Hence, although it is clear that we can sometimes have tangible evidence of what is professionally untoward about such liaisons – there can be unjust or unfair distribution of attention through favouritism (or even penalisation of the loved one) and professionals do lay themselves open to a range of pressures from special pleading to blackmail – any unprofessionality involved is not always so readily apparent. Indeed, given the usual scope for human error, it is hardly possible for professionals to avoid considerable distributive injustice in their judgements and actions for all too much of the time. But since professionals cannot but be aware of how easy it is to get things wrong in their dealings with clients, it is clearly professional folly to give further hostages to fortune via unprofessional liaison, as well as a matter of urgency to cultivate the professional virtues required to limit the damage that is already inevitable in the regular course of professional engagement.

## Interim reflections

Initial reflections upon the normativity of teaching and learning in this chapter led us to a consideration of the reasons (if reasons are needed) why it seems right to regard such conduct as sexual abuse and corporal punishment as unequivocal harms to children and young people – and as hence quite beyond the professional pale. In turn, via a more general consideration of the wrongs of 'unprofessional' professional–client liaison, we were led to broader reflection upon the nature of professional justice, which it was argued is less a function of the application of general ethical rules, or calculation of particular moral consequences, and more a matter of the cultivation of professional virtues apt for the maintenance of proper personally engaged, yet properly detached, relations with clients. These points, of course, sit very comfortably with earlier analyses of professional reason and judgement as a function of the cultivation of non-technicist qualities of situation-specific moral reflection and sensibility, but they also look forward to later discussions of the specific moral character of the teacher's role, and of the contribution of ordinary moral virtues to that role. However, following on from the present examination of what we might reasonably hold to be professionally *unacceptable* conduct – on the grounds that it involves harms at potential or actual variance with any reasonable conception of human rights – we need to look more closely in the next chapter at the issue, fundamental to educational philosophy and theory, of what might constitute substantial educational *benefits*. It is one thing to have descried what professionals should generally avoid in the way of actual harms to their clients, but another to discern the general form and direction of any benefits they aspire to bestow upon their clients in the course of legitimate professional endeavour. In the case of doctors, then, we suppose not only that they are professionally obliged to avoid harming their patients, but that they are also in the business of healing them, and that they have some idea of what this means. By the same token, however, our account of educational professionalism to date now urgently requires some general idea of what *substantial* ends – beyond avoiding the psychological, physical or sexual brutalisation or degradation of pupils – teachers are in business to serve.

# 10

# AIMS OF EDUCATION, SCHOOLING AND TEACHING

## The radical contestability of educational aims

It is the task of medical practitioners to cure patients and/or promote their health, that of lawyers to try to preserve justice under the law and to defend the legal interests of clients. Moreover, despite some room for professional disagreement about the proper processes of medicine and law, there would also seem to be reasonably objective criteria for determining the extent to which these aims are being met: if the health of patients deteriorates or they die, or innocent people are gaoled on false evidence, while the guilty are set free, there is something clearly awry in the states of medicine and law. But what, in general, can we say about the overall aims and purposes of educationalists and teachers, upon which a professional conception of education might go to work? From previous arguments, it might seem that since even the most general aims of education are subject to radical contestation, education and teaching are normative or evaluative enterprises 'all the way down'. But then, as also previously indicated, this consideration would have some fairly serious implications for any conception of education and teaching as *professional* enterprises. Thus, for example, if education is regarded as a matter of culture-specific induction into local habits and practices, how could there be any objection to a given personal or cultural practice on principled professional grounds. Faced with a local episode of witch-doctoring which, psychological or religious considerations aside, has no evident health-promoting basis in objective physio-logical or bio-chemical fact, a physician is clearly in a strong position to denounce the practice as indefensible from a profes-sional medical perspective. But how would I successfully complain on the basis of professional educational principle about a particular practice of would-be education, the teaching, say, of astrology or alchemy, in the teeth of the objection that education is simply local cultural initiation, and this is what we happen to believe around here? Are there any general aims of education, or objective goods it sets out to promote, which might give us grounds for judging that any failure to meet or provide them was a matter of *professional* dereliction?

By way of first response to this challenge, reasons have already been given in this volume for regarding any wholesale postmodern assimilation of facts to values, and values to local cultural practices or perspectives, as fairly implausible. Indeed, with regard to the run of civilised professional and other practices, it could hardly be clearer that there are abundant objective matters of fact upon which we may determine what we ought or need to do. From this viewpoint, we appeal to facts of a fairly basic observational kind in denouncing the witch doctor's hocus-pocus as both medically irrelevant and *unprofessional* (in so far, at any rate, as the witch doctor claims to be physician rather than priest). Thus, what presumably we need to discern with respect to teaching are *objective* grounds, analogous to those of health promotion in the case of medicine, for accepting or rejecting professional practices as consistent or otherwise with general educational goals. In a nutshell, the basic problem here is that while it seems difficult to understand teaching other than as the promotion of human development and learning, it is nowadays tantamount to an article of faith in those philosophical, sociological and anthropological circles which have influenced the present-day postmodern intellectual climate, that there cannot *be* any culture-neutral notion of human development and learning. But, in that case it is not just that there can be no *non-relative* criteria (however locally interpretable) of education upon which to ground an *objective* conception of good or effective teaching, but also that there cannot in consequence be any *professional* conception of education or teaching. This question now needs to be addressed with some care.

## Teaching, human development and culture

Are human learning and development, then, wholly socially constructed or culturally determined? A little thought serves to show us that the best answer to this question (apparent paradox notwithstanding) is, yes and no. The question seems to present us with a *dilemma* to which postmodern or historicist affirmation of the social determinedness of learning and development responds by firmly grasping one horn. Learning cannot *both* be *and* not be culturally determined, it seems foolhardy to claim that it is not, therefore we can hardly deny that it *is* so determined. The trouble, as usual, with any such sweeping conclusion is that it is liable to be ambiguous, and hence, by implication, dangerously overstated. Where, then, lie the ambiguities in this case? First, if we take the question of whether or not development is socially conditioned to be asking if there is any human development or learning which does not take a specific socio-cultural form, then the answer to *that* question is clearly that there is *not*; for how could there ever be any *human* learning which did not occur in and/or reflect the values of some specific socio-cultural context? But we also know, from the findings of modern field sociologists and anthropologists, that cultures vary to the point of mutual *contradiction* in their beliefs, values and practices. Moreover, it is not particularly troublesome to accept as one general consequence of this point that what may be perfectly appropriate for inclusion in the educational curriculum of one culture may not be so appropriate in another. This may also be true of a range of rather different things. First, I have no doubt that we would be likely to object to the substitution of French for British history in the UK national curriculum. Second, it may be appropriate to include certain economically-grounded forms of vocational training in the curriculum of some developing countries, which might well be out of place in the curricula of developed economies. Third, we may well be willing to concede the legitimacy in separate religious schools of certain kinds of moral instruction – concerning the sanctity of marriage, the right to life and the evils of non-heterosexual congress – which we personally find, from a secular-humanist position, at least illiberal if not actually mistaken.

But does it thereby follow that nothing can be said concerning the overall shape and form of human development which is *generally* applicable to human beings, as members of a species rather than of some particular cultural constituency? One of the troubles with radically sceptical epistemologies, as we have continually seen, is that they invariably presuppose what they purport to deny. Thus, just as idealist or phenomenalist claims that human knowledge can only be a matter of subjective experience appear to presuppose some sort of distinction between subjectivity and objectivity – to which such theories are not entitled – so postmodern claims to the effect that there are no facts of human nature – or that any science which might presume to teach us such facts is simply one myth or narrative among others – invariably smuggle in a great many assumptions about the nature of human life and development to which they are equally not entitled. What grounds, for example, could postmodernists have for holding what they do about the diverse influence of different conceptual schemes on different ways of life, other than what field sociologists and anthropologists claim to have discovered concerning the vital role played by enculturation in assisting the particular purposes of survival (or whatever) of *essentially* rational and social animals. To be sure, post-structuralist and hermeneutic challenges[1] to our received concepts of person and agency are well taken if they aim to show that such concepts might be shaped or informed by different *conceptions* of reason or moral association, but they go too far if they claim to show that concepts of person and agency are *themselves* merely figments of social construction. Indeed, in the absence of some fairly substantial and stable species relative and cross-cultural notions of person and agency, the sociological claims could make hardly any sense at all.

Indeed, alternative medicine and rational medical disagreement apart, we have already seen that it would be foolhardy for any postmodernist to gainsay the anatomical and physiological facts of proper human functioning which both give rise to and vindicate professional medical practice.[2] It is surely not insignificant that when post-structuralists and hermeneuticists fall ill they are invariably inclined to seek the help of state-of-the-art western medical practice, rather than consulting African witch doctors: this, moreover, is not cultural colonialism, it is just good sense. But then we only require it to be acknowledged, as postmodernists who make so much of the role of ideas and concepts in shaping any human perspectives must also surely acknowledge, that there is a *psychological* as well as a physical dimension to human health and development. From this point of view, it is not unreasonable to suppose that minds as well as bodies can become disordered, and that people may fall mentally as well as physically ill. But then it becomes very hard to see how *any* human educational, moral and legal practices might be sustained in default of certain crucial distinctions between different folk-psychological levels of dysfunctional character and personality: between the responsible and the irresponsible, the mature and the immature, the wicked and the deranged, and so forth. Once again, it is crucial here to distinguish any reasonable claim that particular received *versions* of these distinctions are questionable, from the rather less plausible claim that these distinctions *as such* are no more than local cultural fictions. From this perspective, it may well be that we have not always (or not yet) managed to fix some of these distinctions in the best or most useful of ways: there may be grey areas which leave us hard put to know whether someone should be characterised for medical, educational or legal purposes as mad or bad, emotionally disturbed or intellectually retarded.[3] Equally, however, to the extent that *some such* distinctions are the very cornerstones of all intelligibly recognisable human practices or institutions of education, medicine and law, it would hardly make much sense to speak in their absence of human society and culture at all.

It may therefore be doubted whether postmodern and/or other forms of epistemological scepticism offer more than self-undermining reasons for abandoning any of those basic folk-psychological categories and distinctions evidently presupposed to any intelligible account of human society and culture. Indeed, it is likely that even a thoroughgoing scientific determinist or elimina-tivist would be more disposed to *redescribe* or redefine (as perhaps involving different kinds or levels of determination) our workaday distinction between responsible and irresponsible human agency, than to abandon it altogether.[4] In summary, then, it is reasonable to suppose that such basic psycho-functional categories and distinctions must have enormous significance for any *professional* definition and articulation of the aims, purposes and processes of education and teaching. Just as some sort of distinction between health and disease seems presupposed to the identification of needs or deficits which medical intervention may be required to remedy, so distinctions between knowledge and ignorance, sense and nonsense, reasonable belief and superstition, maturity and immaturity, interest and obsession, may serve to identify human needs which it is the *general* business of education to address. Indeed, we may reasonably regard education and schooling as generally concerned, irrespective of any local social forces which might give particular cultural shape to such generalities, with answering a fairly straightforward array of basic human needs and interests in respect of a fairly uncontroversial view of human weal and woe. In this connection, just as we can be sure that it is better for people to be physically well rather than diseased, so we can be confident, irrespective of any philosophical controversies about truth, that ignorance is more a benighted and disabling, than blessed or enabling, human condition. We can also be confident that, however much cultures interestingly differ in their conceptions of maturity and in their child-rearing practices, intellectual and emotional maturity is an *acquired* rather than an innate characteristic, and that most if not all cultures have a concept of development from childhood to maturity implying some requirement (however well or badly respected in practice) for parental nurture and guidance, especially in early years, towards such maturity.

We may also be reasonably certain that since the logic and evidence of human psychology is linked to that of sociology – it is virtually a commonplace of contemporary philosophy of mind and culture that there could hardly *be* individual human psychology apart from human society – the needs and interests which education and schooling are called upon to address must also reflect the crucial socio-economic dimension of any significant human flourishing. Indeed, educational philosophers have recently been at pains to indicate the importance of *work*, including co-operative work with others, in people's lives with particular regard to re-affirming the important role of schools in equipping people with *vocational* and other practically and socially useful skills.[5] Moreover, although much recent work on this topic has been sensitive to the more problematic economic status of paid work in modern developed economies, and has therefore sought to stress the broader human developmental as well as the narrower economic value of work, the urgent need for schools to promote economically significant vocational skills in less developed countries should scarcely need great emphasis. If it is bad for humans to lack the more general forms of knowledge by which we may distinguish educated from uneducated individuals, it is clearly just as disastrous for individuals to lack the basic economic skills needed to provide for themselves and their dependants, especially in circumstances where there may be no recourse to the benefits of state security.

## The diverse developmental purposes of schooling

One important lesson to be drawn from such observations is that teaching is implicated in a *variety* of purposes including, as well as the more general business of rational emancipation, basic socialisation and vocational training. However, although these different purposes need not be seen as *necessarily* conflicting, this does to some extent make the school curriculum a field of difficult negotiation between different human developmental interests. Indeed, I suspect that post-war educational philosophers, falling foul of a particular fallacious line of reasoning, sometimes made rather heavy weather of this point. Hence, it is tempting to suppose that if teaching is concerned to promote education, and education is what goes on in schools, we would have to determine what *education* is in order to see what merits inclusion in the school curriculum. From this perspective, however, it becomes a matter of trying to decide which of several competing views of the purposes of education is the correct one. Thus, in the early years of analytical philosophy of education, perhaps the greatest influence was wielded by those – let us call them *non-instrumentalists* – who argued that education concerns the promotion of human knowledge and understanding *for its own sake*, irrespective of any practical purposes to which individuals might in due course come to put it.[6] There can be no doubt that non-instrumentalism was widely taken to imply, especially in the light of its explicit denigration of practical skills as of merely *extrinsic* or instrumental value, the reduced curricular status of subjects which were not obviously concerned to promote understanding of the world for its own sake. Much ink was therefore spilt by teachers of practical subjects, concerned to salvage the curricular value of their area of expertise, in desperate efforts to show how home economics, physical education, technical education, or whatever, might be said to promote *intrinsically worthwhile* knowledge. On the other hand, curricular *instrumentalists* of utilitarian and other persuasions sought to show the *opposite*: that no subject could be considered *really* educationally worthwhile, and therefore be regarded as fit for inclusion in a rational school curriculum, unless it could be shown to be instrumentally *useful* in personal, social or economic terms.[7]

I do not doubt that close scrutiny of recent educational philo-sophical literature would serve to confirm that some such issue between instrumentalism and non-instrumentalism is still fairly widely regarded as central to the debate about the proper direction of education, and at least one contemporary educational philoso-pher of reputation has written as though the tedious survival of this controversy indicates the irresolvable postmodern condition of educational debate.[8] Perhaps a postmodernist might regard instrumentalism and non-instrumentalism as rival educational narratives between which different social constituencies are free to choose on grounds of what best suits their socio-cultural context or, more postmodernly, on no grounds at all. It takes little thought, however, to see that since the very idea that there might be genuine controversy of this kind about the purpose of education rests on a fairly elementary conceptual mistake, any society or state which inclined to such an either-or conclusion on this important issue would be really rather irresponsible. Moreover, the confusion in question is the already familiar one between *education* and *schooling*. For, of course, just as it does *not* follow from the fact that a subject or activity is *non-educational* (drawing here upon the rationally emancipatory sense in which 'education' has been construed in post-war educational philosophy), that it has no place in the school curriculum, so it does not follow either from the fact that the school curriculum serves a socio-economic purpose that all school subjects must be of *instrumental* value. It is therefore of the utmost import to recognise that school (unlike education) is a social *institution*, that it exists to serve purposes of *vocational training* and *socialisation* which are at once both more and less than the acquisition of knowledge for its own sake, and that *education* is therefore only *one* of the ends which any school curriculum exists to serve.

However, despite the central theoretical and practical importance of the distinction between schooling and education, it has been quite seriously fudged of late in a variety of ways. Thus, for example, although the distinction appears to be recognised in the earlier noted arguments of 'deschoolers' to the effect that education *is* different from schooling – that the latter, on this view, actually impedes the purposes of the former – it should also be clear from the focus of such radical theorists on the socio-economic and survival value of practically worthwhile skills, that they are little more than unreconstructed *instrumentalists* who fail in sometimes fairly philistine ways to recognise the value of non-instrumental knowledge and understanding. Clearly there is something dangerously illiberal or unemancipatory about the idea that because some young people in straitened contemporary circumstances of socially deprived and/or crime-infested urban ghettos are not readily appreciative of a rational understanding of the world which goes beyond the present and the particular, we ought therefore to confine them to a diet of street survival skills. It seems both more reasonable and just to recognise that for schooling to serve the variety of purposes for which human learning is needed, it needs to provide opportunities for rational initiation which extend significantly further – precisely in the direction of what liberal educationalists have conceived as learning 'for its own sake' – than the acquisition of vocational and other coping skills.

More surprisingly, however, such recognition also seems to have been rather lost in some highly influential latter-day attempts to bridge the alleged gap opened up by modern educational theorising between the 'intrinsic' personal emancipatory purposes of education and the 'instrumental' socio-economic goals of schooling.[9] Such attempts begin reasonably enough from the observation that early post-war analytical philosophy of education was guilty of unwarranted conflation of a number of rather different distinctions. In brief, it is complained with some justification that the philosophical pioneers of liberal traditionalism[10] greatly compounded confusion: first, by aligning the distinction between education and training with those of intellect and skill and theory and practice; second, by a mapping of these onto a further distinction between what is of value for its own sake and what is only of instrumental value. The dire consequences of such wholesale conflation are that what is of educational value can no longer be considered useful, that the spheres of theory or intellect and practicality cannot be regarded as other than mutually exclusive, and that whatever is of practical value cannot, by that very token, be considered educationally valuable. It is, to be sure, hard not to agree in finding all of this conceptually mistaken and at odds with common sense. Thus, the fact that science may be studied for the non-practical purpose of understanding the world for its own sake does not preclude its practical or technical application, most if not all human activities involve significant interplay of theory and practice, and qualities of great practical value – for example, moral virtues – seem to be of undeniable intrinsic educational worth. The trouble is, however, that the largely pragmatist (Dewey) inspired reconstruction of the idea of educational value developed in the light of these observations falls foul of its own peculiarly fallacious reasoning.

## The errors of pragmatism

The interest of new pragmatists in distinctions between education and training, intrinsic worth and instrumental value, theory and practice, appears to be focused upon a range of perennial questions concerning the relation of pupil interest and ability to the wider social and economic purposes of the school curriculum. Indeed, the new pragmatist arguments seem essentially to amount to a liberal educational restatement of a range of concerns which had already surfaced in the wake of post-war British educational reforms – most notably, perhaps, the raising of the school-leaving age and educational comprehensivisation – about how it is appropriate to conceive the schooling of large numbers of young people of apparently non-academic bent. In the 1960s and 1970s, it was argued by what I have elsewhere called 'conservative traditionalists' – a tradition owing much to the educational writings of such earlier literary figures and cultural critics as T.S. Eliot and D.H. Lawrence – that large numbers of especially working-class children were unsuited to the academic learning of liberal education and ought rather to be equipped by schools with some form of practically useful non-academic training in domestic, artistic and vocational skills.[11] In so supposing, the 'alternative curriculum'-mongers seem to have been influenced by much the same psychometric ideology which informed the official educational policy of the 1944 Education Act – an approach which sought to sort and grade children, in the light of alleged scientifically verifiable differences of aptitude and ability, for the rather different purposes of separate schooling. Indeed, with the wisdom of hindsight, it seems little surprising that the post-war educational reforms of a notoriously class-ridden Britain seemed to have no difficulty endorsing an essentially Platonic conception of education for an inherently caste-based social and economic system. Thus, for post-war (rear) guardians of received cultural and social distinctions, education was functioning best when it taught each and every person to know his or her place, as defined on some absolute scale of class, ability or gender-determined ability or inclination.

One risks some injustice in associating vocationalists of the new pragmatism with the socio-cultural prejudices of conservative traditionalist advocates of alternative curricula. At the same time, it is difficult to overlook the tendency for their somewhat more enlightened and sophisticated arguments to proceed to not dissimilar conclusions. As far as one can tell, then, new vocational reasoning seems to proceed in something like the following way. First, new pragmatists reject assimilation by such post-war educational philosophers as R.S Peters[12] of the distinction between education and vocational training to the theory–practice distinction – maintaining that any such identification reflects not only an unwarranted academic bias against the practical and vocational, but also a highly *artificial* distinction between the academic or theoretical and the practical or vocational. Hence, as already indicated, one can hardly deny that theory (principled reflection) is invariably implicated in intelligent practice, or that practical pursuits have frequently significant consequences for the understanding of theory. Indeed, recalling a previously noted Aristotelian distinction between truth-focused theoretical enquiry and value-driven practical enquiry, it is surely hard to deny the educational significance of those forms of practical engagement presupposed to acquiring moral virtue or creating works of art. But then, is it not just as true that the practice of vocational skills can also have significant *educational* implications? Apart from the fact that the practice of such skills is often a route to the acquisition of virtues of patience and persistence, the educational value of which has just been conceded, one's intellectual understanding of the world, oneself and other people stands to be considerably enhanced by vocational initiation. But in that case (so the story goes), why cannot practically focused forms of vocational and other training be properly regarded as providing, at least for some young people, a valid educational experience – a 'practical education'[13] – which is equal in status to any 'academic' education?

Unfortunately, however, in so far as this apparently plausible argument plays extremely fast and loose with (among other things) rather different senses in which practice can be a source of theoretical understanding in the education of young people, it requires to be dismissed as invalid. The trouble, once again, lies in a failure to distinguish crucially different senses in which theory is involved in practice (or vice versa), or either of these notions is implicated in education. On the one hand, then, if the argument is no more than the familiar point of pragmatist pedagogy that pupils may often be more effectively taught science by engaging in practical experiments, than through the taking of notes or memorisation of laws and theorems, this, whilst true, indicates only another approach to *theoretical* learning, and falls well short of supporting any substitution of hands-on practical experience for educational understanding more broadly construed. On the other hand, however, if it is meant to show that there is a way of learning skills which focuses less on the rote learning of practical procedures and more upon the acquisition of those principles which inform their intelligent practice, this, whilst also true, equally fails to license the substitution of such principled skill-learning for forms of educationally significant understanding. In short, any inference from intelligent practice (of vocational skills or whatever) to educational value goes through only at the cost of ignoring a rather important difference between the educational status of that principled understanding – however practically acquired – which constitutes scientific knowledge, and the grasp – however 'intellectual' – of any principles which inform effective hairdressing. One cannot 'liberalise' home economics or bestow educational value upon volleyball by a more precise articulation of the principles which enable us to engage in such activities intelligently, because it is not upon such principles that education in the more substantial rational emancipatory sense of the post-war pioneers of liberal education is built. Indeed, to employ such reasons to argue that we might, in the education of some less able pupils, substitute a critical appreciation of cookery or typing for a critical understanding of science or history, is clearly the royal road to elitism if not worse. Doubtless, then, the distinctions of Peters and others between education and training, theory and practice, and intrinsic and instrumental value, stand in need of more careful mapping and refinement; but, in so far as they serve to steer us well clear of any such educationally pernicious conclusions, their importance could hardly be clearer.

Again, according to the story so far, it should be clear that what lies at the heart of this confusion is persistent failure to observe a crucially important distinction between education and schooling. We have already seen how the non-instrumentalist assumption that the only purpose of schooling (here confused with education) is to transmit intrinsically worthwhile educational knowledge and understanding is as potentially damaging to educational theorising as the opposite instrumentalist or utilitarian assumption that the only purpose of education (now confused with schooling) is to promote vocational or other life skills. Post-war liberal traditionalists such as Peters and Hirst fell foul of these confusions; so did their utilitarian critics; so did radical advocates of 'deschooling'; so did the anti-liberal educational prophets of 'alternative curricula'; and so do those new 'liberal' vocationalists lately given to questioning the education/vocation and theory–practice distinctions. In their own way, then, new vocationalists side with instrumentalists in considering the main task of schooling (here confused with education) to be the preparation of young people for the adult life of post-school work and social relationships, against the non-instrumentalist construal of education (there confused with schooling) as exclusively concerned with the initiation of children into intrinsically worthwhile and rationally emancipatory forms of knowledge and understanding. However, if we map the education–vocation distinction onto the distinction between education and schooling, it should be apparent that although the instrumentalist is largely right to claim what he does of schooling, and the non-instrumentalist is quite correct about education, both would be quite *wrong* if they put matters the other way around. In short, it would be quite *untrue* to say either that education is primarily about equipping young people with life skills, or that schooling is exclusively about the initiation of individuals into a personal understanding of themselves and the world for its own sake.

Hence, if we duly recognise that schooling and education are distinct, albeit practically related, enterprises and that education is only *one* (albeit a crucially important one) of the many purposes of schooling, then we may come to see that the problem is not so much that of seeing how vocationalism might be made educational or education vocationalised, but that of how to do justice to both education and vocational training within a coherent overall conception of the diverse purposes of institutionalised schooling. More particularly, however, while recognising that the acquisition of knowledge and understanding with which both schooling and knowledge are concerned has practical as well as theoretical aspects, we need to keep firmly in mind that not all sorts of knowledge, theoretical or practical, are centrally concerned with the rationally emancipatory purposes whereby education has been reasonably distinguished from the other ends of schooling. As the early pioneers of analytical philosophy of education argued, education is concerned with acquisition of the sort of knowledge which is capable of affording a broad cognitive and explanatory perspective on the world and one's place in it, more than with training (however principled) in the know-how of practical skills.

## The possibility of self-determination

The distinction drawn between education and training (and other forms of socialisation or preparation for adult life) by post-war philosophers of liberal education, and the conceptual connection they descried between education and an appreciation of knowledge and truth for its own sake, also played a crucial role in establishing a certain ideal of rational *autonomy* or *self-direction* as the key aim of distinctively educational endeavour. In this connection, the new liberal educationalists claimed continuity with philosophers from classical antiquity to modern times[14] in maintaining that the very idea of human freedom was barely intelligible apart from an education conceived, more or less Socratically, as a rational initiation into *objective* knowledge and truth. On this view, it is only through the clearest possible understanding of how things actually *are*, rather than how they take them or would wish them to be, that human agents have any hope of escape from Plato's cave[15] of ignorance and superstition into the sweetness and light of responsible self-determination. From this perspective, it would be the main aim of education as a prime function of schooling to equip young people with intellectual resources for understanding themselves, the world and the general human predicament through substantial initiation into flower of human achievement in the arts and natural, social and moral sciences. But, by the same token, any form of schooling which misguidedly sought to provide some young people with an 'alternative curriculum' of practical and vocational subjects allegedly more suited to their less academic needs and interests would be liable for censure as inimical to the development of those capacities for self-direction traditionally considered a *sine qua non* of peculiarly human development and agency: all the more in so far as it may be reasonably suspected that arguments in favour of a more vocational or utilitarian training or life preparation for the masses have often concealed a deliberate intent to deprive some human beings of the possibility of such development. At all events, the now familiar 'forms of knowledge' conception of education which advocated rational initiation into a range of forms of rational appraisal of the world – natural scientific, social scientific, mathematical, moral, religious, aesthetic and philosophical – was expressly formulated with a view to the promotion of such individual rational autonomy.

However, it is just these conceptions of rational knowledge and objective truth – and associated notions of rational autonomy – which have come increasingly under attack in educational philosophy over the past quarter of a century or so. The attacks, as previously indicated in this work, have been inspired by wider mainstream developments in both analytical and non-analytical traditions of philosophy. On the one hand, then, certain powerful anti-realist trends in epistemology and the philosophy of science seem to have disposed of the very idea – which may at least have been implicit in forms of knowledge theorists' talk of 'testability against experience'[16] – of a mind-independent reality against which our statements or judgements about the world of experience may be tested for their truth or falsity. On the other, certain powerful historicist and communitarian trends in moral and social theory have served to undermine the idea – which may also have seemed inherent in the basically deontological conceptions of moral development at the heart of many liberal educational views of moral autonomy – that moral knowledge or understanding is primarily a matter of the grasp of certain abstract universal ethical principles accessible from some socially detached or culturally disinherited 'view from nowhere'. These rather different epistemological and social/moral-theoretical perspectives have of late been widely combined in the heady cocktail of postmodernism, and the general product of this juxtaposition is catchily summed up in the now familiar claim of one of the leading gurus of this movement that there are 'no overarching meta-narratives'.[17] Truth is irredeemably, on this account, both *particular* and *perspectival*. In educational philosophy, moreover, there can be no doubt that the familiar liberal educational aim of rational autonomy or self-determination has been a chief casualty of these postmodern attacks. On the classical view of post-war analytical philosophy of education, the notion of autonomy was linked to ideas of reason and truth as both referentially objective and universal in scope. But if postmodern epistemology denies rational objectivity, and postmodern social and moral theory denies the universality of reason, what remains of rational autonomy?

First, since I believe that post-war philosophers of liberal education were quite right about the conceptual connection between rational autonomy and objective truth, I have to concede that if these sceptical postmodern doubts about the very possibility of knowledge as traditionally conceived are true, they must be quite fatal to any coherent notion of rational autonomy. But although a very great deal would need to be said in order to do full justice to this issue,[18] we have already said enough here to defuse any extreme forms of such scepticism. Thus, with regard to the anti-realism of much postmodern epistemologising, we have seen that it is mostly confusion to take the inherently conceptualised nature of any intelligible human experience to preclude our judging this or that state of affairs to be, as matter of objective *fact*, thus and so – or to imply that all our judgements about the world have to be relativised to this or that conceptual scheme or perspective. Thus, whether I am right or wrong that there is a cat sitting on this mat depends less upon the theoretical coherence of this report with other judgements of mine, and more on whether there is or is not a cat on the mat. However, all that we need for this crucial degree of objectivity is that modest Aristotelian correspondence which maintains that it is speaking truly to say of what is, that it is, and speaking falsely to say that it is of what is not: we do not in the least require any wholesale correspondence theory of the kind which would require impossible comparison of entire conceptual schemes with some completely unconceptualised reality. Moreover, any such conception of objective truth is clearly quite consistent with the *provisional* status of knowledge construed more explanatorily. From this viewpoint, I need not in the least deny that my objective knowledge of the expansion of heated metals (assuming this to be true knowledge which is not liable to falsification via the discovery, should this be intelligible, of a metal which does not so expand) may be susceptible of better or worse understandings in the light of evolving scientific explanations of physical properties. It is quite bizarre, however, to suppose that I cannot know whether there is a cat on the mat, or whether metals expand when heated, because I cannot be certain whether there is any objective reality to which these statements refer. In sum, even if human knowledge can never be certain in the sense envisaged by some traditional epistemology, there could be no intelligible talk of explanation barring the possibility of objective truth as a goal of explanation. In short, if all science is narrative and all narratives are works of fancy, then there could be no such thing as scientific or other *explanation* – as opposed to fiction or fancy.

Again, we have argued that the communitarian idea, widely subscribed to by virtue theorists, ethical realists, feminists of the ethics of care school and others, that genuine moral identity, integrity and agency are more products of particular cultural inheritance and context-sensitive sensibility than of the grasp of socio-culturally dislocated moral universals, is not necessarily fatal either to the idea of moral objectivity. Whilst it may sometimes have appeared that contemporary debates between liberals and communitarians have faced us with a stark choice between procrustean context-insensitive moral absolutes, and some utterly promiscuous moral relativity of socio-cultural diversity, we have indicated that the dilemma is more apparent than real, and that it is not necessary to grasp either horn of it. To a large extent, the problems arising here are simply a special case of the general epistemological difficulties just aired. We seem to be faced with a choice between an impossible goal of mind-independent truth – in this case routed through the idea of absolutely valid moral rule or principle – and a hopeless perspectivalism according to which morality is what the individual or society chooses to make of it. A moment's reflection serves to show that objective moral truth lies in neither of these directions. In the first place, the objectivity of morality does not obviously seem to need Kantianly routing through the idea of universality. I can come to *know* with the wisdom of painful hindsight, in the light precisely of considerations of which I was at the time insufficiently appreciative, that a decision once made on the basis of a consistent commitment was quite *objectively* wrong. But although I can now also see that the wrongness of this decision was not in the least due to my lack or otherwise of *principle* – for observance of this or that principle need not be what is at stake here – its wrongness need not be related either to any compromise of culturally inherited values. In this connection, it hardly needs saying that moral error may follow as easily from uncritical subscription to the faith of one's fathers as from rigid adherence to the rule of moral law.

## Schooling, education and training

In the final analysis, of course, autonomy or self-direction is itself a *moral* quality, and since – as critics of liberal theory have fairly decisively shown – moral qualities may not be exhaustively understood in terms of some purely 'cognitive' or intellectual grasp of rules or principles, much post-war analytical educational philosophy seems to have been mistaken in its attempts so to construe it. But although self-direction undoubtedly requires the educational cultivation of sensibilities and qualities of perception which are no less affective than cognitive, even those non-cognitive faculties upon which it rests are nevertheless focused on the discernment of objective truth. In order to act wisely and well in this world, we need to be as undeceived in our perceptions and feelings as in our cognitions, and it is again education, understood as the capacity to pursue and value knowledge and truth for its own sake, which is crucially presupposed to the development of such correct discernment. From this viewpoint, all the same, although practical activities may well contribute to the promotion of educational understanding and illumination in precisely the way that scientific experiment or technology can contribute to scientific knowledge, or the movements of the dancer express the meaning of the dance, the practical skills of experiment or dance need not in themselves necessarily issue in any educated understanding or rationally autonomous appreciation of the objective value and place of science or dance in human affairs. It is therefore of the utmost educational importance to observe a proper, albeit unfashionable, distinction between *education* and *training* in science, dance and other activities.

To this end, moreover, we should also be clear that although the capacity to pursue and value knowledge or activities for their own sake has been regarded as an important *necessary* condition of education, it is by no means a *sufficient* one, so that it would also be a mistake to regard various sports and games, invariably pursued for no other reason than the sheer enjoyment of them, as educational ends in themselves in anything like the sense of history or science. For whereas rational reflection on nature or enquiry into the human past are well-nigh paradigm cases of what it means to have one's understanding of the world educationally enlarged, it is less plausible to claim that hockey or netball contribute comparably to any educated appreciation of the human natural, cultural or social predicament. This is certainly not meant to downgrade any non-educational aspects of human development and learning, or to argue that practices and skills of a more utilitarian or vocational kind have a less secure place in the school curriculum. On the contrary, although such practices and skills may have little to contribute to the rational emancipation of individuals as such (no matter how much their practice may presuppose the grasp of practical rational principles), they have nevertheless an indispensable part to play in *schooling* with respect to such other highly important and legitimate purposes of schools as vocational training, health and fitness promotion, recreation and leisure preparation, and so on.

# 11

# THE MORAL ROLE OF THE TEACHER

## The moral educational dimension

In the previous chapters we have already indicated a dimension of ethical involvement which sets teaching significantly apart from such standard professions as medicine and law. By way of illustration, let us suppose that parents are seeking medical assistance for a child afflicted with some ailment. Getting the best medical care largely comes down to finding someone who is appropriately informed or skilled in the relevant field. However, it might be that the best qualified person here is not from a personal-moral point of view a very nice or good man. In his private life he is dishonest, spiteful and dissolute; he is mentally and physically cruel to his wife as well as persistently unfaithful; he repeatedly betrays his friends and exploits acquaintances, and so on. None of this may matter to parents, of course, so long as the doctor has the required medical expertise. On the other hand, however, if parents in search of a good education for their child discover that the best available in terms of academic knowledge and pedagogical skills is someone who is known personally to be a liar and an adulterer, as well as disloyal, shifty, sarcastic and bullying, they may well – regardless of his or her approved academic knowledge and technical skill as a teacher – have serious reservations about placing their child in the care of that person. It is therefore arguable that it cannot be a matter of total indifference either to professional educationalists or parents what a teacher is like as a private person in the sense that it is a matter of (relative) indifference what a surgeon or lawyer is like, precisely because educational goals cannot be disentangled from wider considerations and ideals of personal moral development. It may therefore be a cause for concern if teachers exhibit values or personal characteristics apparently at variance with what seems to be educationally desirable, which is why parents are inclined to worry, understandably if sometimes unnecessarily, about such aspects of the lives of some teachers as homosexuality, extra-marital cohabitation, political and religious affiliations, and so forth.

It is also hard to deny that *all* teachers are directly involved in moral education, as we *might* deny their involvement in the transmission of other sorts of values. Thus, in the face of a not implausible claim that aesthetic education is a cross-curricular issue, the protest of mathematics teachers that it is really not their business to promote aesthetic values, so long as they effectively communicate mathematical understanding, might nevertheless attract a measure of sympathy (whether or not misplaced). I suspect, however, that we should be less sympathetic to any protest on the part of such or other teachers that it is no part of their job to encourage children to behave decently towards others and to observe certain standards of honesty, fairness and probity.[1] In short, I would expect to be able to count upon a fair level of professional consensus that education and teaching are inherently moral enterprises, and that teachers in general would be disinclined to deny that much of what they do in the classroom, in the context of whatever else they teach, is liable to have a broadly moral influence on the attitudes, beliefs and conduct of pupils.

## Moral education and social control

Assuming such general agreement about the moral significance of education and teaching, however, I suspect that there is also no small confusion and uncertainty among teachers about the extent of their moral role and responsibilities, and I shall concentrate in this chapter mainly on trying to identify the root sources of such difficulties. In the first place, I believe that much common thought about the nature of moral education unhelpfully blurs a significant distinction between *moral education* and *social control*:[2] that, indeed, although there is undeniable overlap between these two concerns, it is nevertheless important to keep the differences between them clear. Second, however, I shall argue that getting reasonably clear about the difference between social control or moral training and moral education gives rise to further problems of understanding the nature of moral *education*, precisely in so far as it is possible to identify different and *competing* conceptions of moral education, and of the teacher's role in moral development. In this connection, I shall identify two common conceptions of moral education, which also seem to be largely (if not entirely) at odds with one another, despite the fact that it is also common for teachers to move uncertainly between them in their moral educational thought and practice. However, while conceding that each of these conceptions enshrines important truths about moral life and education, I shall also argue that in so far as they cannot be consistently combined, both are generally unsatisfactory and in need of replacement by a more satisfactory view.

But first, what of the potential for confusion between moral education and social control? This largely follows, I believe, from a common tendency – repeatedly noticed in this volume – to regard education itself in predominantly *instrumentalist* terms: to confuse, one might say, the intrinsic purposes of education with the extrinsic purposes of schooling. Thus, if we ask politicians, employers or the public at large what they want from 'education', understood broadly as schooling, they will *rightly* say that they want well-trained and informed young people capable of getting on with others and of shouldering the burdens of adult responsibility. In the more specific domain of moral education this is likely to mean, first and foremost, general conformity to the commonly accepted values of society. Hence, when parents complain that schools no longer seem to be upholding moral standards, what they usually have in mind is that children no longer seem to have respect for authority or for the property of others, and this may be accompanied by calls for the return of the sterner sanctions of the 'good old days'.

Similarly, when politicians start to take an interest in the moral aspects of formal education or schooling it is usually in response to public concern about one form of juvenile misdemeanour or other, and, once more, teachers are liable to be the focus of criticism for having let standards of discipline decline.[3] Moreover, although I believe that scapegoating schools and teachers for the current moral discontents and maladies of society is for the most part misdirected, dishonest and mischievous, I am not at all inclined to ridicule or belittle the genuine concerns of parents and the general public about the uncivil and anti-social behaviour of many young people which our schools so often seem unable to counteract. Hence, while we need not doubt that by far the great majority of teachers in our schools both acknowledge that it is a prime function of schools to try to foster attitudes and conduct of basic honesty and respect for others in young people, and do their utmost to promote them, we should not – in view of the immense difficulty of this task in contemporary circumstances – lose sight of the fact that this *is* a crucial function of schooling. In so far as this is so it would be well for politicians, educational managers and administrators and the larger public to ensure – before they leap to cast the specks from others' eyes – that they have done all within *their* power to support schools and teachers in this particular regard.

All the same, while there is everything to be said for, and little against, inculcating positive attitudes to the lives, rights and property of others, there clearly *is* more to be said about moral education than is adequately captured by the idea of training young people to be obedient to current social requirements. At one level, this is a merely *formal* point about the relationship of training to education as such. Although it is no doubt true that training is presupposed to education[4] – that one cannot come to an educated appreciation of certain subjects until one has acquired certain basic skills – education is *not* reducible without remainder to such training. For example, while at one level school mathematics (or arithmetic) has the purely utilitarian concern to equip young people with the skills required to count their change in commercial exchanges, at another, if (as Galileo maintained) the universe is a book written in the *language* of mathematics, mathematical education may also assist understanding of the mysteries of the universe for its own sake. Similarly, whereas woodwork may at the most basic level be simply a training in certain functional self-coping skills, it might at another level – under the guidance of a master of the craft – be regarded as a matter of *educational* initiation into an entire world of aesthetic sensibility and crafts-manly virtues. However, it is also crucial to observe that though it is difficult, if not impossible, to educate without training, it *is* possible to train without educating.[5] Indeed, given our familiar utilitarian concerns with schooling, it is not uncommon for instrumental learning to be emphasised at the expense of the pursuit of knowledge for its intrinsic educational worth.

Indeed, not only is this common, it is sometimes inevitable, and, in any case, may not always or necessarily matter. For example, given that the mental preconditions for advanced conceptual understanding of mathematics as a 'language' seem to be somewhat unequally distributed, we may well have to rest content with training the majority of young people in our schools in the basic arithmetical operations required for various functional purposes. In the same pragmatic spirit, we may reasonably propose to teach elementary home economics skills to all children to assist them with the chores of adult domestic life, while recognising that few of them may ever appreciate the intrinsic worth of culinary arts, or acquire the aesthetic sensibilities of a master chef. Thus, a rough-and-ready distinction between training and education may be consistent with appreciating that no very deep injustice need have been done if the initiation of some young people into some subjects occasionally falls short of a fully *educational* one, so long as young people are not actually *denied* opportunities to pursue what they might have a genuine aptitude for or inclination towards.

However, it is equally important to recognise that there are some areas of learning in which it is quite *inappropriate* to think like this, and in which no such rough-and-ready line can or should be observed. Areas in which no very meaningful distinctions between education and training *can* be observed are, I think, history and literature; but an area in which no such distinction *ought* to be observed is that of moral education; all the more so, because it does seem *possible* to draw a quite significant distinction between moral training and moral education. Indeed, in meaning to speak of the second of these functions we all too often get no further than speaking of the first. Thus, when parents complain that schools are failing to *educate* morally, what they may mean is that schools do not seem to be training young people to be very respectful of social values, their elders, or authority in general. But whilst one should neither despise this complaint nor deny that it is vital for children to be trained in habits of self-control, courtesy and respect for others, it also needs to be appreciated that an effective moral *education* may well be one which actually encourages children to *question* certain social values and the sources of authority by which they are sustained. Parents and other concerned adults are invariably taken aback, of course, when young people start to engage in independent and principled questioning of received assumptions or entrenched prejudices, and may well wish, when it comes to the crunch, that teachers would do more to knock such impudence out of their pupils. All the same, the desire to return this particular genie to the bottle is a questionable one, precisely because – to whatever degree the former is presupposed to the latter – a moral training can be no substitute for moral education. Indeed, it may well be that some kinds of moral habituation are actually *inimical* to moral education, an obvious example being precisely that of respect for authority which, though doubtless having certain salutary consequences for social harmony and public order, can often and otherwise merely reinforce a debilitating, even intolerant, moral conservatism. Moreover, we have abundant as well as terrible evidence from recent history of how the political exploitation of widespread habits of deferring to authority have greatly facilitated the perpetration of appalling crimes against humanity.

## The role of rule, principle and habituation

Still, a certain degree of basic moral habituation does seem presupposed to effective moral education in a not dissimilar way (as Aristotle first recognised[6]) to that in which a good musical education requires the acquisition of certain basic musical skills: for essentially the same reason, that acquiring moral qualities or virtues, like becoming good at music or any other worthwhile pursuit, is a matter of practical *difficulty*. Thus, the 'discovery' of modern cognitive psychology[7] that the early years of human life are characterised by a certain egocentricity should come as no great surprise to parents: one lesson young children need to learn for the development of effective moral agency is how to 'decentre' in such a way that they can come to appreciate the viewpoints of others, as well as their own, in their deliberations and behaviour. And while one aspect of acquiring this capacity of concern for others consists in nurturing a child's natural inclinations and instincts for positive human association, another large part must consist – since we should not want young people to respect or be polite only to those they happen to *like* – in getting children to respect others as a matter of *principle*. But since grasping principles is generally a matter of following rules, it would seem that to register principles at a reflective level – in moral life as elsewhere – a child needs to be given ample practice in such rule-following as well as to be corrected if he or she goes wrong. Thus, Kylie should not speak to auntie Sharon like that, even if she detests her, because her aunt is a person with feelings and the same right to respect as uncle Kevin whom she worships. On this account, a morally principled approach to the world would appear to be constructed upon a basis of rule-following grounded in training, much as a principled grasp of mathematics can only reasonably be expected to follow from a basic grasp of simpler arithmetical operations as a result of similar training.

In the light of previous observations, of course, it could be complained that such training is likely to *impede* or obstruct rather than assist subsequent educational development; is it not true that the rote learning of musical or mathematical skills sometimes stifles musical creativity or proves impedimental to the growth of mathematical insight, and might not the same be true of moral training in relation to moral education? But whilst conceding that there is some truth in this, we should be clear that this is only an argument against *some* forms of training – mindless rote learning perhaps – and not against training as such.[8] For the point that one cannot expect to understand higher mathematical functions unless one has mastered basic arithmetical skills and operations is a purely *formal* one, entirely consistent with the observation that there may be better and worse modes of basic mathematical, musical or moral habituation. But what is undoubtedly true is that no mere training in the skills of a discipline can add up to education, without the development of certain further qualities or capacities of *understanding* or insight into its intrinsic nature, meaning and purpose: without, as it were, having come to some appreciation of the *raison d'être* or wider human significance of that discipline.

To the extent this is so, however, there can be no question of our restricting the moral initiation of young people to some narrowly defined repertoire of moral habits as there might be of our confining the mathematical education of at least some children to the mastery of basic arithmetical skills of counting, weighing, measuring, and so on, for a number of important reasons. The most significant of these, of course, is that morality is not just another *subject* discipline; indeed, to the extent that it enters constitutively into any coherent conception of self-definition and flourishing, it is intrinsic to the conduct of worthwhile human life as such. From this point of view, to whatever degree we are free to reject the consolations of philosophy, music or tennis, we may not in the same way disengage from the concerns and requirements of morality. This has sometimes been expressed, quite strongly, in terms of the *overriding* nature of moral imperatives. It has been said, for example, that one can hardly dismiss counsel to treat others more decently as one might so ignore advice to improve one's performance at some game, recreation or skill, presumably because the idea of improving oneself morally ought to carry more weight with us than improving at some sport or pastime.[9] Moreover, even if we are sceptical about this on the grounds that people *do* often put their personal pleasures and interests before moral duty, it is still true that all rational human agents, no matter how vicious or corrupt they might be, are logically bound to evaluate their own actions under some conception, however distorted, of what conduces at least to their own fulfilment or flourishing (even Satan himself, so the poet tells us, said evil be thou my *good*[10]). To the extent that this is so, however, it is arguable that even wicked agents could not *rationally* exempt their actions from the demands of wider ethical accountability.

So although young people may choose or refuse to become mathematicians, sportspersons or accountants, they cannot in the same way decline the role of moral agency since this is, by and large (and for good or ill), their human inheritance. By the same token, of course, it is open to them to *choose* good *or* ill, or to be morally good or bad agents: to be sure, being able to choose well and to assume responsibility for worse choices is largely what we mean by mature moral agency. However, this crucially important aspect of moral choice constitutes a second important reason why, although a degree of moral training is presupposed to effective moral education, such training cannot be the whole story, and why it is not ethically permissible (except in certain exceptional pathological cases) to restrict a young person's moral initiation to training rather than education. For example, while we may rightly wish to promote a certain respect for elders on the part of youth, we should also expect morally mature agents to be capable of courteous dissent from views they find prejudiced or unprincipled, to say nothing of actual non-co-operation with unjust practices, whatever the source of their authority. Thus, although moral training may instil blanket respect for authority as such, what we ought educationally to be aiming for in the interests of moral health is a *principled* or discerning respect for well-grounded authority, which is also likely to mean, of course, a training in those settled habits of honesty and courage which serve to reinforce resistance to the threats and blandishments of *unjust* authority.

Beyond any sort of training, then, full realisation of one's humanity in moral association must be a function of *education*, of having acquired some measure of that moral insight or understanding which is a *sine qua non* of wise moral choice or decision. It is only via understanding of the moral superiority of some ways of living over others – for example, that participation in the higher human goods of love and friendship is crucially dependent upon the moral improvement of the individuals involved in such association – that people may really come to love and be committed to various personal and interpersonal virtues for their own sake. But now, what are the conditions for the growth of this moral understanding or insight? In the spirit of Kant we may acknowledge that the development of human understanding is generally a matter of the interplay of two processes – *reason* and *experience*. Essentially, Kant regarded the deliverances of sense experience, or what he called 'intuitions', as the raw data of knowledge upon which the conceptualising capacities of human cognition go to work. As he put it: 'thoughts without content are empty, intuitions without concepts are blind'.[11]

However, what might count as experience for the basis of moral understanding? It might be thought an initial problem here that in the case of moral learning – unlike cases of learning in such theoretical disciplines as nature study or geography – there does not seem to be much in the way of experiential moral data or 'information' upon which moral reasoning might go to work. However, if we bear in mind that morality is more a practical than a theoretical sphere of human activity, there is at least one important source of experience: precisely that practical experience of rule-following acquired from childhood via various forms of early socialisation. In short, we may now be free of all remaining doubt that moral training is itself partly constitutive of moral understanding, for it is only through elementary moral rule-following that children can come to acquire basic first-hand experience of the meaning and value of, for example, generosity or co-operation: that is, some idea of the reciprocal benefits of dispositions for positive human association. Arguably, then, the primary data of principled moral reflection are the moral habits in which we have been encouraged and accustomed to engage from our earliest years by those in the family and wider community who have cared for us. However, as the further experience of ripening years multiplies occasions for moral reflection and response, we continue to need the assistance of guides and mentors – parents, friends and teachers – to find better and ever more finely-tuned ways of expressing those basic moral dispositions of early training. For example, we may need help to assess moral priorities in circumstances of value-conflict; to know whether bearing witness should here take precedence over keeping a confidence, or honesty should come before hurting another person's feelings

## Morality, reason and relativism

Nevertheless, it is by no means unproblematic to construe moral understanding exclusively in terms of reflection upon the received values of a given social or cultural context – upon, as it were, how to express the virtues and values into which we have already been effectively socialised – given the common assumption that human communities *differ* markedly in their conceptions of what is of moral value or priority. Thus, at the very least, encouraging young people to reflect only upon how to express more effectively responses in which they have already been trained may seem little more than indoctrination. Moreover, as already seen, contemporary communitarians[12] have argued that since moral values and virtues are indexed to local socio-cultural perspectives, there can be no common conception of moral growth of the kind envisaged by such modern structuralist cognitive developmentalists as Piaget and Kohlberg. On a more optimistic interpretation of this position, this would seem to preclude any possibility of substantial moral instruction in the kind of culturally pluralist contexts in which many modern teachers find themselves. On a more pessimistic view, it would seem to preclude any possibility of moral *education* (as distinct from moral socialisation) at all. This raises, at the very least, crucial questions of how different we should take the moral perspectives and values of different social groups to be, and of the extent to which these differences should be considered susceptible of rational appraisal or arbitration.

Roughly, as also previously indicated, those who believe that the moral values and codes of different societies diverge to the point of incommensurability or mutual unintelligibility are generally known as moral *relativists*, whereas those who hold that moral values are not rationally-grounded (but rather, perhaps, based on personal taste or preference) are moral *subjectivists*. Commitment to relativism does not necessarily, it should be said, entail subscription to subjectivism (or vice versa) – there is, indeed, a real case for regarding these viewpoints as incompatible – but the two positions are commonly found together. Despite the popular appeal of both viewpoints, we have already given reasons in this work for finding neither position overly persuasive. First, apart from the implausibility of assimilating judgements of moral value to expressions of personal preference – for, on the contrary, it is clear that we give *reasons* for and argue for our moral values in a manner we should find inappropriate with regard to personal tastes – the very possibility of moral education is undermined on any subjectivist view of moral values. But, of course, we do ordinarily suppose that we can be assisted to greater understanding of or insight into our moral problems through educated reflection: indeed, that many such problems are a direct result of human ignorance or thoughtlessness.

However, if it is false that we cannot entertain rational grounds for our moral judgements, it would seem to be equally dubious to suppose with relativists that any moral reasons we might give could not be applicable or appreciated (or might even be unintelligible) across different social or cultural contexts.

Certainly, it is neither moral betrayal of our ethical inheritance to recognise that the way in which the civil codes of another culture treat certain racial minorities, women, the elderly, the criminal or the insane, are actually considerably *more* enlightened or humane than our own, nor ethnocentric cultural imperialism to insist that the persistent acquiescence of another social order in slavery, child exploitation or ritual mutilation of women requires *condemnation* as unethical or barbaric (though this may not give us the right to impose our views upon them economically or by force of arms). Indeed, the perennial error of the relativist is to suppose that intimate connections between social-cultural and moral norms, the liability of moral responses to local cultural expression, mean that it is impossible to separate the two, ignoring the extent to which moral values are responses to general considerations of harm and flourishing to which we are all heir by virtue of a common human inheritance. Moreover, to affirm moral relativism is effectively to preclude any possibility of moral progress; to deny not only that some cultures have morally surpassed others in their conceptions of human rights and social duties, but also that our own current social conceptions of decency and justice may stand in dire need of improvement and development. In short, further controversy and debate about the quality and character of human decency and justice is forever silenced if moral judgements are held to be exclusive expressions of norms to which one is irretrievably committed on social or cultural grounds.

From this perspective, of course, it must be an intrinsic goal of moral education, as it has been said of liberal education in general,[13] to transcend the present and the particular in pursuit of standards of decency and justice which are not immovably tied to a set of purely local customs and prejudices. But the main difficulty about the possibility of moral education now turns essentially on understanding how an individual achieves the transition from a moral experience which is rooted in early training, habituation and obedience to local custom, to an appreciation of conceptions of virtue and justice which transcend this by dint of some degree of detachment from and/or critical judgement upon moral inheritance. In this connection, we may discern two broad accounts in ethical theory of how this comes about, both of which have positive points and shortcomings. Moreover, though it is tempting to assume that these two rather different accounts represent *more* and *less* up-to-date or enlightened conceptions of moral education, both have considerable contemporary philosophical currency, and one may readily encounter either of the educational approaches which they entrain (or a confused mixture of both) in contemporary contexts of schooling. Thus, while we shall refer to the first approach as traditional or *paternalist* and the second as progressive or *liberal,* this should not be taken to imply any judgement concerning the greater contemporary truth, utility or relevance of one position over the other.

## Two approaches to moral education

First, the traditional or paternalist view of moral education takes it to be, like any other sort of education, a sort of initiation into certain specifiable beliefs and dispositions; in this instance, a range of moral attitudes and virtues of honesty, integrity, loyalty, courage, and so forth. The hallmark of such traditional moral initiation, however, is essentially its commitment – in the light of some religious, cultural, rational or other authority – to the basic *truth* of these moral beliefs and values. On this view, then, although a young person may well need to acquire those capacities of rational autonomy and moral freedom needed to assist him or her to resolve unavoidable value-conflicts, or to express some moral virtue effectively, the morality or immorality of some kinds of conduct would be essentially beyond question. For example, in many traditional religious contexts of schooling, children will be brought up to believe that marriage is a sacred and unmixed blessing, and that divorce and adultery are therefore unalloyed evils. It is, of course, characteristic of the traditional or paternalist view to flourish best in those circumstances of cultural and evaluative homogeneity which do not, by and large, prevail in modern developed societies, which explains why such a perspective is sometimes thought to be inapplicable to contemporary circumstances. However, although I shall also proceed to suggest that a strictly traditional view is far from entirely correct, I suspect that this is a mixture of prejudice and conceptual error. As we can see from contemporary ethical debates between communitarians and liberals, it remains a significantly open question whether a traditional conception of moral education is or is not viable in modern circumstances. Moreover, some of the enduring positive effects of such initiation appear to be very widely appreciated, not least by those non-religious parents who are inclined to send their children to religious schools for the firm moral discipline they are held to provide.

At the opposite pole from a traditionalist or paternalist view of moral education, however, is what we may call a liberal, progressive, or, at the extreme end of the spectrum, a libertarian, conception of moral initiation. Clearly, as the label suggests, a liberal view is more inclined to focus on those aspects of moral development concerned with individual choice and freedom. From this point of view, liberals are inclined to attribute supreme moral value to such attitudes and dispositions as *tolerance* and *open-mindedness*, as well as to deplore what they regard as the more dogmatic and doctrinaire moral instruction of paternalist educational practices. Indeed, classical liberalism[14] is inclined to regard any interference in the basic right of others to do what they choose with their lives as a benchmark of moral offence, especially since none but a bigot can claim to have privileged access to truth in such an essentially contestable sphere as that of moral conduct. Thus, liberal perspectives are inclined to be deeply *agnostic*, if not downright sceptical, concerning claims to moral truth of the sort apparently presupposed to traditional or paternalist views, and this agnosticism tends to be reflected, even enshrined, in much liberal moral pedagogy. In the first place, for example, liberal conceptions of moral learning have, under the influence of modern cognitive psychology, taken a discernibly *constructivist* turn, in which the emphasis largely shifts from training in modes of conduct to the development of cognitive strategies for the resolution of artificially and somewhat abstractly construed moral dilemmas.[15] Indeed, moral education seems sometimes to have been modelled more upon the pattern of what might go on in a moral philosophy seminar than on that of what is liable to occur whenever a teacher firmly intervenes in a school-yard brawl.

Second, however, correspondingly different (and not obviously compatible) views of moral *instruction* have developed in the light of traditional-paternalist and liberal-progressive conceptions of moral education and development. On the traditional view, for example, it is natural to hold that since there are definite moral rights and wrongs, and moral conduct largely consists in obedience to the authority of moral truth, real moral authority can only be effectively expressed and exercised through the example of teachers:

only individuals who themselves exhibit the qualities they wish the young to acquire can be expected to have much success in promoting such qualities in others. But now, however, to the extent that all teachers are moral educators, it follows that a good teacher needs not only to have knowledge of a given field of enquiry, and/or to possess a range of teaching skills, but also to be a certain kind of *person*. On the other hand, liberals and progressives are prone to extreme caution, for fear of indoctrination, on the matter of teachers communicating their own values to pupils. In this connection, one strand of the theoretical literature of liberal moral education has been devoted to exploration of an ideal of teacher 'neutrality'.[16] Thus, on one extreme (and rather implausible) view of this matter, the 'neutral teacher' would be required, even in the throes of encouraging discussion of controversial issues, to sit firmly on the fence about those views. Likewise, it would not appear to be greatly at odds with a liberal view of the distinction between the personal and the professional to hold that so long as teachers treat their pupils fairly and respectfully in the classroom, and refrain from imposing their own values on them, they are entitled to live their own lives much as they please. To this extent, although it would be unacceptable under a traditionalist dispensation which condemns alcohol, drugs and marital infidelity for teachers to be alcohol or drug abusers and adulterers in their private lives, such teachers might, at least *theoretically*, pass muster under a liberal dispensation, so long as they taught skilfully, did not allow their personal habits to undermine the effectiveness of their practice, and kept their private affairs to themselves. Indeed, it would seem at least an implication of some liberal constructivist conceptions of moral development that moral education is not really the concern of the ordinary classroom teacher, and should properly be given into the hands of experts specially trained in psychological and other techniques of moral pedagogy.

One should also be clear that, at any serious level, paternalist and liberal conceptions of moral education do represent different conceptions of moral *education*: one should not, in short, make the mistake of equating a liberal conception with moral *education*, and of assuming that the paternalist view is only a view of moral *training*. For although the traditional or paternalist conception strongly emphasises the importance for the growth of moral understanding of authority, discipline and training, it can nevertheless entertain cultivation of capacities for wise, rational and informed moral and evaluative choice as an ultimate goal of such training. It does, however, regard moral freedom as importantly predicated upon basic discipline, much as the freedom to reflect conceptually about mathematical questions presupposes some basic training in arithmetic. Likewise, a liberal need not be construed as one who embraces absolute freedom at the expense of authority and discipline. On the contrary, a certain conception of moral authority as rooted in the fundamental obligation to tolerate the opinions and respect the rights and liberties of others, as well as an ideal of discipline as voluntary self-restraint in the service of this basic duty, is central to the liberal account. Any difference between these two positions, then, is by no means a matter of simple conflict between advocates of absolute authority and unbridled freedom, more a complex difference between rival correlative notions of authority and freedom.

## Liberalism and paternalism: an irresolvable dualism?

In the face of an apparent dualism of this kind, of course, it is natural to ask which of these two positions is correct; and, of course, if the parties to this particular issue were totally contradictory, one of them would *have* to be correct. However, although the broad perspectives of moral paternalism and liberalism are certainly inconsistent, they do not seem to be flatly contradictory, and it is probably safer to regard both of them as mixtures of truth and falsehood. Certainly, both paternalism and liberalism are sources of genuine insight into the nature of moral life and education. The deep truth behind liberalism seems to be that morality is a sphere in which *freedom* of thought and conduct is of utmost significance. From this viewpoint, any moral education worthy of the name must therefore be one in which young people are equipped with capacities for wise and principled decisions about how to live, as well as with some sense of personal responsibility for their own decisions and actions. But in the course of affirming the moral primacy of freedom and resisting anything which might impede it, liberal views seem sometimes to have gone overboard in endorsing a certain agnosticism about moral truth, occasionally to the point of moral subjectivism or relativism. At worst, it may sometimes have been mistakenly inferred that because human agents are entitled to authentic moral choice, no one has any right to pass moral judgement on the choices of others, so that any one personal choice is as morally valid, and deserving of the same respect, as any other. Moreover, when this idea is combined with the equally suspect view that if the choices of young people are to be *really* free, then we should refrain from their instruction in *any* moral attitudes and conduct on pain of jeopardising that freedom,[17] we have a very potent cocktail of nonsense indeed.

By and large, traditional-paternalist views of moral education are successful in avoiding such errors as these. Thus, they appear to be resolute in maintaining that to whatever extent morality implies freedom, it is nevertheless appropriate to speak of moral right and wrong, good and evil, in some objective or non-relative sense: that, indeed, if one could not speak in this way it would be literally meaningless to speak of *moral* freedom, which, after all, ordinarily means the capacity to choose between *better* and *worse* alternatives. In this connection, moreover, it is reasonable to argue that whatever the degree of moral difference between cultures, the cross-cultural character of certain moral values and virtues is virtually guaranteed by a common human condition. Thus, it is hardly surprising that we encounter a fundamentally shared moral grammar of attitude and value behind surface socio-cultural differences: common subscription to the moral importance of honesty, loyalty, self-control, fairness, courage, compassion, and so on. It may be in view of this, however, that traditionalists are also clearer about the crucial moral-educational role of training and habituation for any more principled, reflective or critical acquisition of moral traits: that far from impeding further development of moral understanding, training in such basic dispositions of honesty, self-control, fairness, and so on, is actually a *sine qua non* of such development.

Still, if a principal mistake of liberals is to assume that due recognition of the individual right to moral freedom must preclude clear specification of objective criteria for the moral evaluation of individual choices, traditionalists are prone to the converse error of supposing – in the manner of that great pioneer of moral paternalism, Plato[18] – that because we can in many circumstances distinguish reasonably well between right and wrong, we can thereby assume that such clarity of moral vision gives us the right to impose it on others, regardless of their perspective on the matter. For what is here not true of ethics and moral education is not true of any other branch of human enquiry either. The fact that anyone who wishes to do serious science will begin by acquiring a certain amount of correct information, or a certain repertoire of reliable experimental skills and virtues, does not mean that he or she already possesses everything needed to answer finally all the large questions about the nature of the universe that he or she might want to ask – as well as some of those which, without further work, he or she will not even know how to ask. In the moral realm, as in any other area of human enquiry, the present state of human knowledge is such that we cannot ever hope to have attained final truth. But it is an equal and opposite error to suppose that because at present we see through the glass only darkly, we cannot therefore be said to see at all, or to have any access to reliable criteria of understanding for further moral development and progress.

In sum, however, to the extent they both enshrine conceptually flawed views of the nature of moral knowledge and enquiry, it should be clear that there can be little hope of reconciling, or finding some coherent position of compromise between traditional-paternalist and liberal-progressive conceptions of moral authority and freedom, in education or elsewhere. What is rather needed for the promotion of healthy moral life is the replacement of such simple conceptions by something more finely nuanced which more accurately charts the creative interplay between authority and freedom, knowledge and criticism, in moral enquiry and conduct. It should also be clear, however, that in so far as this is a requirement of healthy moral practice in general, it must be all the more required of those whose professional responsibility includes assisting others to some measure of moral maturity: a developed understanding of these matters should be, one might well argue, a *sine qua non* of the professional development of teachers. In this connection, however, it is interesting to observe that one common feature of what we have called paternalist and liberal moral educational conceptions is that both go a long way towards taking responsibility for moral reflection altogether *out* of the hands of teachers, as though such reflection was really none of their business. On the paternalist view, then, it seems to be the teacher's task to communicate a set of predetermined moral values to young people, and, on at least one influential liberal account, the teacher is required to observe complete moral neutrality on pain of potential indoctrination.

From this viewpoint, however, what is urgently needed by way of antidote to such morally paralysing paternalist and liberal positions is a conception which reaffirms the moral authority and responsibility of all who are liable to be professionally implicated – for better or worse – in the problematic process of the moral formation of youth. Thus, although trainee teachers may well need some assistance in coming to see that there is no inherent inconsistency in being both committed to a set of values and virtues which are morally objective, yet *also* undogmatic, open-minded and sympathetic to alternative moral possibilities – and a degree of philosophical help with the complexities of ethical reflection may well be of some assistance in this matter – it is above all imperative for them to appreciate that any professional moral educational effectiveness ultimately depends upon the quality of *their own* personal engagement with moral issues and questions. In this sphere, above all, a training in the sort of professional dependency culture in which one is invariably brought to rely on the authority and responsibility of others for knowing what to say or do, is as unlikely to serve the interests of professional effectiveness, as it is to serve *personal* moral effectiveness. At the level of professional teacher education and training, however, it should be clear that there can be no reasonable alternative to such dependence in the absence of that broader education in ethical sensibility, which, though it ought to be the foundation of any proper professional preparation, has been dangerously marginalised in recent vocational emphases on the development of more instrumental teaching skills and competences. But in view of the undeniable implications for moral formation of education and teaching, it is hardly an overstatement to say that such initiation can be nothing less than an overriding requirement of the professional preparation of teachers.

# Part V

# PARTICULAR ISSUES

# 12

# ETHICAL ISSUES CONCERNING THE ROLE OF THE TEACHER

## Towards the particular case

Thus far we have argued that teaching may be regarded as a professional enterprise, along with such traditional professions as medicine and law, to the extent that it is implicated in the promotion of ethically contestable and morally problematic goals of human flourishing. It is because this is so that it seems misguided to try to account for professional educational preparation in the technically reductive terms of competence models. It is not just, as often argued by contemporary 'particularists' about the art of teaching, that teaching is a highly context-relative or situation-specific activity which resists articulation in terms of some simple set of mechanical rules, but that – since what is to count as an educational method is variously determined by different conceptions of the ends or purposes of education – it is also difficult to talk of fundamental all-purpose pedagogical strategies in quite the way required by any pure competence conception of professional training. Hence, we saw in Part IV that although there is broad professional agreement that it is the aim of teaching to secure certain human developmental ends of socialisation, preparation for life and work and rational emancipation, there is apt to be some disagreement concerning the several natures and respective weightings of these goals in the context of schooling. In the last chapter, moreover, we observed that despite broad professional agreement that teaching has moral educational implications, there is also much scope for diverse interpretations of these implications, and about where any line, if any, ought to be drawn between the private and public aspects of a teacher's life.

The final section of this book is devoted to a brief consideration of some general ethical or moral questions, difficulties and dilemmas which are prone to arise in relation to education and teaching. In this chapter, I will mainly consider issues related to the already indicated public–private interface of teacher professionalism; in Chapter 13, I will concentrate more upon the strains and tensions to which educational and other principles are heir in institutionalised contexts of schooling. However, before we turn to these particular issues, it is worth saying a few words – with perhaps particular regard to the prospects of ethical progress with present analyses – about the purpose of so doing. It should already have been gathered from previous arguments and observations that we need to avoid either overly ambitious or unduly pessimistic perspectives on this question. First, we have so far taken great pains to emphasise that one should not regard problems of ethics and moral practice as resolvable in the manner of *technical* problems. A potential error here is to suppose that there are rationally neutral strategies of ethical analysis, of, perhaps, Kohlbergian dilemma resolution or utilitarian calculation,[1] which would allow us to return unequivocally positive or negative responses to given ethical questions, or decisively adopt one course of action over another in the teeth of moral conflict or dilemma. However, although there are certainly better and worse strategies of ethical reasoning – well explored by past and present philosophers and logicians – it is unlikely that there are any which are apt for application in any context-free way. It is not just that whereas something close to, for example, utilitarian reasoning might be admissible in some contexts, there are others in which such reasoning would be quite beyond the pale,[2] but that different forms of ethical ratiocination (such as arguments from principle and arguments from utility) are liable to be given weightings on different ethical perspectives, not to mention that different parties to debates about abortion or divorce are likely to give priority to different potential consequences.

## The uses of moral reason

We have also seen how observations of this sort may all too readily give rein to sceptical postmodern despair about the very *possibility* of reason in ethics. Thus, the communitarian end of postmodernism (or perhaps the postmodern end of communitarianism) seems sometimes to give ground to the idea, via repudiation of 'metanarrative' and dubious assimilation of morality to local cultural practices, that moral traditions are not just rival but *incommensurable* to a point of complete invulnerability to external moral criticism.[3] But this is to throw out the indispensable baby of moral reason with the bathwater of some unattainable ideal of ethical foundationalism. To be sure, we should need no extravagant postmodern denial of metanarratives (whatever that means) to remind us that it is in the nature of much moral dilemma for there to be no easy appeal to any higher court of moral absolutes, in circumstances where one feels the pull of competing and equally compelling moral imperatives. But does this mean that no actual or apparent moral disagreements, problems and dilemmas are susceptible of resolution, or that reason is (as Hume more or less said[4]) entirely impotent in matters of morals? At the very least, any such sweeping claim blurs too many significant differences between types or levels of moral disagreement or dilemma. Clearly the existence of disagreement does not in and of itself imply irresolvability. Disagreements in scientific and historical enquiry are rife, but they are often resolved when one theory or hypothesis appears to be the clear best option, or its rivals turn out to be no options at all. Someone may now say, of course, that whereas there can indeed be talk of resolution in cases of historical or scientific dispute because such enquiries must at least yield to the facts, moral difference is hardly amenable to any such resolution, lying as it does in the realm of subjective or relative values. But in the light of earlier observations that values may have a perfectly objective evidential basis (leaving aside the postmodern or pragmatist irrelevance about the value-ladenness of facts), it should be clear that this claim is a mere *petitio principii*. Hence, if I claim that good dentistry must be of value to any victim (human or other) of caries and you deny that it is, then, bar your falling foul of some trivial ambiguity of 'X values Y', you are at best mistaken and at worst confused.

It is at least arguable, for example, that there are value disagreements in respect of, say, matters of justice, which *are* resolvable, either because some claim to justice was driven by unjust motives, in which case no such claim was ever actually moral, or because it was sincerely made on mistaken logical or evidential grounds. A good educational illustration of this, I think, is to be found in proposals of previously considered social and educational theorists[5] to provide an 'alternative' non-literary or vocational schooling for some young people on grounds of their allegedly non-academic bent or inferior ability. Would such alternative schooling constitute an 'alternative' conception of educational justice? Clearly something here depends upon the intentions behind any such proposal. If, as Marxists and others have argued (and it may often have been the case), it has been the cynical intent of those who have so argued merely to maintain the privileges of some through the suppression and exploitation of others, then what might here seem to be an *alternative* vision of society is certainly not a vision of a *just* society. On the other hand, however, it is entirely plausible to suppose that some who have been driven to argue along these lines have been motivated by a *sincere* concern for the proper realisation of diverse forms of human potential in different forms of educational provision. But one may no less plausibly maintain that, irrespective of their sincerity, such arguments have been bedevilled by discernible failures to distinguish between, or give due weight to, what is owed to human need in respect of rather different aspects of human formation and flourishing, sometimes under the influence of highly questionable psychometric theories of intelligence, ability and reason.[6] In short, certain 'alternative' accounts of educational justice, though well intentioned enough to qualify as 'rival' *moral* accounts, may nevertheless turn out to be flawed on fairly straightforward logical and empirical grounds: the conceptions of fair due which they enshrine are not adequately supported by the 'evidence' to which they appeal. As we see from the kind of considerations which are the basis for any talk of human rights, moreover, there are clearly forms of human conduct which are connected so closely with human woe – torture, enslavement, starvation, and so on – that no 'alternative' conception of human justice which countenanced them, however sincerely held, could represent anything less than serious failure to comprehend properly the nature of human weal. On this view, as already argued, one may be hard put to see how any moral – as opposed to merely pragmatic – defence might seriously be given of corporal punishment in schools. It is also reasonable to suppose that any progress which has been made by so-called civilised societies from their own barbarous pasts – and it would be hard to maintain that none has – has been marked by a concern to reduce much more basic kinds of human misery.

Someone might yet say, all the same, that such cases are not especially typical of human moral dilemma, since the typical moral cases are all too often the result of conflicts which cannot be resolved by straightforward preference of this moral course over that. What, then, of cases in which it seems for one reason or another arbitrary or gratuitous to give priority to one set of moral values over another set? The qualification 'for one reason or another' is of some moment here, however, since there are surely very different kinds of conflict which might be said to resist such resolution. First, there are the familiar cases – perhaps first raised by Socrates and Plato – where one cannot simultaneously fulfil the equally compelling demands of, say, honesty and welfare. Thus, in the example presented in the *Republic*,[7] any socially responsible answer to the madman whose weapons one has borrowed seems dishonest, but any honest response is likely to be harmful. In such a case it is clear enough that whatever course of action we take is bound (in so far as compromise of one value is an inevitable consequence of fidelity to the other) to entail a measure of moral loss. But there is also the quite different sort of case where some alien human group engages in social or cultural practices which are quite contrary, even repugnantly so, to our own. It is not especially illuminating here to focus upon such grotesque cultural extremes as female circumcision or wife burning, since such practices do precisely involve the violation of basic human rights, which we need not suppose that *any* morally right-thinking people of *any* religion or culture would have committed. Perhaps a rather better example is to be found in the different kinds of matrimonial arrangements which have from time to time obtained in different parts of the world. Clearly many people in western liberal democracies (though clearly not in Utah) would find African polygamy or Tibetan polyandry repugnant to the point of (at least local) unacceptability. At the same time, however, any attempt on the part of Christian missionaries to encourage monogamy in societies where men and women have lived contentedly with polygamous or polyandrous arrangements from times long past may be liable to criticism from many liberal *monogamists* as culturally imperialist. Moreover, whereas most right-thinking people from any culture would want to do all in their power to stamp out *suttee*, it is not at all clear in cases of alternative matrimony that any charge of cultural imperialism would be misdirected. For what right, after all, have we to object to a culturally socio-economic practice which others claim to have served them well, just because people of our different sort do not happen to approve of it?

## More on the uses of moral reason

Although these are different cases of value conflict, it might be thought that what they have in common is that rational deliberation is utterly *impotent* to resolve them. Consider the first case: if whatever I do betrays some moral value, then it hardly matters what I do, and reason is entirely powerless to help me act morally for the better. But the Platonic example already provided needs little thought to show that any such despair over the uses of reason is quite premature; for the fact that whatever I do involves substantial moral loss does not preclude the possibility, via sensible attention to context, of considerable moral damage limitation. Of course, since effective moral deliberation in this case will doubtless focus mainly upon implications for practical weal and woe of this or that moral trade-off, it is also liable to be in some sense *consequentialist* – though it may or may not be *utilitarian* as such. But surely it would be nothing short of insane to refuse – on the grounds that lying is *always* wrong (which it is) – to give false intelligence to the enemy if such dissemblance might save several thousand military and civilian lives. On the other hand, however, we may be right to insist upon more principled fidelity to honesty, upon trying to get someone to face up to the painful truth about their betrayal by a friend or spouse, even when we know that the plain truth may hurt them. In yet other cases it may be harder to estimate clearly the moral costs and benefits of a particular decision or course of action, and since there is no moral algorithm which can guarantee right choice in hard cases, decisions may turn out with hindsight to have been mistaken. But this perfectly sensible and familiar way of putting things testifies well enough to the importance of deliberation in such circumstances. The point is that we can often see with hindsight that a specific decision was the right one, or that if only we had then more clearly perceived the facts of the matter we would best have done otherwise.

But what of the second case: if different moral loyalties are engendered in different cultural contexts, and there are no obvious considerations of human weal and woe by reference to which we might find those of alien cultures morally wanting, then surely there can be no rational warrant for our preferring this set of commitments to that? We earlier conceded that some of the rules by which people choose to live may be rules of 'club membership', suited perhaps to our particular natural endowments or social conditioning, but not obliging those who are not members of our club to abide by them. Moreover, it may be no more than a contemporary egalitarian prejudice to suppose that justice is invariably served by denying or ignoring the existence of certain natural and circumstantial differences. To take a trivial case, there is not much to be gained from extending membership of the Mothers' Union to those lacking obvious qualifications for motherhood, or who are unlikely to share the particular interests or encounter the specific problems of mothers. (This is *not* to deny the truth that potential fathers need parenting skills, only to recognise the fact that fathers cannot be mothers.) Likewise, it is hardly open to *anyone* to play cricket for Yorkshire, or qualify for membership of MENSA. And again, although I regard my fidelity to Roman Catholicism as, among other things, a binding moral commitment – and might even wish that the whole world would convert to the Roman faith – it would be unreasonable of me to try to impose my views upon those whose conscience otherwise inclines them (although I am likely to regard those who do not agree with Catholic views on abortion, divorce and contraception as morally mistaken, if not corrupt).

But then, surely, in such cases of moral commitment by club membership, where moral loyalties are determined less by deliberate choice and more by natural endowment, socio-cultural circumstance or even aesthetic sensibility, reason can have little or no place in resolving differences between those who belong and those who do not (or are otherwise excluded)? Perhaps, however, we should not be quite so hasty. In the first place, we cannot know in advance of some sort of ethical *reflection* whether such moral relativities or incommensurabilities are genuine or only *apparent*, and it may well be part of the ongoing project of ethical clarification to distinguish genuine from bogus cases of moral club membership. Take, for example, the case of monogamy versus polygamy or polyandry, which we earlier gave as a possible instance of cultural alterneity whose attempted suppression by western monogamists could be considered improper cultural imperialism. It is itself, however, an unresolved ethical problem whether this is so. Indeed, it is arguable that polygamy and polyandry have historically emerged more in response to local economic exigencies than to true personal and interpersonal moral need, and that such arrangements – whatever support they may receive from those party to them (one should recall that slavery has often been defended by slaves) – may well involve considerable gender-based power imbalance, and/or distortion of human association and relationship. To this extent, it makes all the difference in the world whether we regard polygamy and polyandry as quaint local practices licensed by cultural inheritance and affiliation, or as morally corrosive forms of repression, from which those who are more male or female concubines than true wives or husbands have some moral entitlement to liberation.

At all events, this is something that we cannot know in advance of further anthropological enquiries of both conceptual and empirical kinds. We should not therefore too hastily conclude from the reasonable observation that *some* moral commitments are largely or entirely matters of personal choice or social loyalty, that we know precisely which these are, thereby prematurely closing off important avenues of ethical research. As previously indicated, moreover, there can be little doubt that questions of this kind are deeply implicated in professional disputes about the proper direction of education. It makes all the difference whether a given educational practice – a progressive or radical education which allows children unbridled freedom, or a traditional one which imposes rigid discipline – represents acceptable parental choice of upbringing within tolerable, liberal limits of freedom of lifestyle, or whether such an approach constitutes a distortion of the proper course of human development which it behoves educationalists to try with all available professional expertise, irrespective of parental choice, to correct. We have argued in this work that this is perhaps the most critical question for teachers as professionals in the contemporary climate of liberal theorising about polity, morality and human flourishing, a question upon which the very possibility of conceiving teaching as a profession may well turn. In the rest of this chapter, however, we shall explore a number of not unrelated particular difficulties which are liable to arise on any professional conception of teaching as concerned with moral influence through personal example.

## Virtuous and vicious speech and attire

In a discussion paper entitled *Spiritual and Moral Development*, published in 1993 by the British National Curriculum Council, it is observed that:

> Values are inherent in teaching. Teachers are by the nature of their profession 'moral agents' who imply values by the way they address pupils and each other, the way they dress, the language they use and the effort they put into their work.[8]

This statement not only endorses the general claim of the previous chapter that teaching, at least in the standard professional contexts

214

of institutionalised schooling, has moral educational implications, but also proceeds in a fairly authoritative way to detail some of the precise respects in which teachers should avoid letting the side down. Thus, teachers are to be mindful of the way they dress and speak, to exemplify industry and diligence and to set the right tone, presumably of proper respect for persons, in their dealings with colleagues and pupils. Certainly, these could seem – if we ignore for the moment the official source of these prescriptions (not to mention the *de haut en bas* suggestion that it might need someone in authority to remind teachers of their duties in these respects) – to be fairly unexceptionable claims. On closer scrutiny, however, it appears that they are susceptible of rather different, more or less controversial, interpretations. Take, for example, the matter of dress and speech:

A young teacher is inclined to very casual or 'trendy' forms of personal dress and presentation (jeans, 'irregular' hairstyle, facial jewellery) and/or speech (a tendency to vernacular, slang or street idioms) which other staff do not find acceptable. The teacher is popular with pupils and his/her example is beginning to be imitated by them.

Despite the apparent moral triviality of modes of attire as such – indeed, it may be that outrageous popular fashions often camouflage, especially among the young, extremely conventional, conservative, if not downright puritanical, moral views – there cannot be much doubt that questions of 'correct' dress and speech are liable to arouse powerful emotions, not least cross-generationally. Dress and speech are bound to be educationally contentious, however, given the influential traditional view that it is the main duty of education to ensure a measure of cultural continuity via transmission of yesterday's wisdom to tomorrow's generations. Since, on this view, 'culture' inevitably implies a particular conception of established authority and order, educational initiation is easily conceived as a matter of imposition of moral and other disciplines constitutive of this order. Granted this, however, it is difficult to think of more potent symbols of traditional order than dress and, more particularly, speech. Taking speech first, it is virtually a commonplace of contemporary philosophy and social theory that language is key to culture, and that initiation into a particular language constitutes the most effective rite of passage into the hard-won wisdom and experience of elders and ancestors. Since 'correct' spoken and written language is the very measure of the best that has been hitherto thought and said in the world, it seems that we neglect, ignore or reject it at our intellectual and practical peril. From this viewpoint, it is small wonder that appointed guardians of received culture will often react strongly to abuse or wilful neglect of received usage, especially on the part of those professionally charged with the task of sustaining and transmitting culture. Moreover, although it is possible to go to over-zealous conservative extremes about usage, teacher educators seem on safe enough ground in insisting that professional teacher trainees uphold and observe, at least in their work with pupils, the standard conventions of received grammar and orthography.

Although sartorial innovations may seem less culturally threatening than linguistic lapses or abuses – after all, the way one dresses may have no effect whatsoever on the way one thinks or upon one's moral character – they have nevertheless often enough seemed even more potent symbols of rebellion and nonconformity. Revolutionaries are readily given to bohemian deviations from bourgeois convention, and the young invariably turn to new clothes for new ways of distancing themselves from the staid middle-aged values of tired parents, even when it often seems little more than replacing one uniform by another. So it is hardly surprising that educationalists, particularly in conservative, culturally homogeneous places and times, have often made a fair amount of fuss about professional dress. In this connection, indeed, one may observe a marked shift in attitudes to professional dress in British teacher training institutions in the four decades or so since the end of the Second World War, perhaps reflecting Britain's general progress (some might say decline) from a colonial power, secure in the culturally superior ethnocentric knowledge and values of its ruling order, to a more liberal, egalitarian and pluralistic society in which it is less easy to impose received customs and conventions upon teacher trainees.

There can be little doubt, however, that colleges of professional teacher training, unlike (or rather less than) universities, were formerly cast in a rather paternalistic mould, and that it was common well into the post-war years for students both on and off campus to be closely monitored with regard to personal conduct and demeanour. It was widely held that the teacher's role as moral exemplar warranted quite close, even personally intrusive, scrutiny of individual pre-professional behaviour. Thus, trainees were liable to censure for all kinds of alleged nonconformity – ranging from relatively serious alcohol abuse or sexual misconduct, to such relatively trivial offences as growing hair too provocatively long (males) or wearing hair too wantonly loose (females) – many of which would today be regarded as matters of personal or private concern. Nowadays, indeed, it could well be teacher trainers who risked professional censure for interrogating the sexual conduct or orientation of their students, and it is certainly hard to know what yesterday's teacher educators would have done in the position of today's placement supervisors nervously and delicately attempting to break the news to students that this Mohican hairstyle or that abundance of facial piercings might not especially endear them to their hosts on some school practice. But whilst one is doubtless right to feel that there is something quite unacceptable, even morally repugnant, about more extreme past climates of professional preparation – indeed, there may seem to be something particularly ill-advised about fostering slavish conformity to rules rather than responsible self-direction on the part of those professionally charged with promoting mature responsibility in others – there is just as clearly something to the idea of reasonable professional standards of dress and speech which is hard to give up altogether.

In the event, of course, there are more or less pragmatic strategies for forestalling potential problems of unacceptable garb in contexts of teacher education. Most students embarked upon professional courses will be prepared to abide by some not too stringent dress code and, in the absence of such a code, it seems reasonable to advise trainees seeking to know how they should dress to conform to what is acceptable to the headteacher of any school to which they have been posted for placement. Moreover, the fact that what is sartorially acceptable would appear to vary from school to school may in itself appear to testify to the outdatedness of notions of professional dress in teaching. It is not just that schools differ in general ethos but that the professional roles and functions of teachers will often vary widely both within and between schools. In the nature of their work, then, teachers of art, craft and chemistry require various kinds of protective clothing, PE teachers will sport tracksuits, and in the rough and tumble of nursery, infant and primary work it may be neither economic nor practically convenient to ply one's trade in clothing which is not quite beyond the pale for other presentational purposes. However, despite the fact that all of this makes it practically difficult to impose a universal dress code across the board of professional practice, the issue still seems to generate considerable concern, especially in more conservative educational quarters, and one may not feel entirely unsympathetic towards those who still wish to insist that teachers should observe *some* standard of sartorial respectability.

Moreover, any suspicion of intellectual affectation notwithstanding, it is arguable that such an apparently trivial matter as professional dress invites considerable clarification of some fairly complex problems at the interface of philosophical anthropology, politics, ethics and aesthetics. Indeed, one might begin by asking whether dress *is* generally merely a matter of personal taste or has any larger moral or ethical implications. What could possibly incline us to question the plausible claim that clothing is a matter of personal aesthetic with no moral implications whatsoever? The most potent source of any such doubt, I think, would be the idea that, contrary to some modern theorising about such matters, there is *no* conception of the aesthetic which is *entirely* devoid of moral implications. In relation to matters of garb, moreover, one should not necessarily construe ethical or moral significance too *narrowly*, as concerned *only* with aspects of interpersonal relationship. On the face of it, the way I dress can do no actual violence to anyone else and, although my clothing may well offend others, that may well be their problem, and no good reason for me to divest at their bidding. But might not my clothing harm me? If it should be that the way I dress or my sartorial attitudes have adverse implications for my character or personality, then there might be some basis for saying that I *ought* not to dress as I do, even if I so desire. It is a case somewhat along these lines, I suspect, to which those who make a fuss about dress are inclined. They would precisely claim to discern connections between certain attitudes to appearance or fashion and such virtues as seriousness, sobriety, neatness, self-respect and modesty, traits which also seem reasonably characterisable as *universal* virtues or values. Hence, if such connections could be established in some objective non-question-begging way (not, that is, according to definitions of sobriety and modesty which comprehend a tendency to dress in a particular sort of way), then one might have a basis of argument that it is good for the development of young people to undergo some dress discipline, and only right for teachers to set pupils an appropriate example in this respect. One might, in short, have an argument for school and/or professional uniforms.

To a considerable extent, the difficulty here recapitulates earlier explored issues about whether education is a matter of initiation into universal rules or rules of club membership. If dress is only a matter of personal taste with no wider social, moral or human implications, I might wish as an aesthetic parent to choose an education for my child which allows him or her the maximum possible sartorial self-expression. If, on the other hand, I was privy to evidence that such licence encouraged dissolute or slovenly attitudes or habits, I might well want to avoid any educational initiation with such adverse consequences. Even then, of course, any resolution of this question would not yet settle the further political issue, particularly in liberal polities where the aims of education are themselves contested with regard to questions of balanced human development, of whether schools should be required to promote the proven virtues of sober apparel. If one supposes that it is the main (if not the only) goal of schooling to adapt individuals to the purposes of a particular socio-economic ideal, one might above all want people to acquire the virtues of sobriety and conformity. If, on the other hand, one sees personal fulfilment as the main (if not the only) goal of schooling, one might regard it as ultimately up to parents, if not to young people themselves, to decide what should count as optimal individual development or flourishing. All of this, of course, would have clear implications for the issue of professional dress.

## Teacher character and personality

Questions of virtuous attire or, at any rate, of whether the matter of professional dress has any wider ethical implications, lead us on fairly naturally to a consideration of other personal/professional characteristics which also seem apt for assessment in the terms of virtue and vice. Consider the following case:

A teacher, popular with pupils and respected by colleagues as someone who is efficient and gets results, is given to persistent use for discipline purposes of sarcasm and ridicule of his or her pupils. Moreover, the pupils are now observed to be using this kind of verbal harassment among themselves.

The apparent frequency with which we can recall the personalities and characters of our teachers long after we have forgotten what they actually taught us, greatly reinforces the suspicion that teachers have, by personal example, something of a modelling effect on the development of young people. Of course, we need to be wary of over-simplistic assumptions about the nature, direction or strength of any such causal links. Just as watching the odd horror movie on television is unlikely to turn the casual viewer into a mad axe murderer, so almost inevitable contact with at least one teacher who is a thoroughly bad lot is unlikely to corrupt and deprave those with whom he or she comes in contact. Indeed, one should not discount the possibility of thoroughly unprincipled, mean, spiteful and vindictive teachers having a morally *beneficial* influence on pupils, who *repelled* by their example determine to be as *unlike* them as possible. Indeed, experience seems to show that extremely bad and unpleasant parents can have delightful children, and sometimes – perhaps by way of perverse reaction to a one-sided diet of probity – vice versa. In this light, the dangers of adverse influence are perhaps more to be feared from pupil attachment to people who are, in the general human run of things, neither especially virtuous nor particularly vicious and, from this point of view, there may be nothing too far-fetched about the above example.

In this connection, moreover, there can be few teachers – the best as well as the worst – who are in any position to cast the first stone with regard to use of more or less humiliating verbal put-downs for purposes of class control and maintenance of authority. Indeed, with the removal from schools of the 'ultimate' deterrent of physical punishment, such tactics may well appear to many basically decent teachers to represent the last really effective means at their disposal by which they might hope, by virtue of superior wit and verbal facility, to gain the edge over loud-mouthed classroom demagogues. Nor should one underestimate the sheer righteous pleasure of 'justly' humbling those of whom one might fairly say that they had it coming. We will mostly be ready to admit, if pressed, that verbal bullying and humiliation are not very nice. But if we can defend such conduct as serving certain wider purposes of classroom justice and fairness – after all, if we do not silence the smart alecs (and the stresses of teaching at this point can be intolerable) the learning of the other ninety-five per cent of decent children will suffer – then it may seem that in this instance the end more than justifies the means. From this point of view, much latter-day professional emphasis on teacher development as mainly a matter of the cultivation of skills of, among other things, effective class management,[9] might even encourage us to regard such punitive verbal manipulation as a perfectly reasonable disciplinary technique in certain straitened circumstances.

There, however, is the rub. One trouble with conceiving the role of the teacher primarily in terms of managerial and other skills is that it is precisely liable to encourage the kind of instrumental or consequentialist thinking about education which opens a dangerous space between ends and means. However, on that virtue-ethical perspective which seems equally appropriate when considering the effects of character on others, such negative traits or dispositions to ridicule and sarcasm may also appear to have consequences which are as damaging to the character of the teacher – and hence to the overall moral climate of authority and relationships in the class or school – as they are to those on the more immediate receiving end. Still, it might be said, is this not something of a mountain out of a molehill? Are teachers to be forever on their guard against the casual friendly jibe that might be taken in a wrong or hurtful way? Surely not all classroom banter is of a hostile and demeaning kind, and it might even be considered damaging to the kind of healthy rough and tumble classroom climate which good teachers often do manage to establish with their classes, that they are ever required to be self-consciously vigilant in this way. But the proper response here, none the worse for being obvious, is that there is normally nothing to fear from friendly banter between teachers and pupils who *have* established a non-threatening climate of mutual respect and trust. What rather calls for attention is the deliberate use of any device, including the use of ridicule and sarcasm, which serves to promote the kind of atmosphere which militates against such respect and trust. In this light, it seems a sound point of general principle that deliberate deployment of superior verbal facility to demean and belittle can never serve the interests of wider school justice, even if it achieves a temporary resentful cessation of hostilities. In this connection, if circumstances should dictate that classroom control requires the injury of force, then it is surely better that the insult of humiliation is not added to it.

## Professional persona and personal probity

Such observations regarding the implications of personal character and demeanour for the role of the teacher, however, now lead us naturally on to issues concerning the private–professional interface of teachers' lives; indeed, given their unavoidable role as moral exemplars, we have already been given grounds to suspect that this may be more of an issue for teachers than other professionals. Consider the following case:

---

It is widely known that a head of department in a school is having an extra-marital affair with a younger teacher. This is known to be causing great personal and familial distress and is also clearly the subject of much gossip among pupils as well as staff.

---

Schools are social institutions, teachers are (despite what pupils and parents often seem to think) human beings, and it would be unrealistic to suppose that school staff-rooms are any less likely than offices, hospitals, department stores, police stations or factories to exhibit the familiar tapestry of human virtue and vice, including the usual quota of irregular or unofficial attachments. Despite this, we have already argued that it may sometimes be appropriate for teachers as moral exemplars to try to modify their characters or personalities in the light of professional demands. Indeed, moral exemplification aside, it is surely no less reasonable to require teachers to control their tendencies to short temper, laziness or misanthropy, than it is to require the same of doctors or nurses. But what of a teacher's personal life and circumstances? Despite the evident personal dimension of much professional engagement – the need for certain kinds of character traits in addition to certain sorts of skills – it would be unreasonable to deny the entitlement of professionals to some measure of private life. From this perspective, although personal 'in-house' involvements between doctors and nurses, police sergeants and detectives, accountants and actuaries, may well attract much shop-floor gossip and no small disapproval, they are also likely to be regarded as no one else's business, just so long as such liaisons have no obvious adverse professional consequences (of, for example, breaches of confidentiality). In the case of teachers, however, there is good reason to suppose that parents do often worry about the personal lives or private conduct of teachers, precisely with a view to the potential influence of such agents on their children. Such worries also doubtless vary a good deal in respect of both prevalence and seriousness, though the fact that a worry is of *any* parental concern must make it a matter of *some* professional concern. All the same, parental complaints about a male teacher wearing an earring or a ponytail could hardly be considered a disciplinary matter in this day and age. Knowledge of the cohabitation, homosexuality, unmarried pregnancy or sexual promiscuity of teachers is invariably taken in the stride of most contemporary non-religious state schools, as well as by the secular-liberal parents whose children attend such schools, although such conduct is more likely to raise questions in the houses (for perhaps rather different reasons) of religious and private education. However, other conduct such as alcoholism, drug addiction or affairs between teachers and even over-age consenting pupils, could well, as we have seen, give rise to professionally instigated disciplinary action.

But into which of these categories of seriousness, if any, should extra-marital affairs between teachers fall? Have such liaisons any professional or educational implications whatsoever, and are they the business of anyone other than the parties involved? First, it seems unlikely, as we have seen, that such involvements would be regarded as having significant professional implications in other professional contexts; second, it appears that known affairs and cohabitation, even between teachers working in the same school, are at least routinely tolerated (it would also seem that the majority of secular-liberal state schools are disinclined to make much professional fuss about extra-marital involvements as such). Is there anything, then, to distinguish the educational case here from similar cases in other professional or occupational contexts? One feature, of course, by which adulterous liaisons stand to be distinguished from other non-marital affairs and involvements is that they explicitly involve *betrayal* (of promises as well as people) and injury to a third party or parties, and it is surely upon this that any clear adverse moral implications will turn. Thus, it is not just – as I have sometimes heard it said in discussion of such cases – that such involvements are more likely to create the personal disruption and dislocation which impedes professional effectiveness. To be sure, in the rather narrow sense of professional effectiveness which is here implied, it should be clear that an adulterous affair need be no more damaging to day-to-day efficiency than a marriage on the rocks, or an out of house love affair which is otherwise poisoned by betrayal. The point about adultery would be rather that there cannot, in circumstances where the life of a teacher is compromised by betrayal in such a conspicuously public way, be professional effectiveness in the rather wider sense with which we have been concerned in this work.

From this perspective, it may seem a rather bitter ethical pill to swallow that, from a personal moral (virtue-ethical) point of view, the adulterous teacher may happen to be a much better and more serious person, deserving of greater sympathy, than the unmarried Lothario in the classroom next door who routinely spends his time pursuing casual and shallow sexual conquests. But although a school may easily turn a professional blind eye to the private extramural capers of classroom Casanovas, it may seem more professionally problematic for schools to appear entirely unconcerned about the adulterer, on pain of appearing to condone cavalier disregard of the kind of public human contract for which schools ought to be teaching some regard, even if no formal professional censure is forthcoming. An ever present temptation here, of course, is to sit on the fence and try to observe a kind of value neutrality. It might be said that marital infidelity is one of those facts of life with which children have inevitably to come to terms, and to which they are in any case witness whenever they turn on their (doubtless personal) television sets. But to the extent that it is proper to conceive education as primarily concerned less with teaching young people to accept facts of life, more with helping them to discern the difference between good, principled and admirable behaviour, and bad, wrong or disreputable behaviour (and it is once again a *conceptual* point, not merely a matter of subjective opinion, that adultery falls into the latter category), any such attempted neutrality cannot but be problematic. How, then, should such cases be handled in professional terms? I think we should say that they should at least be treated with as much human sympathy, compassion and understanding as they deserve: perhaps with much more than they deserve, not least when they do not deserve it. But since such infidelity raises questions of human right and wrong over which it is merely derelict of educational establishments to equivocate, understanding ought not to be confused with condoning, or compassion with indifference. The heart of any school's moral influence on children is the moral example of teachers; to that end, if teachers often fail to be just, it is none the less professionally incumbent upon them, as far as possible, not to appear *conspicuously* unjust. As teachers we fail as humans and as humans we fail as teachers, and when we fail it is proper to ask for understanding and forgiveness; but as educators we only further compound our failures if we refuse to acknowledge them for what they truly are. In the next and final chapter, we shall examine some of the larger issues of fairness and justice which are prone to arise in relation to the nature of schools as institutions.

# 13

# ETHICAL ISSUES CONCERNING EDUCATION AND SCHOOLING

## The character implicatedness of teacher professionalism

In the previous chapter we looked briefly at a range of issues concerning the role of the teacher, with particular respect to issues of the interplay of the personal/private and professional/public aspects of teachers' lives. On the face of it, teaching seems to differ from many other professions and occupations in so far as the kind of person a teacher is, and the way he or she is inclined to live, appear to have considerable implications for professional practice, not least in respect of that further ethical dimension of moral exemplification which is less conspicuous, if not entirely absent, in the case of such standard professions as medicine and law. In this respect, as we saw at the outset, teaching seems to exhibit some of the features of such traditional vocations or vocation-professions as religious ministry. Just like a teacher a minister or clergyman is in role liable to attract censure for aspects of his or her lifestyle which might be considered irrelevant to effective professional practice of law or medicine, precisely because it also seems that effective religious ministry cannot be conceived independently of the development of a certain kind of character. Indeed, it may be only a relatively recent inclination to construe the professional teacher's role in terms of the acquisition of a set of off-the-peg skills or competences which seduces us into thinking of good teaching as conceivable apart from more personal qualities. However, it should need little further reflection to see that many of the skills featured in competence models of professional training – abilities to match general curricular prescriptions to individual needs, to hold the attention of a class or to maintain good order – depend precisely upon the cultivation of situation-specific capacities and sensibilities of empathy, care, patience, fairness and persistence which are neither themselves skills, nor apt for acquisition in quite the manner of skills.

One can recognise, of course, that the inclination to hive off the professional from the personal and private aspects of individuals lives is often based on an ostensibly laudable desire to protect the integrity of professional practice from the vagaries and caprices of human character and personality: to uphold a standard of professional conduct which is precisely impartial by virtue of being 'personality-proof'. It may be thought that so long as the teacher, doctor or lawyer observes the stated rules and skills of sound professional practice, all will be well in practice. It is a key claim of this book that this is not obviously so, at least in the case of teaching. Indeed, it is not just that any character-proof conception of professional expertise must be devastating for any practice which crucially concerns the moral formation of others, but that it fails to recognise that any *general* professional principles depend precisely for *particular* interpretation upon capacities for wise judgement grounded in appropriately educated qualities of understanding and affect. But such failure to think in a more rounded and robust way about the professional role of the teacher, to recognise that to the extent that effective teaching depends on competences, such competences are in turn grounded in personal qualities which are not themselves expressible in the manner of competences, often appears to be replicated in more *institutional* thinking about education and teaching. Thus, just as one may be tempted to think that we can insure, via professional regulation of the teacher's role, against human vice or arbitrariness at the level of particular classroom engagement, so one might seek to insure against injustice, unfairness or downright inefficiency at more institutional levels, via articulation and imposition of some set of moral or economic rules or procedures. In this respect, it is notable that just as competence conceptions of professional preparation have lately been promoted in the training of individual practitioners, so a new managerialism has recently come of age for similar purposes of rationalisation of the organisation and administration of schools as publicly-funded social institutions.[1] Nowadays, then, it would appear that erstwhile heads of academic communities are widely encouraged to regard school government and administration, the just and/or efficient administration and organisation of educational institutions, as a matter of quasi-scientific rationalisation of economy and ethos: as a matter of the putting in place of the right sort of rules and procedures.

## The hazards of managerialism

Once again, one might well ask what is especially wrong with attempts to rationalise, even quasi-scientifically, the management and administration of institutions? I suppose that one general objection to managerialism – understood as a scientific or 'rationalistic' approach to educational management – is that it is somehow *dehumanising* or careless of the significant moral and ethical dimensions of the life of many if not most public institutions. Thus, television soaps have accustomed us to think of hospitals as combat zones in which big-hearted doctors and nurses struggle vainly to uphold basic human values against a faceless bureaucracy of soulless administrators intent only on sacrificing patients on the altar of Mammon. However, although balancing the budget is doubtless a real enough concern of today's headteachers in all too often straitened economic circumstances, issues of appropriate educational *ethos* have received considerable attention of late,[2] and opportunities for serious reflection on ethical issues are often – if perhaps not often enough – available in courses of professional training for headteachers and administrative assistants. Thus, deliberations about efficient school organisation or cost-effective timetabling need not *necessarily* be divorced from reflections about what might be fair or just in some wider moral sense. Another related objection, however, is that managerialism is bound to entail an unacceptably *undemocratic* or 'top-down' approach to school management, in a field of public service which is notoriously line management ridden and has frequently been said to place far too much autocratic power in the hands of headteachers.[3] But first, significant questions need to be asked about the extent to which schools can and should be conceived as democratic institutions; second, there seems to be no obvious reason why professional courses of training in school management could not explore strategies for the greater democratisation of educational institutions, allowing greater scope for the involvement of other staff, and even pupils, in the formulation of school policy.

Hence, although neglect of the ethical and moral dimensions of institutional life, or generally undemocratic policies and procedures, may be side-effects of more extreme forms of managerialism, they need not be, and I suspect that any real difficulty runs a little deeper than these objections suggest. Indeed, given proper attention to ethical considerations, or policies for workplace democracy or employee participation, it is not obvious that rational strategies of a kind popularly associated with managerialism are at all inappropriate to a wide range of familiar human occupations. So what, if anything, is inappropriate about any such rationalisations in the sphere of educational management? I suspect that the heart of the difficulty lies in considerations already aired in our criticisms of competence approaches to teaching, and which in turn reflect communitarian or virtue-ethical objections to any understanding of justice and morality in decontextualised terms. However, it is not that impersonal moral or managerial rules or imperatives can never have any application, more that they have most appropriate application in moral, political and occupational contexts in which individual differences of personality, background and value are not centrally implicated in the purposes of the project. Thus, for example, the moral universalisms of political liberalism may be judged fairly adequate for the purpose of value-neutral arbitration between the competing interests of different cultural constituencies in plural societies, where the task is precisely to develop a set of rules or constraints to which individual or cultural differences constitute no exemption. Likewise, in such industries or commercial enterprises as automobile manufacture or sales, in which personal values and relationships are either irrelevant or largely subservient to the achievement of corporate goals, the moral or economic rationalisations of managerialism may well be real grist to the literal mill.

However, in an enterprise such as education or teaching in which the personal touch, human relationships and the cultivation of personal values are not just instrumental to achieving certain ends, but more or less *constitutive* of them – social work, nursing and religious ministry may well represent other instances of such enterprises – general professional rules, principles and strategies will be liable to diverse context-sensitive evaluation, negotiation and compromise. As communitarians are wont to argue, this seems true of moral communities in general. This is why, on the virtue-ethical perspective adopted by many communitarians, the moral universals of political liberalism, no matter how successful they may be in policing border clashes between diverse cultural constituencies and interests, seem impotent to provide any substantial account of moral formation, commitment or even argument and dispute. But is it not also natural to conceive of schools, parishes and dioceses, or community centres as moral communities in which personal values and relationships are constitutive of, rather than merely instrumental to, the aims of such institutions? To the extent that this is so, although schools, parishes and community centres will need to be managed, they will also require of their managers just those situation-specific sensibilities which we have already supposed to be needed by classroom teachers: more, at any rate, than acquaintance with those moral and economic abstractions to which managerial rationalisation often aspires. In short, just as the generalisations of teaching competence are likely to lack pedagogical purchase if not rooted in deeper resources of character and personality, so the *episteme* and *techne* of managerialism can hardly be effective in the moral contexts of educational institution if not rooted in qualities which go rather beyond what is contained in managerial *episteme* and *techne*.

In fact, one might maintain that any talk of management in connection with education and teaching, not least of headteachers or college principals as managers, is as insensitively solecistic as speaking of schools as businesses, regarding parents and pupils as clients or customers, or treating academies as limited companies. It is not so much, as we have conceded, that management is not part of the wider role of headteachers or parish priests, more that any managerial duties which such ministers may be required to undertake are *secondary* to and derivative of their primary non-managerial responsibility for the moral and/or spiritual growth and well-being of those under their stewardship: in short, the primary duty of headteachers or parish priests is to forge communities conducive to moral and spiritual growth. But although good headteachers or parish priests may need to be effective managers of available resources in promoting such growth, and such resources will also include assistant teachers and curates, such resources are themselves key members of the communities whose overall moral and spiritual welfare their leaders are in business to promote, and hence more than just objects of management. From this viewpoint, it is as hazardous to foster a managerial mentality on the part of heads of schools or colleges, if this means encouraging them to conceive school management as the rationalisation of school life according to externally determined quasi-scientific moral or economic imperatives, as it is to encourage competence attitudes to professional expertise on the part of individual teachers. This is not because there is no need for management or rules – even, from time to time, for bringing pupils and teachers into line with the rules – but because good management in such contexts is a matter of sensitive collegial appreciation of the diversity of individual and personal perspectives and contributions out of which the moral project of schooling is itself constructed. Thus, if a positive school ethos is crucial to good schooling, and ethos is a function of good community, then the best personal attitudes and values of teachers as members of school community are not just *instrumental* to, but *constitutive* of, schooling's purposes.

## Equality and difference

It is ever tempting, not least in a modern climate of social thinking deeply influenced by the behavioural sciences, to believe that institutions may run more effectively if they are mechanically regulated, if, so to speak, they run like 'clockwork', and it may well be true of some human production that efficiency rises with the elimination of individual difference. However, educational institutions are not industries but *cultures*, and harmonisation, arbitration or negotiation of differences of perspective, personality and value are not merely incidental to, but of the very essence of, cultural growth. Thus, just as the good teacher is one whose classroom impartiality is moderated by sensitive recognition of the different needs of individual pupils, a good school leader is one who can without fear or favour deploy staff, in the best overall interests of the institution, in the light of wise appreciation of diverse individual strengths and weaknesses. From this viewpoint, creating positive school ethos should begin with the cultivation of positive relationships of trust and respect, rather than conclude with the writing of school mission statements of commitment to strict observance of justice, respect and equal opportunities. Indeed, as noted in Chapter 12, behaviour which could appear disrespectful, abusive or sexist in some contexts, perhaps certain kinds of verbal cut and thrust, may be no such thing in contexts characterised by trust and mutual good-will between teachers and taught. It takes the right sort of sensitivity and perception, however, to see which is which.

But what are the limits of such reflective accommodation of 'universal' moral principles to particular cases? Suppose, for example, we want to ensure that a class of children all feel that they are treated fairly or equally, but one particular child is liable to become upset or disobedient if made to join in a common activity for personal-psychological or cultural reasons. How are we to know where lines should or should not be drawn in such cases? The trouble is that one naturally seeks advice on such matters in the form of a rule or set of rules which would dictate whether we have got things right or wrong. But if justice is itself less a matter of straightforward application of rules, more of sensitive situation-specific interpretation of them, how could there be any *further* particular rule which tells us how to apply a given general rule? The absence of any such rule does not, of course, mean that we *cannot* get matters right or wrong, for we are quite often able to judge with hindsight that we did the right or (perhaps more commonly) the wrong thing. But in virtue-ethical terms it is not so much the mark of a just man that he strictly observes rules of justice, but the mark of justice to do precisely what a just person would do.[4] In turn, however, this crucially means cultivating the characteristics and qualities of a wise judge: that proper balance of fairness, compassion, sympathy, understanding, courage and self-control which facilitates accurate perception of the precise needs of the moment. All the same, there is no short cut to the development of such qualities. Thus, the trouble with any search for a simple rule is precisely that it is a quest for a short cut: precisely for that moral *techne* which is sometimes promised, but never delivered, on liberal-theoretical cognitive-developmental conceptions of moral development.[5]

The absence in principle of any general prescription which might serve to short cut fine moral decision is also, of course, what gives rise to the difficulty of discussing abstract case studies in works concerning practical ethics of roughly the kind presented here. The trouble is that such cases can never be specified in the amount of detail required to deliver a satisfactory, even interim, decision about what should be done in a specific situation. Indeed, one danger of such works is that they may be picked up by school managers and administrators concerned (understandably) with knowing how to troubleshoot moral problems, in rather the way a mechanic would have recourse to a vehicle maintenance manual in order to fix a problem of internal combustion. It might be tempting to treat a particular case study in the manner of a wiring diagram, and to suppose that once one has sorted this problem one can move onto the next. But the differences between moral and technical problems should by now be clear. First, there cannot be quite the same finality to any description or evaluation of a moral issue, of a kind often to be had in the technical case. A technical fix can be quite 'good enough', and if it is not we may be able to go back to fix it properly. But later revision of initial moral diagnosis (the wisdom of hindsight) will often uncover moral saliences which we had missed at the time, and we are not in any technical way able to retrieve our moral mistakes. Indeed, it is a commonplace that past moral mistakes are liable to have a formative influence on the kind of people we turn out to be in a way that technical mistakes have not. This is not simply the triviality that we learn morally from experience – to which the obvious reply is that we also learn technically from experience. The point is rather that a past betrayal is part of me in the way that a past botched plastering job is not. On the one hand, I was taken to task over the plastering, I repaired the job, all was mended and the event is forgotten; on the other hand, I was rebuked for the betrayal and went back and apologised – but not all was mended, and it is greatly to my moral shame and discredit if I have now forgotten.

The trouble with moral textbook cases, then, is that they are seldom more than initial shallow and near-sighted glances at *types* of problem which cannot be seriously addressed in default of the situation-specific detail which might lead us to quite different ethical judgements regarding different *tokens* of such types, if not to quite different later moral assessments of the same tokens in the light of the wisdom of hindsight. It is just this, of course, which is liable to engender serious moral agnosticism or scepticism among the more moral philosophically faint-hearted. How can we ever get it right, and what is the point of deliberation in circumstances where we can never know all we would need to know to ensure correct moral decision? In that case, are not the interests of justice best served by procrustean adherence to rules which, applied without fear or favour, might cut the Gordian knot of situational complexity? It is important to see, however, not just that we can and do often get things morally right through sensitive judgement and sincere concern for others, but that we can also improve our virtue-ethical sensibilities and capacities for judgement and concern quite appreciably through the bitter experience of getting things wrong. In short, it does not follow from the fact that there is no rational decision procedure for ensuring moral success, that there *is* no moral success or failure. Any moral understanding, moreover, has to start somewhere: to this end, even general case studies – of the kind we are about to consider – may assist recognition of some key moral saliences in some broad areas of moral concern.

## School administration: democracy versus autocracy

As the main concern in this chapter has so far been with educational management and the nature of schools as moral institutions, we may now examine the following issue:

---

Dinwiddie High is widely regarded as an orderly and well managed school with a headteacher who knows what she wants and is popular with parents, staff and pupils. She is not, all the same, given to a markedly democratic or consultative management style and her generally paternalist and autocratic approach is reflected throughout the school in relations between heads of departments and assistants and teachers and pupils.

---

Should schools be democratic institutions? Significantly, with the distinguished exception of Plato,[6] almost all notable past educational philosophers have argued for a conception of education as initiation into the kind of qualities of open-mindedness usually associated with democratic association.[7] According to this broad consensus, ideas of education and open society are connected to the extent that there must be something suspect about any educational climate which actually runs counter to the democratic spirit. Still, despite broad philosophical agreement that any education worthy of the name should equip young people with intellectual capacities and attitudes apt for democratic participation, there is some controversy over the extent to which educational institutions would, in the interests of fostering such capacities, themselves need to be arranged democratically. An extreme line on this was taken by modern radical or progressivist educationalists such as A.S. Neill and (his mentor) Homer Lane who considered democratic participation in school government on the part of all (including very young) pupils to be the *sine qua non* of personal emancipation and social responsibility. In this connection, Lane and Neill regarded the trappings of coercion and control of educational and other social institutions (including, in all probability, the family) to be the cause not only of the anti-social resentment of authority of problem youngsters, but of the failure of most young people to achieve the responsible liberty of personal maturity. In their own

Rousseauian way, they held that children could never come to appreciate the value of social rules and legitimate authority, without some opportunity to exercise freedom and learn experimentally from the consequences of making and breaking rules. Hence, the notion of the self-governing school, realised to some degree both in Homer Lane's The Little Commonwealth and at A.S. Neill's Summerhill.

On the other hand, however, it has been a central claim of the liberal traditional orthodoxy of post-war educational philosophy that any proper development of those qualities of rational self-direction also valued by progressives actually presupposes a fair measure of coercion or compulsion.[8] For many traditionalists, the qualities most needed for responsible democratic citizenship are those of personal *discipline*, and schools can be thought to play a major part in shaping such qualities in at least two major respects. First, the compulsory core curriculum of intellectual and practical disciplines which the school provides plays an indispensable role in moulding the qualities of mind and character needed for sound judgement and unswerving commitment to the deliverances of such judgement. Thus, in the absence of a sense of identity rooted in some grasp of one's historical and geographical place, or the powers of logical reasoning acquired in mathematics and science, or the ordered affect of artistic and aesthetic appreciation, or the physical discipline and co-operation to be gained from participation in sports and games (without which, as Plato declared, a man may have less backbone than is decent[9]), individuals must lack the basic capacities and sensibilities presupposed to responsible democratic participation.

But, second, it may be held that schooling itself also has a part to play in the formation of responsibility by providing young people with their first taste of co-operation and competition with others in a public space which lies beyond the cosy security of the pre-school world. On this account, school is the key rite of passage from family membership to wider civic participation, and learning to abide by its interpersonal rules and constraints is a crucial mark of any such successful transition. From this viewpoint, however, coercion and subjection to external discipline may appear to be the very *raison d'être* of schooling, and there may therefore seem to be every reason why schools should *not* be ordered on democratic lines. Indeed, conservative traditionalists will often point out that life 'in the real world' is mostly and inevitably a matter of learning to take one's rightful place in some 'received' social and economic scheme of things. Children may be told by parents and teachers that they will not be able to behave thus or so when they have to leave school to enter an office or factory, and advised that any adult authority to give rather than follow orders is the rightful inheritance only of those who have learned the importance of responsible obedience.

All the same, in the view of educational progressives and radicals, who also value capacities for responsible self-regulation and self-direction, it is not just that there do not seem to be any clear ethical grounds for the repressive subjection of children to compulsory schooling, but that any such powers are more apt to be stifled than promoted by the processes of top-down authority and discipline beloved of educational traditionalists. Notoriously, for example, A.S. Neill took the strong libertarian and child-liberationist line (whilst still recognising, it has to be said, the need for safety rules for the protection of small children against their own immaturity) that the psychological damage caused by the repression of compulsory schooling and conventional education could lead only to the uncreative conformity of individuals effectively incapable of that responsible personal initiative presupposed to democratic citizenship. It was the view of Neill, largely influenced by Homer Lane, that there could be no real understanding of the social importance and significance of following rules in the absence of some understanding of the freedoms and burdens of responsible authority: the two were considered to go hand in hand. Hence, Neill advocated and implemented at his school Summerhill an extreme form of democratic school government in which, from the outset, the smallest of children had equal rights of participation with the oldest of teachers.

Neill's views in general and educational practice at Summerhill (and similar schools) in particular, of course, have been the subject of much heated educational controversy and criticism and are widely regarded as extreme, if not quite beyond the pale.[10] All the same, these different perspectives on the place of authority, compulsion and freedom in education and schooling have obvious implications for any question of the proper extent to which schools should be democratically organised. I suspect that it is also probably safe to say that in the case of this particular educational issue (though not, by any means, in the case of *all* educational issues) the answer lies somewhere in the middle. On the one hand, although there is doubtless much in the idea that a positive attitude to rules and authority is liable to be assisted by a proper grasp of what rules are for, which may even be reinforced by some imaginative role play in assuming authority, the often anarchic free-for-all of Summerhill may seem to be a rather extravagant way of promoting such understanding. Moreover, the method of self-government which Neill inherited from Lane was originally devised as a form of therapy for problem children, those whose negative experiences of (often brutal) parental and other authority had created reaction formations only susceptible to the most radical of socio-psychological remedies. Much in the manner of Freud, then, who also seems to have sought to extend to human character and personality, in general, theories originally devised to explain only extreme cases of neurotic personality, Neill appears to have somewhat dubiously supposed that strategies developed for dealing with the behavioural consequences of disordered personality were equally applicable to the 'normal' case.[11]

On the other hand, however, although there may indeed be something to the idea that schools are crucial agencies for the acquisition on the part of young people of the basic discipline (or disciplines) required for effective flourishing in a world where they will often need in the general interest to do as they are told, buckle down and get on with it, there is clearly also a need, emphasised by progressives, for young people to develop initiative through the burdens of responsibility. But this arguably requires more opportunities for the promotion and exercise of individual initiative than seem to be readily available in the average state comprehensive. From this viewpoint, moreover, it would seem desirable to provide young people in this as other moral spheres with clear patterns or examples of free democratic association of a kind which are not readily available within institutions run on largely hierarchical, autocratic or top-down lines. Thus, if adult members of the school community operate according to a strict line management in which some dictate to others without consultation, and others follow orders without question, it is unlikely that the right ethos or climate of responsible democratic engagement will be set from the outset. This is where earlier points about the inappropriateness to collegial life of the sort of managerial approach to administration which might arguably suit some spheres of industry and commerce comes into its own. Despite the highly complex economic character of modern educational institutions, it should not be forgotten that schools and colleges are not factories or businesses, and that they are centrally more concerned with the preservation and promotion of culture, than the promotion of economic growth. This, generally speaking, must mean imparting to young people the highest ideals of human association of a culture. In the special case of liberal democratic culture, however, it must particularly mean promoting capacities for free and equal rational negotiation of diverse needs and interests in a climate of respect and tolerance. Thus, notwithstanding the benevolence of any school despot, and bearing in mind the perfectly proper point that contemporary headteachers will often have to take tough economic decisions which leave little space for consultation, the conceptual connection between *real* education and democratic sensibility seems such as to preclude any overly autocratic or non-collegiate style of school management. Thus, it arguably behoves headteachers to exemplify from the top, as far as possible, the kind of 'bottom-up' climate of association they should want to be characteristic of any human community.

## Intra-school value conflict

But if democratic sensibilities are to include giving a serious hearing to dissenting views and policies, how far can such dissent be allowed to go without dangerously undermining the effective prosecution of school business? What, for example, of the following possibility:

A teacher is well known for her radical, progressive and libertarian political and educational views. However, her highly sceptical and critical attitudes to the system and authority now appear to be influencing some pupils to question the authority of other teachers, with serious adverse consequences for discipline.

This case is by no means fanciful. In the British education system there have been notorious instances, particularly in the 1960s and 1970s, when radical educational ideas were allowed to slip the leash in the state sector, of schools being brought to a virtual standstill by the near-anarchist activities of individuals whose apparent sole aim was to buck the system.[12] From a professionally top-down or paternalist point of view, of course, one might be disinclined to recognise any real problem here at all. According to the more centrally prescribed conceptions of professional standards which seem to have overtaken professional preparation in teaching and other fields under the pressure of recent British administrations (both Conservative and Labour), such teachers would be simply liable to professional censure and discipline in the light of strictly laid down professional principles, values and standards. Throughout this work, however, we have consistently argued that any such conception of professional life may be less than faithful to that openness to sincere departure from orthodoxy which should, at least in principle, lie at the heart of both serious professional reflection and liberal-democratic association. In short, there seems to be something rather untoward about a conception of professionalism which insists on absolute conformity to this or that ideological perspective, even if (perhaps *especially* if) any such perspective currently enjoys official sanction. From this point of view, it might be said, the professional garden should be one in which a thousand flowers are allowed to bloom. Moreover, although such a view is by no means inconsistent with the elimination of educational weeds (crackpot views held without much rational warrant) we have repeatedly observed that there is much *genuine* and *serious* professional dispute about the ends and means of rational educational practice. In this respect, indeed, there may be something to radical or progressive claims that schools often do seem to serve purposes of social control rather than education; promoting mindless conformity to, more than critical questioning of, received injustices and inequalities.

However, the trouble with this line of argument – precisely the trouble which attracts centralised top-down approaches to professional regulation – is that it seems to generate paradoxes. Indeed, the main professional paradoxes to which it gives rise are possibly variants or special cases of the central paradox of democratic freedom.[13] Genuine democracy goes hand in hand with liberal openness to and tolerance of intellectual and/or value diversity: with, in short, individual freedom of thought, speech and conduct. Of course, such freedom is subject to the liberal harm condition; individual freedom is permissible only to the extent that it does not violate or unduly restrict the freedom of others. Thus, I have liberty to play heavy metal music on my stereo so long as it does not seriously discomfort my neighbours, and precisely the same applies to them. It is in realms of freedom of conscience and speech, however, that problems of liberal freedom arise in an acute form. In cases of verbal intimidation or incitement to racial violence, the liberal harm condition would seem to apply well enough (although one should not ignore the important complication that a *potential* harm is easy neither to identify nor to legislate for). But some of the most serious of adverse consequences of free speech may be for the very idea of democratic freedom as such. Consider, for example, the left- or right-wing extremist – or, for that matter, a Platonic 'republican' – who stands at Hyde Park corner proclaiming the decadence of democracy. On this occasion, he preaches no race hate, only the comforting message that if the people give him supreme power to run the country with a firm hand, he will remove corrupt politicians, put an end to social service scrounging and make the trains run on time. All this, however, can only be achieved via the removal of parliamentary democracy and a range of civic liberties (the right to vote out the government, withdraw labour, and so on). The obvious bind here is that if liberal democracy takes measures to silence such anti-democratic propaganda, it will certainly be acting contrary to its own most basic tenets and principles. On the other hand, if it gives free rein to anti-democratic sentiments, it runs the risk of assisting the forces which seek to overthrow it, and we know from recent painful political history how vulnerable to such countervailing forces democracy can be.

School-place democracy is prey to related dangers. Considered as human academic communities schools and colleges ought surely to encourage the greatest possible openness to the diversity of views and values which come their way. Teachers *qua* educationalists should encourage frank and free discussion of any and every topic of interest and concern to children and young people, and headteachers ought to welcome the wide diversity of ideas and perspectives of their staff members. But, as already noted, schools are not just concerned with the promotion of education; they are also complex economic institutions accountable to larger socio-cultural and economic aims. Hence, although it may not be an *educational* aim of the headteacher to balance the books, it is nevertheless a valid headteacher aim, and although it may not be an educational aim of schools to get children through examinations and into jobs, it is nevertheless a proper aim of schooling. From these and other perspectives, however, the ideas of some teachers may be unrealistic if not plain crazy. It is likely that many teachers in posts which do not involve budgetary responsibility will assume that the educational money pit is bottomless and be inclined to demands for resources which are hardly apt for sane and sensible debate. Moreover, the fact that such demands may come from the *majority* of staff in a school does not make them more (democratically) reasonable; on the contrary, the greater such demands are, the better the case for despotically refusing them. Again, however, some radical teachers and educationalists have held that education in the context of schooling would be more effective without the pressure of examinations. But whilst this idea is by no means crazy (on the contrary, it may very well be *true*), it fails to recognise that schools are charged with the promotion of a wider range of capacities, powers and entitlements than those we might strictly wish to call educational. There are therefore clear logistical and pragmatic limits to the possibility of serious discussion of even plausible and interesting educational ideas in public institutions where we also require the locomotives of education and training to run on time.

What, then, is to be done in the case of radical, anarchist or non-conformist staff members? In principle, the difficulties of such cases probably reflect those which generally confront liberal-democratic polity in accommodating the often strident demands of radicals who want total reform now. Thus, any general answer is certainly going to be in terms of some sort of pragmatic accommodation, although more would need to be known about the particular case to determine precise policy. We have already claimed in relation to the case of the undemocratic head, that a democratic approach to staff relations is the only one really consistent with the very idea of school as *community*, and such an approach, one which aims to reduce confrontation and keep open lines of communication, is almost certainly in principle the best one in cases of radical intra-school value conflict. If the actions or inflammatory speeches of school radicals are seriously rocking the boat, then their views should be openly confronted, in a spirit of reasonable compromise, with arguments which appeal to the long-term good of the school as a whole. If radical actions seriously undermine the school's effective fulfilment of its responsibilities to parents and the wider community, then disciplinary procedures invoking considerations of professional negligence may well be in order. If the rebels are in a small minority, then a combination of reasonable dialogue, rational consensus and disciplinary action may be sufficient to keep the show on the road; but if they make up a significant proportion of the staff, or are in the majority, then the school may well be in the kind of trouble that only external intervention can remedy. No one need doubt that even minor unresolved internecine strife can seriously undermine the effective functioning of educational institutions, and as already noted, it is a sad fact that such ferment has actually torn schools apart within recent British educational memory.

## Educational principle and anti-educational interests

To end this volume on a suitably controversial note, however, should we say that a teacher's stubborn allegiance to deeply held educational principles and convictions should always play second fiddle to wider considerations of public accountability? It is of some interest here that professional educationalists, not least those inspired by the post-war liberal educational ideal, have always been keenly aware of the potential *threat* to education represented by such external agencies and pressures as parents, the state and the economy. Indeed, it seems to have been in just this spirit that Paul Hirst many years ago argued for a conception of education 'based on the nature and significance of knowledge itself, and not on the predilections of pupils, the demands of society, or the whims of politicians'.[14] Thus, what should we say to someone who protested that currently fashionable commitment to wider public accountability was undermining the very possibility of education? Consider the following example:

McGuigan Academy is generally committed to the overall aim of promoting rational autonomy and critical capacities on the part of pupils and Ms Prufrock, the RE teacher, is second to none in her attempts to assist pupils to think for themselves. She is currently under criticism, however, from the parents of a local religious community who believe that their children should follow the teachings of the prophet without question.

Is this a matter for compromise of deeply held educational principle? Should schooling ever be made subject to the kind of pressures which make accountability to such external agencies as community, economy and state the be and end all of their existence? While the above example is somewhat overdrawn for the sake of a fine point, it is nevertheless clear enough that schools have lately been encouraged to enter the market place in free competition for client satisfaction in a way that has potentially serious implications, not only for the economic running of such institutions, but for the very concepts of education and teacher professionalism as such. The idea that open competition for custom in the sphere of education will have the same benefits – of improving quality, forcing down prices and eliminating efficiency – as it is alleged to have in the commercial sector, trades on analogies between quality of educational and other productivity which are deeply questionable. There is also by now a very extensive contemporary debate on the theme of education and the markets into which I shall not enter here, other than to note that there may be some danger in the literature of treating this question as a merely socio-political one – as a question of pure economic strategy.[15] In fact, I suspect that what may lie behind market thinking are rather deeper metaphysical and epistemological concerns over the nature of human flourishing and knowledge itself.

The particular question of whether there can be the same kind of open enquiry into meaning and truth in the sphere of religion as there can in the field of science clearly matters for religious education.[16] If there can be no such enquiry, there can be no religious education in any robust (emancipatory) sense of this term, but also no profession of religious education worthy of the name (only shamanism). There are very many people, believers and non-believers, who would deny that religious belief does rest on any such enquiry. Both fundamentalist and non-fundamentalist believers may take it to be a matter of faith rather than reason, and secularists and atheists will hold it to be a matter of superstitious nonsense. But, as we have also seen in this work, there are strong contemporary currents of epistemological scepticism which have tended to cast doubt on the possibility of rational enquiry as such, in *any* field of human enquiry. In a situation in which we appear bereft of any possibility of objective knowledge or understanding beyond individual or social human expediency, it may seem hazardous to ground our educational practices in considerations other than state-dictated economic interest or local individual or cultural predilection. From this viewpoint, it is hardly surprising that a national education system should come to exhibit the rather incongruous mixture of centralised and market thinking which has been the focus of some recent educational sociological interest.[17] In a postmodern climate of the demise of metanarrative, we may no longer believe in scientific truth, but as an economic competitor in a world market we must believe in literacy, numeracy and technology, and ensure a state system of educational provision in which vital skills and information are imparted. In a multicultural climate in which it is bad political form to proclaim the absolute truth of these values over those contrary ones, however, the state must also respect diversity and provide a market place in which parents can choose according to taste the kind of educational formation which is most consistent with their personal or cultural predilections.

But if there is anything to the arguments put forward here, it should be clear that no substantial *professional* conception of education could be based upon any such radical epistemological scepticism; in this connection, it is noteworthy that both these conceptions of education and schooling, the market and the centralised, are the source of marked deprofessionalising tendencies. In conceiving education as exclusively a matter of transmission of uncontroversial information and instrumental skills, the centralising approach inclines to construe the teacher as no more than classroom technician, the effective (or ineffective) deliverer of 'top-down' curriculum packages. In tailoring educational provision to this or that client demand for socialisation or training, the school may succumb to sophistical pressures to provide the client only with what flatters his or her prejudices rather than conduces to the health of his or her soul. Indeed, it was Socrates, the founding father of western philosophy, who first recognised in his opposition to the epistemological scepticism of the sophists the profound issues at stake here.[18] In promoting the health of the body, the professional physician is answerable not to what the client wants, or to what is socio-economically expedient, but to what is medically desirable. In order properly to address the needs of the patient the doctor has to discover what is wrong with the patient by reference to objective physiological facts, and to judge which of several possibly competing remedial strategies is likely to be most beneficial. There can, of course, be no certainties here: the physician may get either the diagnosis or the treatment wrong, and the patient may get worse or die. But the possibility of medical professionalism surely depends upon faith in the objective correctness or otherwise of diagnosis, and upon the possibility of real improvement of medical strategies and enhancement of professional wisdom with respect to their use. It seems clear enough that Socrates thought very much along these lines about the educationalist with respect to his or her prime professional function of curing the soul of ignorance and delusion. The teacher may not know (in general or in particular) what exactly the wisdom which frees us from ignorance is, anymore than the doctor may presently know what health is: but so long as there is some objective touchstone for distinguishing truth from falsity, reason from superstition, the teacher has a compass to follow and education has a coherent professional goal. Without such objective standards, however, the teacher may seem to be – like the medicine man or snake oil salesman – no more than a dealer in sophistry and delusion.

# NOTES

## 1 TEACHING AND EDUCATION

1 On this point, see Hirst, P.H., 'The logical and psychological aspects of teaching a subject', in P.H. Hirst, *Knowledge and the Curriculum*, London: Routledge and Kegan Paul, 1974.

2 Substance could be given to this point by reference to a wide range of educational trends and professional, theoretical and policy literature, and there is by now an extensive critical literature on this issue in post-war philosophy of education. For some exemplary recent resistance to the widespread incidence of skills talk in education, however, see Johnson, S., 'Skills, Socrates and the Sophists: learning from history', *British Journal of Educational Studies*, 46, 1998, pp. 201–14.

3 See Carr, D., 'Education, learning and understanding: the process and the product', *Journal of Philosophy of Education*, 26, 1992, pp. 215–25.

4 Points along these lines are made in Passmore, J., *The Philosophy of Teaching*, London: Duckworth, 1980.

5 For interesting work of a particularist bent, see Schon, D.A., *The Reflective Practitioner: How Professionals Think in Action*, New York: Basic Books, 1984; Dunne, J., *Back to the Rough Ground: 'Phronesis' and 'Techne' in Modern Philosophy and in Aristotle*, Notre Dame: University of Notre Dame Press, 1993.

6 For some recent British policy documentation which clearly does hold teachers responsible in this way, see National Curriculum Council (NCC), *Spiritual and Moral Education: A Discussion Paper*, National Curriculum Council, UK, 1993; Ofsted, *Spiritual, Moral, Social and Cultural Development: An Ofsted Discussion Paper*, Office for Standards in Education, UK, 1994; Schools Curriculum and Assessment Authority (SCAA), *Spiritual and Moral Development*, Schools Curriculum and Assessment Authority, UK, Discussion Paper No. 3, 1995; SCAA, *Education for Adult and Moral Life*, Schools Curriculum and Assessment Authority, UK, Discussion Paper No. 6, 1996.

7 The highly inflamatory proposals for a 'mums army' of non-graduate early years teachers was made by the Conservative education secretary John Patten in 1993. The proposal was resisted almost unanimously by the profession and came to nothing.

8 Matthew Arnold, 'Preface to *Literature and Dogma*', in J. Gribble (ed.), *Matthew Arnold*, London: Collier-Macmillan, Educational Thinkers Series, 1967, p 150.

9 Radical literature enshrining scepticism about educational professionalism of this kind is extensive: see, for example, Illich, I., *Deschooling Society*, Harmondsworth: Penguin, 1973a; Illich, I., *Celebration of Awareness*, Harmondsworth: Penguin, 1973b; Illich, I., 'Disabling professions', in I. Illich, *Disabling Professions*, London: Marion Boyars, 1977; Goodman, P., *Growing Up Absurd*, London: Gollancz, 1960; Goodman, P., *Compulsory Miseducation*, Harmondsworth: Penguin, 1971; Postman, N. and Weingartner, C., *Teaching as a Subversive Activity*, Harmondsworth: Penguin, 1971; Reimer, E., *School is Dead*, Harmondsworth: Penguin, 1971.

10 For this idea, see Neill, A.S., *Summerhill*, Harmondsworth: Penguin Books, 1968.

11 The distinction between 'thin' (liberal) and 'thick' (communitarian) ethical concepts and perspectives seems first to have been drawn by Bernard Williams, in Williams, B., *Ethics and the Limits of Philosophy*, London: Fontana Press/Collins, 1985, Chapters 7 and 8. For communitarian views and perspectives see Sandel, M., *Liberalism and the Limits of Justice*, New York: Cambridge University Press, 1982; MacIntyre, A.C., *After Virtue*, Notre Dame: Notre Dame Press, 1981; MacIntyre, A.C., *Whose Justice, Which Rationality?*, Notre Dame: Notre Dame Press, 1987b; MacIntyre, A.C., *Three Rival Versions of Moral Enquiry*, Notre Dame: Notre Dame Press, 1992; Taylor, C., *Sources of the Self: The Making of the Modern Identity*, Cambridge: Cambridge University Press, 1989. Most of these views represent some sort of reaction to the kind of liberal view presented by, for example, John Rawls in Rawls, J., *Theory of Justice*, Cambridge: Harvard University Press, 1985.

12 The distinction between restricted and extended professionalism seems first to have been made by Eric Hoyle. See Hoyle, E, 'Professionality, professionalism and control in teaching', *London Education Review*, 3, 1974, pp. 13–19. See also Kirk, G., *Teacher Education and Professional Development*, Edinburgh: Scottish Academic Press, 1988, Chapter 1.

13 The literature on home and school and partnership between schools and parents is extensive; see, for example, Bastiani, J., *Working with Parents*, London: Routledge, 1989; and Armstrong, D., *Power and Partnership in Education: Parents, Children and Special Educational Needs*, London: Routledge, 1995.

14 For recent critical work on education and the market, see Bridges, D. and McLaughlin, T.H. (eds), *Education and the Market*, Lewes: Falmer, 1994; Jonathan, R., *Illusory Freedoms: Liberalism, Education and the Market*, Oxford: Blackwell, 1997.

15 Peters, R.S., 'Reason and habit: the paradox of moral education', in *Psychology and Ethical Development*, London: George Allen and Unwin, 1974, p. 272.

16 For the idea of Socratic midwifery, see Plato's *Theaetetus* (149e–151d), in E. Hamilton and H. Cairns (eds), *Plato: The Collected Dialogues*, Princeton: Princeton University Press, 1961.

## 2 PROFESSIONS, PROFESSIONALISM AND PROFESSIONAL ETHICS

1 There is a large amount of literature on professions and power and on professional status-seeking. See, for example, Freidson, E., *Professional Powers: A Study of the Institutionalization of Formal Knowledge*, Chicago: University of Chicago Press, 1986; Illich, I., 'Disabling professions', in *Disabling Professions*, London: Marion Boyars, 1977; Jackson, A.J. (ed.), *Professions and Professionalisation*, London: Cambridge University Press, 1970; Johnson, J.T., *Professions and Power*, London: Macmillan, 1981; Larson, M.S., *The Rise of Professionalism: A Sociological Analysis*, London: Marion Boyars, 1977; Parsons, T., 'Professions', in D.L. Sills (ed.), *International Encyclopedia of the Social Sciences*, New York: Free Press, 1968; Reader, W.J., *Professional Men: The Rise of the Professional Classes in Nineteenth Century England*, London: Weidenfeld and Nicolson, 1966.

2 On the idea of semi-professions, see Etzioni, A. (ed.), *The Semi-Professions and their Organization: Teachers, Nurses and Social Workers*, London: Collier-Macmillan, 1969.

3 Kant, I., *Groundwork of the Metaphysic of Morals*, in H.J. Paton (ed.), *The Moral Law*, London: Hutchinson, 1948.

4 Aristotle, *The Nicomachean Ethics*, Book III, Section 3, in R. McKeon (ed.), *The Basic Works of Aristotle*, New York: Random House, 1941.

5 Ibid., Book VI and generally.

6 For discussion of competence models of education and teaching, see Burke, J.W. (ed.), *Competency Based Education and Training*, Lewes: Falmer Press, 1989. For a more critical discussion, see Hyland, T., 'Competence, knowledge and education', *Journal of Philosophy of Education*, 27, 1993, pp. 57–68; Hyland, T., *Competence, Education and NVQ's: Dissenting Perspectives*, London: Cassell, 1994; Carr, D., 'Questions of competence', *British Journal of Educational Studies*, 41, 1993, p. 3; and 'Guidelines for teacher training: the competency model', *Scottish Educational Review*, 25, 1993, p. 2.

7 Kohlberg, L., *Essays on Moral Development: Volumes I–III*, New York: Harper Row, 1984.

8 This position, again, is associated with various forms of contemporary communitarianism; see, for example, Sandel, M., *Liberalism and the Limits of Justice*, New York: Cambridge University Press, 1982; MacIntyre, A.C., *After Virtue*, Notre Dame: Notre Dame Press, 1981; MacIntyre, A.C., *Whose Justice, Which Rationality?*, Notre Dame: Notre Dame Press, 1987b; MacIntyre, A.C., *Three Rival Versions of Moral Enquiry*, Notre Dame: Notre Dame Press, 1992; Taylor, C., *Sources of the Self: The Making of the Modern Identity*, Cambridge: Cambridge University Press, 1989.

9 For a well-known examination of this notion, see Nagel, T., *The View From Nowhere*, New York: Oxford University Press, 1986.

10 See Carr, D., 'Towards a re-evaluation of the role of educational epistemology in the professional education of teachers', in S. Tozer (ed.), *Philosophy of Education, 1998*, Urbana, Illinois: The Philosophy of Education Society, 1999.

## 3 TEACHING AND PROFESSIONALISM

1 For examples of the extensive lieterature on professional ethics in general and the ethics of educational professionalism in particular, see Campbell, E., 'The moral core of professionalism as a teachable ideal and as a matter of character', *Curriculum Enquiry*, 26, 1996, pp. 71–80; Freedman, B., 'A meta-ethics for professional morality', *Ethics*, 89, 1978, pp. 1–19; Goldman, A.H., *The Moral Foundations of Professional Ethics*, Totowa, New Jersey: Rowman and Littlefield, 1980; Goodlad, J., Soder, R. and Sirotnik, K., *The Moral Dimensions of Teaching*, San Francisco: Jossey-Bass, 1990; Hostetler, K.D., *Ethical Judgement in Teaching*, Boston: Allyn and Bacon, 1997; Koehn, D., *The Ground of Professional Ethics*, London: Routledge, 1994; Kultgen, J., *Ethics and Professionalism*, Philadelphia: University of Pennsylvania Press, 1988; Martin, M.W., 'Rights and the meta-ethics of professional morality', *Ethics*, 91, 1981, pp. 619–25; Sockett, H., *The Moral Base for Teacher Professionalism*, New York: Teacher's College Press, 1993; Soltis, J.F., 'Teaching professional ethics', *Journal of Teacher Education*, 37, 1994, pp. 2–4; Strike, K.A. and Soltis, J., *The Ethics of Teaching*, New York: Teacher's College Press, 1985; Strike, K.A. and Ternasky, P.L. (eds), *Ethics for Professionals in Education: Perspectives for Preparation and Practice*, New York: Teacher's College Press, 1993; Strom, S.M., 'The ethical dimension in teaching', in M.C. Reynolds (ed.), *Knowledge Base for the Beginning Teacher*, Oxford: Pergamon Press, 1989, pp. 267–76.

2 This sort of objection has its source in Socrates' question in Plato's *Euthyphro* about whether the good is good because God commends it, or God commends it because it is good; see Plato's *Euthyphro* in E. Hamilton and H. Cairns (eds), *Plato: The Collected Dialogues*, Princeton: Princeton University Press, 1961. The argument has also been used by modern ethical naturalists against ethical non-cognitivism; see, for example, Geach, P.T., *Logic Matters*, Oxford: Blackwell, 1972, Part 8.

3 See Etzioni, A. (ed.), *The Semi-Professions and their Organization: Teachers, Nurses and Social Workers*, London: Collier-Macmillan, 1969.

4 See Humes, W., *The Leadership Class in Scottish Education*, Glasgow: Bell and Brain Ltd, 1986.

5 For interesting work of particularist inclination, see Schon, D.A., *The Reflective Practitioner: How Professionals Think in Action*, New York: Basic Books, 1984; Dunne, J., *Back to the Rough Ground: 'Phronesis' and 'Techne' in Modern Philosophy and in Aristotle*, Notre Dame: University of Notre Dame Press, 1993.

6 For such anti-professional vocationalism, see Illich, I., *Deschooling Society*, Harmondsworth: Penguin, 1973a; Illich, I., *Celebration of Awareness*, Harmondsworth: Penguin, 1973b; Illich, I., 'Disabling professions', in *Disabling Professions*, London: Marion Boyars, 1977; Goodman, P., *Growing Up Absurd*, London: Gollancz, 1960; Goodman, P., *Compulsory Miseducation*, Harmondsworth: Penguin, 1971; Postman, N. and Weingartner, C., *Teaching as a Subversive Activity*, Harmondsworth: Penguin, 1971; Reimer, E., *School is Dead*, Harmondsworth: Penguin, 1971.

7 MacIntyre, A.C., 'The idea of an educated public', in G. Haydon, *Education and Values: The Richard Peters Lectures*, London: Institute of Education, University of London, 1987a.

8 See, for example, Carter, R., *The Doctor Business*, New York: Doubleday, 1958.

9 Such scepticism about the educational value of much received curriculum content is to be found in Postman and Weingartner, op. cit., 1971.

10 Humes, W., *The Leadership Class in Scottish Education*, Glasgow: Bell and Brain Ltd, 1986.

11 Bailey, C., *Beyond the Present and the Particular: A Theory of Liberal Education*, London: Routledge and Kegan Paul, 1984.

12 See, in particular, Illich, op. cit., 1973a; Reimer, op. cit., 1971.

13 See Cox, C.B. and Boyson, R. (eds), *The Black Papers*, London: Dent and Sons, 1975, pp. 4–5.

## 4 EDUCATIONAL THEORY MISAPPLIED?

1 On this topic I have benefited, in particular, from: Carr, W. and Kemmis, S., *Becoming Critical*, Lewes: Falmer Press, 1986; Carr, W., 'Theories of theory and practice', *Journal of Philosophy of Education*, 20, 1986, pp. 177–86; Carr, W., 'What is an educational practice?', *Journal of Philosophy of Education*, 21, 1987, pp. 163–75; Carr, W., 'The idea of an educational science', *Journal of Philosophy of Education*, 23, 1989, pp. 29–38; Elliott, J., 'Educational theory and the professional learning of teachers: an overview', *Cambridge Journal of Education*, 19, 1989, pp. 81–101; Hirst, P.H., 'The theory and practice relationship in teacher training', in M. Wilkin, V.J. Furlong and M. Booth (eds), *Partnership in Initial Teacher Training: The Way Forward*, London: Cassell, 1990; Smith, R., 'Theory: an entitlement to understanding', *Cambridge Journal of Education*, 22, 1992, pp. 387–98.

2 See, especially, Plato's *Phaedo* and *Republic* in E. Hamilton and H. Cairns (eds), *Plato: The Collected Dialogues*, Princeton: Princeton University Press, 1961.

3 See Descartes' *Meditations* and *Discourses*, in G.E.M. Anscombe and P.T. Geach (eds), *Descartes: Philosophical Writings*, London: Nelson, 1954.

4 See Plato's *Meno*, in E. Hamilton and H. Cairns (eds), op. cit.

5 See, for example, the reference to the Inspectorate visit to A.S. Neill's school Summerhill, in A.S. Neill, *Summerhill*, Harmondsworth: Penguin Books, 1968, pp. 77–86.

6 See, especially, Rousseau, J-J., *Emile*, London: Dent, 1974.

7 See the editor's Introduction to Perry, L. (ed.), *Four Progressive Educators*, London: Collier-Macmillan, Educational Thinkers Series, 1967.

8 See Carr, D., 'Educational enquiry and professional knowledge', *Educational Studies*, 20, 1994, pp. 33–52.

9 For broadly this conception of the contribution of educational theory in educational professionalism, see Hirst, P.H., 'Educational theory', in P.H. Hirst (ed.), *Educational Theory and its Foundation Disciplines*,

London: Routledge and Kegan Paul, 1983; also Peters, R.S., *Ethics and Education*, London: George Allen and Unwin, 1966, pp. 309–10.

10 For Peters' view of the role of philosophy in professional teacher education, see P.H. Hirst and R.S. Peters, *The Logic of Education*, London: Routledge and Kegan Paul, 1970.

11 For some extreme scepticism about the value of educational theory in professional training, see Lawlor, S., *Teachers Mistaught*, London: Centre for Policy Studies, 1990; O'Hear, A., *Who Teaches the Teacher?*, Research Report 10, London: Social Affairs Unit, 1988; and Phillips, M., *All Must Have Prizes*, London: Little, Brown and Company, 1996.

12 Carr, D., 'The uses of literacy in teacher education', *British Journal of Educational Studies*, 45, 1997, pp. 53–68.

13 The literature on action research in relation to education and teaching is considerable. For the idea in general see, for example, McNiff, J., *Action Research: Principles and Practice*, London: Routledge, 1988. It is not infrequently motivated by an extreme 'particularist' belief that the relatively abstract and decontextualised school research of educational academicians is largely irrelevant or insensitive to the actual contexts of practitioner engagement. This sort of view seems central to the highly influential work of John Elliott; see, for example, Elliott, J., 'Educational theory, practical philosophy and action research', *British Journal of Educational Studies*, 35, 1987, pp. 149–69.

14 Ryle, G., *The Concept of Mind*, London: Hutchinson, 1949.

15 Wittgenstein, L., *Philosophical Investigations*, Oxford: Blackwell, 1953.

16 For some interesting work on the notion of practical rationality in relation to teaching, see Fenstermacher, G. and Richardson, V., 'The elicitation and reconstruction of practical argument in teaching', *Journal of Curriculum Studies*, 25, 1993, pp. 101–14; Hostetler, K.D., *Ethical Judgement in Teaching*, Boston: Allyn and Bacon, 1997; Pendlebury, S., 'Practical reasoning and situational appreciation in teaching', *Educational Theory*, 40, 1990, pp. 171–9; Pendlebury, S., 'Practical arguments, rationalization and imagination in teachers' practical reasoning', *Journal of Curriculum Studies*, 25, 1993, pp. 145–51; also Schon, D.A., *The Reflective Practitioner: How Professionals Think in Action*, New York: Basic Books, 1984.

17 Again, this was a prominent feature of the Black Paper thinking of the 1970s. Such thinking was also to inform the subsequent requirement of the English Council for the Accreditation of Teacher Education (CATE), that lecturers in higher education responsible for the professional preparation of teachers should undergo periodical renewal and updating of their practical experience of classroom teaching in schools.

18 On mentoring and related ideas, see Bines, H. and Welton, J. (eds), *Managing Partnership in Teacher Training and Development*, London: Routledge, 1995; also, Furlong, J. and Maynard, T., *Mentoring Student Teachers*, London: Routledge, 1995.

19 Lawlor, op. cit., 1990; O'Hear, op. cit., 1988; Phillips, op. cit., 1996.

20 Carr, D. (ed.), *Education, Knowledge and Truth: Beyond the Post-Modern Impasse*, London: Routledge, 1998a.

## 5 DIFFERENT FACES OF EDUCATIONAL THEORY

1 Aristotle, *The Nicomachean Ethics*, Book VI, Section 5, in R. McKeon (ed.), *The Basic Works of Aristotle*, New York: Random House, 1941. See, also, Dunne, J., *Back to the Rough Ground: 'Phronesis' and 'Techne' in Modern Philosophy and in Aristotle*, Notre Dame: University of Notre Dame Press, 1993; and numerous works by Wilfred Carr – especially Carr, W., 'What is an educational practice?', *Journal of Philosophy of Education*, 21, 1987, pp. 163–75.

2 Aristotle, *The Nicomachean Ethics*, Book VI, Part 2, ibid.

3 Ibid., Parts 4 and 5, *passim*.

4 For an important modern exploration of this distinction, see Wiggins, D., 'Deliberation and practical reason', in J. Raz (ed.), *Practical Reason*, Oxford: Oxford University Press, 1978.

5 The main source of the modern distinction between fact and value is probably Hume, D., *A Treatise of Human Nature*, Harmondsworth: Penguin Books, 1969. But see, also, A.J. Ayer's emotivism in *Language, Truth and Logic*, London: Gollancz, 1967, and R.M. Hare's prescriptivism in *The Language of Morals*, Oxford: Oxford University Press, 1952.

6 At any rate, this view has often been ascribed to, or associated with, the best-known form of consequentialism – utilitarianism. For the classic account of utilitarianism, see J.S Mill's 'Utilitarianism', in M. Warnock (ed.), *Utilitarianism*, London: Collins, The Fontana Library, 1970; and for a useful modern collection of discussions on aspects of consequentialism, see Scheffler, S. (ed.), *Consequentialism and its Critics*, Oxford, Oxford University Press, 1988.

7 For some influential naturalist discussion of the relationship between human purpose and desire and the properties of things, see the essays 'Moral beliefs' and 'Goodness and choice' in Foot, P., *Virtues and Vices*, Oxford: Blackwell, 1978.

8 For a clear account of the defeasibility of practical reasoning, see Geach, P.T., *Reason and Argument*, Oxford: Blackwell, 1976, Chapter 19.

9 Such terms and certainly the idea which I take to underlie them occur in the articles of two of the most influential recent writers on these issues; see, for example, Carr, W., 'The idea of an educational science', *Journal of Philosophy of Education*, 23, 1989, pp. 29–38; Elliott, J., 'Educational theory, practical philosophy and action research', *British Journal of Educational Studies*, 35, 1987, pp. 149–69; and Elliott, J., 'Educational theory and the professional learning of teachers: an overview', *Cambridge Journal of Education*, 19, 1989, pp. 81–101.

10 For action research in relation to education, see McNiff, J., *Action Research: Principles and Practice*, London: Routledge, 1988; and Elliott, J., 'Educational theory, practical philosophy and action research', ibid.

11 See, for example, Peters, R.S., *The Concept of Motivation*, London: Routledge and Kegan Paul, 1958; Taylor, C., *The Explanation of Behaviour*, London: Routledge and Kegan Paul, 1964; and the remarks on psychology at the end of Part 1 of Wittgenstein, L., *Philosophical Investigations*, Oxford: Blackwell, 1953.

12 Carr, D., '5–14: A philosophical critique', in G. Kirk and R. Glaister (eds), *5–14: Scotland's National Curriculum*, Edinburgh: Scottish Academic Press, 1994, Chapter 5.

13 See Bennett, N., *Teaching Styles and Pupil Progress*, London: Open Books, 1976.

14 I have (along with others) argued this point in a number of places. See, especially, Carr, D., 'Guidelines for teacher training: the competency model', *Scottish Educational Review*, 25, 1993, pp. 17–25.

15 Carr, D., 'The uses of literacy in teacher education', *British Journal of Educational Studies*, 45, 1997, pp. 53–68.

## 6 TEACHING AND COMPETENCE

1 See National Council for Vocational Qualifications (NCVQ), *General National Vocational Qualifications*, London: National Council for Vocational Qualifications, 1991a; NCVQ, *Criteria for National Vocational Qualifications*, London: National Council for Vocational Qualifications, 1991b.

2 See various articles in Burke, J.W. (ed.), *Competency Based Education and Training*, Lewes: Falmer Press, 1989.

3 For example, Department of Education and Science, *Reform of Initial Teacher Training: A Consultative Document*, London: HMSO, 1992; SOED, *Guidelines for Teacher Training Courses*, Edinburgh: SOED, 1993.

4 In this connection see, for example, Bridges, D., 'School based training', in D. Bridges and T. Kerry (eds), *Developing Teachers Professionally: Reflections for Initial and In-Service Trainers*, London: Routledge, 1993; also, Hargreaves, D., *The Future of Teacher Education*, Cambridge: Hockerill Educational Foundation, 1990.

5 On mentoring and related ideas, see Bines, H. and Welton, J. (eds), *Managing Partnership in Teacher Training and Development*, London: Routledge, 1995; also, Furlong, J. and Maynard, T., *Mentoring Student Teachers*, London: Routledge, 1995.

6 For the idea of family resemblance, see Wittgenstein, L., *Philosophical Investigations*, Oxford: Blackwell, 1953, Part 1, Section 67.

7 Aristotle, *The Physics*, in R. McKeon (ed.), *The Basic Works of Aristotle*, New York: Random House, 1941, Book II, Chapter 3.

8 Wittgenstein, L., op. cit., 1953, Part 1, Section 154.

9 For a classic dispositional account of human rational agency, see Ryle, G., *The Concept of Mind*, London: Hutchinson, 1949.

10 For a critical account of such fine-grained behaviouristic analyses, see Hyland, T., 'Competence, knowledge and education', *Journal of Philosophy of Education*, 27, 1993, pp. 57–68; also, Hyland, T., *Competence, Education and NVQ's: Dissenting Perspectives*, London: Cassell, 1994.

11 See Elliott, J., 'Educational theory and the professional learning of teachers: an overview', *Cambridge Journal of Education*, 19, 1989, pp. 81–101.

12 Carr, D., 'Education, learning and understanding: the process and the product', *Journal of Philosophy of Education*, 26, 1992, pp. 215–25.

13 Dearden, R., 'What is general about general education?', in R. Dearden, *Theory and Practice in Education*, London: Routledge and Kegan Paul, 1984.

14 Hirst, P.H., 'Liberal education and the nature of knowledge', in P.H. Hirst, *Knowledge and the Curriculum*, London: Routledge and Kegan Paul, 1974.

15 Aristotle, *The Nicomachean Ethics*, Book 6, in R. McKeon (ed.), *The Basic Works of Aristotle*, New York: Random House, 1941.

16 See, for example, Carr, W., 'The idea of an educational science', *Journal of Philosophy of Education*, 23, 1989, pp. 29–38; Elliott, J., 'Educational theory, practical philosophy and action research', *British Journal of Educational Studies*, 35, 1987, pp. 149–69; and Elliott, J., 'Educational theory and the professional learning of teachers: an overview', *Cambridge Journal of Education*, 19, 1989, pp. 81–101.

17 Aristotle, *The Nicomachean Ethics*, Book 6, Chapter 3, in McKeon, op. cit.

18 In my view an attempted reply to this point by David Bridges (in Bridges, D., 'Competence-based education and training: progress or villainy?', *Journal of the Philosophy of Education*, 30, 1996, pp. 361–75) entirely fails to grasp the point about the internal relationship of moral response to moral perspective generally, and of educational conduct to educational conception in particular. While such internality does not imply that there cannot be truth and error in the realm of moral understanding, it does completely undermine any conception of value-neutral professional competence.

19 This mistake is widely appreciated in post-war work influenced by the 'later' Wittgenstein. See, for example, Winch, P., *The Idea of a Social Science and its Relation to Philosophy*, London: Routledge and Kegan Paul, 1958; and Peters, R.S., *The Concept of Motivation*, London: Routledge and Kegan Paul, 1958.

20 Jessup, G., 'The evidence required to demonstrate competence', in H. Black and A. Wolf (eds), *Knowledge and Competence: Current Issues in Training and Education*, Sheffield: Careers and Occupational Information Centre, 1990.

21 Plato's *Parmenides*, in E. Hamilton and H. Cairns (eds), *Plato: The Collected Dialogues*, Princeton: Princeton University Press, 1961.

22 Booth, M., Furlong, J. and Wilkins, M. (eds), *Partnership in Initial Teacher Training*, London: Cassell, 1990.

## 7 PROFESSIONAL VALUES AND THE OBJECTIVITY OF VALUE

1 Hume, D., *A Treatise of Human Nature*, Harmondsworth: Penguin Books, 1969, Part III, Section 1; see, also, Ayer, A.J., *Language, Truth and Logic*, London: Gollancz, 1967, Chapter 6.

2 See, for example, Hudson, W.D., *Modern Moral Philosophy*, London: Macmillan, 1970.

3 This position is associated with such 'non-cognitivist' moral theories as 'prescriptivism'. See Hare, R.M., *The Language of Morals*, Oxford: Oxford University Press, 1952.

4 See, for example, the postmodernism of Wilfred Carr, in Carr, W., 'Education and democracy: confronting the postmodernist challenge', *Journal of Philosophy of Education*, 29, 1995, pp. 75–91; Carr, W., 'Professing education in a postmodern age', *Journal of Philosophy of Education*, 31, 1997, pp. 309–27.

5 Kant, I., *The Critique of Pure Reason*, trans. N. Kemp Smith, London: Macmillan, 1968, p. 93.

6 The most influential of German Idealist successors of Kant in present respects, of course, was Hegel.

7 Quine, W.V.O., *From a Logical Point of View*, New York: Harper and Row, 1953, p. 41.

8 See any of the influential works of Sir Karl Popper; for example, *Conjectures and Refutations*, London: Routledge and Kegan Paul, 1969.

9 Quine, op. cit., pp. 37–42.

10 'Post-structuralism' is that historicist form of constructivism associated with such writers as Derrida, Foucault, Bataille and Levinas. See the editor's introduction to Carr, D. (ed.), *Education, Knowledge and Truth: Beyond the Post-Modern Impasse*, London: Routledge, 1998a.

11 See, for example, Foot, P., *Virtues and Vices*, Oxford: Blackwell, 1978; Geach, P.T., *The Virtues*, Cambridge: Cambridge University Press, 1977; Anscombe, G.E.M., *Ethics, Religion and Politics: Collected Philosophical Papers, Volume III*, Oxford: Blackwell, 1981.

12 Aristotle, *Categories*, in R. McKeon (ed.), *The Basic Works of Aristotle*, New York: Random House, 1941, pp. 31–5.

13 See papers in the educationally-influential Young, M.F.D. (ed.), *Knowledge and Control*, London: Collier-Macmillan, 1971.

14 By 'existentialist theology', I refer to that post-Kantian project of separating faith from reason, begun by Kierkegaard and continued in various ways by such modern (notably) Protestant theologians as Karl Barth and Rudolph Bultmann.

15 By 'structural functionalist sociology', I refer to the sort of social analyses associated with the likes of Talcott Parsons; see, for example, Parsons, T., *The Structure of Social Action*, London: The Free Press, 1949.

16 Matthew Arnold, 'Preface to *Literature and Dogma*', in Gribble, J. (ed.), *Matthew Arnold*, London: Collier-Macmillan, Educational Thinkers Series, 1967, p 150.

17 Liberal traditionalism in this sense is best exemplified by the work of such post-war educational philosophers as Richard Peters and Paul Hirst. See, for example, Peters, *Ethics and Education*, London: George Allen and Unwin, 1966; Hirst, *Knowledge and the Curriculum*, London: Routledge and Kegan Paul, 1974.

18 Hirst, P.H., 'Liberal education and the nature of knowledge', in Hirst, ibid., pp. 30–53.

19 Plowden Report: Central Advisory Council for Education, *Children and their Primary Schools*, London: HMSO, 1966; and Primary Memorandum: SED, *Primary Education in Scotland*, Edinburgh: SED, 1965.

20 MacIntyre, A.C., 'The idea of an educated public', in G. Haydon, *Education and Values: The Richard Peters Lectures*, London: Institute of Education, University of London, 1987a; MacIntyre, A.C., *How to*

*Appear Virtuous Without Actually Being So*, University of Lancaster: Centre for the Study of Cultural Values, 1991.

21 MacIntyre, ibid., 1987a.

22 MacIntyre, op. cit., 1991.

## 8 RIVAL CONCEPTIONS OF EDUCATION

1 This phrase in the context of a rather indiscriminate anti-relativist stance has been a feature of recent public output by Dr Nick Tate, Chief Executive of the English Schools Curriculum and Assessment Authority (SCAA) and associates. For critical response to views of this kind, see Smith, R. and Standish, P. (eds), *Teaching Right and Wrong: Moral Education in the Balance*, London: Trentham Books, 1997.

2 Kant, I., *Groundwork of the Metaphysic of Morals*, in H.J. Paton (ed.), *The Moral Law*, London: Hutchinson, 1948.

3 For the idea of a positional good in relation to education, see Hollis, M., 'Education as a positional good', *Journal of Philosophy of Education*, 16, 1982, pp. 235–44.

4 For some problems of curriculum thinking in relation to this issue, see Carr, D., 'The dichotomy of liberal versus vocational education: some basic conceptual geography', in A. Nieman (ed.), *Philosophy of Education, 1995*, Urbana, Illinois: Philosophy of Education Society, 1996.

5 An important and influential work in this connection is Taylor, C., *Multiculturalism: Examining the Politics of Recognition*, edited by A. Gutmann, Princeton, N.J.: Princeton University Press, 1994.

6 MacIntyre, A.C., *How to Appear Virtuous Without Actually Being So*, University of Lancaster: Centre for the Study of Cultural Values, 1991.

7 Modern fideism of a fairly extreme sort is to be found in the post-Kierkegaardian Protestant theology of Barth, Bultmann, Bonhoeffer, Tillich and others.

8 Alternative education for different faiths has long been a feature of both state and independent sectors of British schooling. Although viewed by some as divisive, it is increasingly called for by some British Muslims, and is supported by communitarian educational philosophers. See, on this issue, Halstead, M., 'Voluntary apartheid? Problems of schooling for religious and other minorities in democratic societies', *Journal of Philosophy of Education*, 29, 1995, pp. 257–72.

9 See Carr, D., 'Traditionalism and progressivism: a perennial problematic of educational theory and policy', *Westminster Studies in Education*, 21, 1998b, pp. 47–55.

10 Phillips, M., *All Must Have Prizes*, London: Little, Brown and Company, 1996.

11 See Carr, D., op. cit., 1998b, pp. 47–55; also, *Educating the Virtues: An Essay on the Philosophical Psychology of Moral Development and Education*, London: Routledge, 1991.

12 Hirst, P.H. and Peters, R.S., *The Logic of Education*, London: Routledge and Kegan Paul, 1970.

13 Neill, A.S., *Summerhill*, Harmondsworth: Penguin Books, 1968, pp. 77–86.

14 On the principal issues here, see Rousseau, J-J., *Emile*, London: Dent, 1974; Piaget, J., *The Psychology of Intelligence*, London: Routledge,

1950; Dewey, J., *Experience and Education*, New York: Collier Books, 1938.

15 See Bennett, N., *Teaching Styles and Pupil Progress*, London: Open Books, 1976.

16 See Alexander, R., Rose, J. and Woodhead, C. (eds), *Curriculum Organization and Classroom Practice in Primary School*, London: DES, 1992.

17 Peters, R.S., *Authority, Responsibility and Education*, London: George Allen and Unwin, 1959, Part III, Chapter 8, p. 104.

18 Rousseau, J-J., 'A Discourse on the Origin of Inequality', in J-J. Rousseau, *The Social Contract and Other Discourses*, London: Dent, 1973.

19 Kant, I., *Groundwork of the Metaphysic of Morals*, in H.J. Paton (ed.), *The Moral Law*, London: Hutchinson, 1948.

20 Aristotle, *The Nicomachean Ethics*, Book 1, Section 6, in R. McKeon (ed.), *The Basic Works of Aristotle*, New York: Random House, 1941.

21 Lane, H., *Talks to Parents and Teachers*, London: Allen and Unwin, 1954; Neill, A.S., *Summerhill*, Harmondsworth: Penguin Books, 1968.

22 Aristotle, *The Nicomachean Ethics*, Book 5, in McKeon, op. cit.

## 9 EDUCATIONAL RIGHTS AND PROFES-
## SIONAL WRONGS

1 The eponymous, pegagogical (anti-) heroine of Muriel Spark's novel *The Prime of Miss Jean Brodie* (Harmondsworth: Penguin, 1965).

2 However, R.S. Downie's article, 'Professions and professionalism' (*Journal of Philosophy of Education*, 29, 1990, pp. 147–59), contains some interesting discussion of the complexities of this issue.

3 On the basis of a report entitled 'Worlds Apart', which was commissioned by the British Office for Standards in Education (Ofsted) and co-authored by Professor David Reynolds and Shaun Farrell of Newcastle University in 1996 (and highlighted in a programme for BBC1's *Panorama*), Chief Inspector Chris Woodhead and others urged a return to direct instructional 'whole class' approaches to teaching (of particularly mathematics) of a kind allegedly conducive to economic advancement in such 'Pacific rim' countries as Taiwan.

4 For theories of punishment, see Honderich, T., *Punishment: The Supposed Justifications*, Harmondsworth: Pelican, 1971.

5 Although unacquainted with systematic research on this issue, I can personally vouch for this circumstance from first-hand acquaintance of school punishment books as a young teacher in northern English state schools which employed corporal punishment during the 1960s.

6 In February 1999, Chief Inspector Chris Woodhead, Head of the Office for Standards in Education, outraged the teaching profession by a comment he made in a speech at Exeter University to the effect that affairs between teachers and pupils might be 'educative'. Woodhead's comment came at a moment when the British Parliament was in the process of considering legislation which would make it a criminal offence for teachers to have sexual relationships with sixteen- and seventeen-year-old pupils. Despite Woodhead's subsequent apology,

these remarks seem to have done little to endear him to a profession from which he has increasingly alienated himself.

7 For some education exploration of this perspective, see various contributions to Carr, D. and Steutel, J. (eds), *Virtue Ethics and Moral Education*, London: Routledge, 1999.

## 10 AIMS OF EDUCATION, SCHOOLING AND TEACHING

1 See various contributions to Carr, D. (ed.), *Education, Knowledge and Truth: Beyond the Post-Modern Impasse*, London: Routledge, 1998a.

2 For similar points, see Luntley, M., *Reason, Truth and Self: The Postmodern Reconditioned*, London: Routledge, 1995.

3 See Reznek, L., *Evil or Ill: Justifying the Insanity Defence*, London: Routledge, 1997.

4 An eliminativist is someone who believes that it is possible to replace the pre-theoretical discourse of folk psychology with a more objective 'physicalist' discourse of brain science. Paul Churchland is a good example of a contemporary eliminativist: see, for example, Churchland, P., *Scientific Realism and the Plasticity of Mind*, Cambridge: Cambridge University Press, 1979.

5 See, for example, White, J.P., *Education and the End of Work*, London: Cassell, 1997.

6 While the distinction is by no means hard and fast, the best examples of non-instrumentalists are doubtless to be found among followers of such modern liberal traditionalist educational philosophers as R.S. Peters, P.H. Hirst and R.F. Dearden.

7 The ranks of instrumentalists would doubtless be swelled by many non-philosophical politicians and educational policy-makers, although such post-war defenders of educational utilitarianism as Robin Barrow might also be included in this camp. See, for example, Barrow, R., *Plato, Utilitarianism and Education*, London: Routledge and Kegan Paul, 1975.

8 Something like this position seems to be taken, so far as one can tell, in Carr, W., 'Professing education in a postmodern age', *Journal of Philosophy of Education*, 31, 1997, pp. 309–27.

9 See, in particular, much recent work by Richard Pring, most notably, *Closing the Gap: Liberal Education and Vocational Education*, London: Hodder and Stoughton, 1995; related views appear to be expressed, however, in Bridges, D., 'Competence-based education and training: progress or villainy?', *Journal of the Philosophy of Education*, 30, 1996, pp. 361–75.

10 The main target here is undoubtedly R.S. Peters, in Peters, R.S., *Ethics and Education*, London: George Allen and Unwin, 1966, Part I, Section 1 and Part II, Section 5.

11 For the distinction between conservative and liberal traditionalists, see Carr, D., 'On understanding educational theory', *Educational Philosophy and Theory*, 17, 1985, pp. 19–28.

12 This much criticised conflation is most evident in Peters, op. cit., Part I, Section 1 and Part II, Section 5.

13 In a report (originally televised on Channel Four) on the contemporary state of British education and published as 'Every Child in Britain' (London: Channel Four publications, 1991), such local educational luminaries as A.H. Halsey, Neville Postlethwaite, S.J. Prais, Alan Smithers and Hilary Steedman criticised British secondary education for its failure to take seriously the idea of a 'practical education'.

14 This lineage is ably explored in Hirst, P.H., 'Liberal education and the nature of knowledge', in P.H. Hirst, *Knowledge and the Curriculum*, London: Routledge and Kegan Paul, 1974.

15 For the allegory of the cave, see Plato's *Republic* (514a–521b), in E. Hamilton and H. Cairns (eds), *Plato: The Collected Dialogues*, Princeton: Princeton University Press, 1961.

16 See Hirst, op. cit., 1974, pp. 43–6.

17 Lyotard, J-F., *The Post-Modern Condition: A Report on Knowledge*, trans. G. Bennington and B. Massumi (eds), Manchester: Manchester University Press, 1984.

18 For further discussion of this issue, see Carr, D., 'Self-direction, values and truth: towards an unpostmodern re-examination', *Journal of Philosophy of Education*, 34, 2000.

## 11 THE MORAL ROLE OF THE TEACHER

1 Such general agreement on the moral role of the teacher was found in the school research of Carr and Landon, reported in Carr, D. and Landon, J., 'Teachers and schools as agencies of values education: reflections on teachers' perceptions. Part I: the role of the teacher', *Journal of Beliefs and Values*, 19, 1998, pp. 165–76.

2 See Carr, D., *The Moral Role of the Teacher, Perspectives on Values 3*, Edinburgh: SCCC Publications, 1996.

3 Such criticism is at least implicit in NCC, *Spiritual and Moral Education: A Discussion Paper*, National Curriculum Council, UK, 1993.

4 See Winch, C., 'Education needs training', *Oxford Educational Review*, 21, 1995, pp. 315–25.

5 The idea that training can be distinct from (even exclusive of) education is central to Peters, R.S., *Ethics and Education*, London: George Allen and Unwin, 1966, Part I, Section 1 and Part II, Section 5.

6 Aristotle, *The Nicomachean Ethics*, Book 2, Section 1, in R. McKeon (ed.), *The Basic Works of Aristotle*, New York: Random House, 1941.

7 Piaget, J., *The Moral Judgement of the Child*, New York: Free Press, 1932.

8 See Spiecker, B., 'Habituation and training in early moral upbringing', in D. Carr and J. Steutel (eds), *Virtue Ethics and Moral Education*, London: Routledge, 1999.

9 Wittgenstein, L., 'A lecture on ethics', *Philosophical Review*, 74, 1965, pp. 3–26.

10 Milton, J., *Paradise Lost*, Book IV, line 108, in *Paradise Lost and Other Poems*, New York: Mentor Books, 1961.

11 Kant, I., *The Critique of Pure Reason*, London: Macmillan, 1968, p. 93.

12 Again, for reasonable representatives of modern communitarianism, see Sandel, M., *Liberalism and the Limits of Justice*, New York: Cam-

bridge University Press, 1982; MacIntyre, A.C., *After Virtue*, Notre Dame: Notre Dame Press, 1981; MacIntyre, A.C., *Whose Justice, Which Rationality?*, Notre Dame: Notre Dame Press, 1987b; MacIntyre, A.C., *Three Rival Versions of Moral Enquiry*, Notre Dame: Notre Dame Press, 1992; Taylor, C., *Sources of the Self: The Making of the Modern Identity*, Cambridge: Cambridge University Press, 1989.

13 Bailey, C., *Beyond the Present and the Particular: A Theory of Liberal Education*, London: Routledge and Kegan Paul, 1984.

14 See Mill, J.S., *On Liberty*, in M. Warnock (ed.), *Utilitarianism*, London: Collins, The Fontana Library, 1970.

15 Kohlberg, L., *Essays on Moral Development: Volumes I–III*, New York: Harper Row, 1984.

16 For a classic exchange on the issue of teacher neutrality, see the symposium of Mary Warnock and John Wilson on 'The neutral teacher', in Taylor, M. (ed.), *Progress and Problems in Moral Education*, Slough, Berks: NFER Publishing Co. Ltd, 1975, Section II.

17 This seems to have been the position of A.S. Neill. See Neill, A.S., *Summerhill*, Harmondsworth: Penguin Books, 1968.

18 See Plato's *Republic*, in E. Hamilton and H. Cairns (eds), *Plato: The Collected Dialogues*, Princeton: Princeton University Press, 1961.

## 12 ETHICAL ISSUES CONCERNING THE ROLE OF THE TEACHER

1 Utilitarian calculation is the assessment of the goodness or badness of an action in terms of its consequences for human happiness or pleasure. For a classical account of the doctrine, see J.S Mill's *Utilitarianism,*, in M. Warnock (ed.), *Utilitarianism*, London: Collins, The Fontana Library, 1970.

2 For a celebrated attack on utilitarian reasoning see Elizabeth Anscombe's 'Modern moral philosophy', in G.E.M. Anscombe, *Ethics, Religion and Politics: Collected Philosophical Papers, Volume III*, Oxford: Blackwell, 1981.

3 One should probably here distinguish between the 'relativity' of 'rival traditions' accounts of moral practice, which do not necessarily preclude the idea of moral truth, and that of moral incommensurability theses which probably do. Critics seem to have been undecided about how to classify MacIntyre's 'rival traditions' account in, for example, MacIntyre, A.C., *After Virtue*, Notre Dame: Notre Dame Press, 1981, according to this distinction.

4 Hume, D., *A Treatise of Human Nature*, Harmondsworth: Penguin Books, 1969, Book III, Part 1, Section 1.

5 For 'conservative traditionalist' theorists of alternative curricula, see Carr, D., 'On understanding educational theory', *Educational Philosophy and Theory*, 17, 1985, pp. 19–28.

6 For a useful collection of essays and extracts from such key figures in the psychometric movement as C. Burt, A.R. Jensen and H.J. Eysenck, see Wiseman, S. (ed.), *Intelligence and Ability*, Harmondsworth: Penguin Books, 1967.

7  For Plato's example, see Plato's *Republic* (331c–d), in E. Hamilton and H. Cairns (eds), *Plato: The Collected Dialogues*, Princeton: Princeton University Press, 1961.

8  NCC, *Spiritual and Moral Education: A Discussion Paper*, National Curriculum Council, UK, 1993.

9  Department of Education and Science and the Welsh Office, *Discipline in Schools* ('The Elton Report'), London: HMSO, 1989.

## 13 ETHICAL ISSUES CONCERNING EDUCATION AND SCHOOLING

1  There is a fairly extensive literature on school management, much of it critical of managerialism. See, for example, Bottery, M., *The Morality of the School*, London: Cassell, 1990; Bottery, M., *The Ethics of Educational Management*, London: Cassell, 1992; Grace, G., *School Leadership: Beyond Educational Management*, Lewes: Falmer Press, 1995; Hodgkinson, C., *Educational Leadership: The Moral Art*, Albany, NY: SUNY Press, 1991; Jackson, P.W., Boostrom, R.E. and Hansen, D.T., *The Moral Life of Schools*, San Francisco: Jossey-Bass, 1993; Sergiovanni, T.J., *Moral Leadership: Getting to the Heart of School Improvement*, San Francisco: Jossey-Bass, 1992.

2  There is a growing school management literature in relation to educational climate and ethos. For an example of government-sponsored research and guidance on this topic, see Scottish Office Education Department, *Using Ethos Indicators in Primary/Secondary School Self-Evaluation: Taking Account of the Views of Pupils, Parents and Teachers*, Edinburgh: SOED, March 1992.

3  A strong complaint of this kind may be found in Peters, R.S., *Ethics and Education*, London: George Allen and Unwin, 1966, p. 254.

4  See various contributions to Carr, D. and Steutel, J. (eds), *Virtue Ethics and Moral Education*, London: Routledge, 1999.

5  The best modern example of such a liberal moral rationalism is to be found in the work of Lawrence Kohlberg. See, generally, Kohlberg, L., *Essays on Moral Development: Volumes I–III*, New York: Harper Row, 1984.

6  Plato's anti-democratic sentiments are perhaps most evident in Plato's *Republic* (for example, 558d–562a), in E. Hamilton and H. Cairns (eds), *Plato: The Collected Dialogues*, Princeton: Princeton University Press, 1961

7  For example, Dewey, J., *Democracy and Education*, New York: Macmillan, 1916; Neill, A.S., *Summerhill*, Harmondsworth: Penguin Books, 1968; Peters, R.S., *Ethics and Education*, London: George Allen and Unwin, 1966; Rousseau, J-J., *Emile*, London: Dent, 1974.

8  For useful liberal traditionalist exploration of the relationship between freedom, authority and discipline see, for example, Hirst, P.H. and Peters, R.S., *The Logic of Education*, London: Routledge and Kegan Paul, 1970.

9  Plato's *Republic* (410b–412a), in E. Hamilton and H. Cairns, op. cit.

10  For some rather negative critique of Neill and other radicals in this vein, see Barrow, R., *Radical Education: A Critique of Freeschooling and Deschooling*, London: Martin Robertson, 1978.

11 For the influence on Neill of psychoanalytic thought in general and Freud in particular, see Carr, D., 'The free child and the spoiled child: anatomy of a progressive distinction', *Journal of Philosophy of Education*, 19, 1985, pp. 55–63.

12 For one such well-known case, see Gretton, J. and Jackson, M., *William Tyndale: Collapse of a School or a System?*, London: George Allen and Unwin, 1976.

13 See, for example, Benn, S.I. and Peters, R.S., *Social Principles and the Democratic State*, London: George Allen and Unwin, 1957, p. 353.

14 Hirst, P.H., 'Liberal education and the nature of knowledge', in P.H. Hirst, *Knowledge and the Curriculum*, London: Routledge and Kegan Paul, 1974, p. 32.

15 For issues and problems concerning education and the market, see Bridges, D. and McLaughlin, T.H. (eds), *Education and the Market*, Lewes: Falmer, 1994; Jonathan, R., *Illusory Freedoms: Liberalism, Education and the Market*, Oxford: Blackwell, 1997.

16 On this issue, see Carr, D., 'Knowledge and truth in religious education', *Journal of Philosophy of Education*, 28, 1994, pp. 221–37.

17 For interesting work on this topic see the insightful work of David Hartley; for example, Hartley, D., *Reschooling Society*, London: Falmer, 1997.

18 See Plato's *Gorgias*, in E. Hamilton and H. Cairns, op. cit.

# BIBLIOGRAPHY

Alexander, R., Rose, J. and Woodhead, C. (eds), *Curriculum Organization and Classroom Practice in Primary School*, London: DES, 1992.

Anscombe, G.E.M., *Ethics, Religion and Politics: Collected Philosophical Papers, Volume III*, Oxford: Blackwell, 1981.

Anscombe, G.E.M. and Geach, P.T. (eds), *Descartes: Philosophical Writings*, London: Nelson, 1954.

Armstrong, D., *Power and Partnership in Education: Parents, Children and Special Educational Needs*, London: Routledge, 1995.

Ayer, A.J., *Language, Truth and Logic*, London: Gollancz, 1967.

Bailey, C., *Beyond the Present and the Particular: A Theory of Liberal Education*, London: Routledge and Kegan Paul, 1984.

Barrow, R., *Plato, Utilitarianism and Education*, London: Routledge and Kegan Paul, 1975.

——*Radical Education: A Critique of Freeschooling and Deschooling*, London: Martin Robertson, 1978.

Bastiani, J., *Working with Parents*, London: Routledge, 1989.

Benn, S.I. and Peters, R.S., *Social Principles and the Democratic State*, London: George Allen and Unwin, 1957.

Bennett, N., *Teaching Styles and Pupil Progress*, London: Open Books, 1976.

Bines, H. and Welton, J. (eds), *Managing Partnership in Teacher Training and Development*, London: Routledge, 1995.

Booth, M., Furlong, J. and Wilkins, M. (eds), *Partnership in Initial Teacher Training*, London: Cassell, 1990.

Bottery, M., *The Morality of the School*, London: Cassell, 1990.

——*The Ethics of Educational Management*, London: Cassell, 1992.

Bridges, D., 'Competence-based education and training: progress or villainy?', *Journal of the Philosophy of Education*, 30, 1996, pp. 361–75.

Bridges, D. and Kerry, T. (eds), *Developing Teachers Professionally: Reflections for Initial and In-Service Trainers*, London: Routledge, 1993.

Bridges, D. and McLaughlin, T.H. (eds), *Education and the Market*, Lewes: Falmer, 1994.

Burke, J.W. (ed.), *Competency Based Education and Training*, Lewes: Falmer Press, 1989.

Campbell, E., 'The moral core of professionalism as a teachable ideal and as a matter of character', *Curriculum Enquiry*, 26, 1996, pp. 71–80.

Carr, D., 'On understanding educational theory', *Educational Philosophy and Theory*, 17, 1985, pp. 19–28.

——'The free child and the spoiled child: anatomy of a progressive distinction', *Journal of Philosophy of Education*, 19, 1985, pp. 55–63.

——*Educating the Virtues: An Essay on the Philosophical Psychology of Moral Development and Education*, London: Routledge, 1991.

——'Education, learning and understanding: the process and the product', *Journal of Philosophy of Education*, 26, 1992, pp. 215–25.

——'Questions of competence', *British Journal of Educational Studies*, 41, 1993, pp. 252–71.

——'Guidelines for teacher training: the competency model', *Scottish Educational Review*, 25, 1993, pp. 17–25.

——'5–14: A philosophical critique', in G. Kirk and R. Glaister (eds), *5–14: Scotland's National Curriculum*, Edinburgh: Scottish Academic Press, 1994.

——'Educational enquiry and professional knowledge', *Educational Studies*, 20, 1994, pp. 33–52.

——'Knowledge and truth in religious education', *Journal of Philosophy of Education*, 28, 1994, pp. 221–37.

——'The dichotomy of liberal versus vocational education: some basic conceptual geography', in A. Nieman (ed.), *Philosophy of Education, 1995*, Urbana, Illinois: Philosophy of Education Society, 1996.

——*The Moral Role of the Teacher, Perspectives on Values 3*, Edinburgh: SCCC Publications, 1996.

——'The uses of literacy in teacher education', *British Journal of Educational Studies*, 45, 1997, pp. 53–68.

——(ed.), *Education, Knowledge and Truth: Beyond the Post-Modern Impasse*, London: Routledge, 1998a.

——'Traditionalism and progressivism: a perennial problematic of educational theory and policy', *Westminster Studies in Education*, 21, 1998b, pp. 47–55.

——'Towards a re-evaluation of the role of educational epistemology in the professional education of teachers', in S. Tozer (ed.), *Philosophy of Education, 1998*, Urbana, Illinois: Philosophy of Education Society, 1999.

——'Self-direction, values and truth: towards an unpostmodern re-examination', *Journal of Philosophy of Education*, 34, 2000.

Carr, D. and Landon, J., 'Teachers and schools as agencies of values education: reflections on teachers' perceptions. Part I: the role of the teacher', *Journal of Beliefs and Values*, 19, 1998, pp. 165–76.

Carr, D. and Steutel, J. (eds), *Virtue Ethics and Moral Education*, London: Routledge, 1999.

Carr, W., 'Theories of theory and practice', *Journal of Philosophy of Education*, 20, 1986, pp. 177–86.

——'What is an educational practice?', *Journal of Philosophy of Education*, 21, 1987, pp. 163–75.

——'The idea of an educational science', *Journal of Philosophy of Education*, 23, 1989, pp. 29–38.

——'Education and democracy: confronting the postmodernist challenge', *Journal of Philosophy of Education*, 29, 1995, pp. 75–91.

——'Professing education in a postmodern age', *Journal of Philosophy of Education*, 31, 1997, pp. 309–27.

Carr, W. and Kemmis, S., *Becoming Critical*, Lewes: Falmer Press, 1986.

Carter, R., *The Doctor Business*, New York: Doubleday, 1958.

Central Advisory Council for Education, *Children and their Primary Schools ('The Plowden Report')*, London: HMSO, 1966.

Churchland, P., *Scientific Realism and the Plasticity of Mind*, Cambridge: Cambridge University Press, 1979.

Cox, C.B., and Boyson, R. (eds), *The Black Papers*, London: Dent and Sons, 1975.

Dearden, R., 'What is general about general education?', in R. Dearden, *Theory and Practice in Education*, London: Routledge and Kegan Paul, 1984.

Department of Education and Science, *Reform of Initial Teacher Training: A Consultative Document*, London: HMSO, 1992.

Department of Education and Science and the Welsh Office, *Discipline in Schools* ('The Elton Report'), London: HMSO, 1989.

Dewey, J., *Democracy and Education*, New York: Macmillan, 1916.

——*Experience and Education*, New York: Collier Books, 1938.

Downie, R.S., 'Professions and professionalism', *Journal of Philosophy of Education*, 29, 1990, pp. 147–59.

Dunne, J., *Back to the Rough Ground: 'Phronesis' and 'Techne' in Modern Philosophy and in Aristotle*, Notre Dame: University of Notre Dame Press, 1993.

Elliott, J., 'Educational theory, practical philosophy and action research', *British Journal of Educational Studies*, 35, 1987, pp. 149–69.

——'Educational theory and the professional learning of teachers: an overview', *Cambridge Journal of Education*, 19, 1989, pp. 81–101.

Etzioni, A. (ed.), *The Semi-Professions and their Organization: Teachers, Nurses and Social Workers*, London: Collier-Macmillan, 1969.

Fenstermacher, G. and Richardson, V., 'The elicitation and reconstruction of practical argument in teaching', *Journal of Curriculum Studies*, 25, 1993, pp. 101–14.

Foot, P., *Virtues and Vices*, Oxford: Blackwell, 1978.

Freedman, B., 'A meta-ethics for professional morality', *Ethics*, 89, 1978, pp. 1–19.

Freidson, E., *Professional Powers: A Study of the Institutionalization of Formal Knowledge*, Chicago: University of Chicago Press, 1986.

Furlong, J. and Maynard, T., *Mentoring Student Teachers*, London: Routledge, 1995.

Geach, P.T., *Logic Matters*, Oxford: Blackwell, 1972.

——*Reason and Argument*, Oxford: Blackwell, 1976

——*The Virtues*, Cambridge: Cambridge University Press, 1977.

Goldman, A.H., *The Moral Foundations of Professional Ethics*, Totowa, New Jersey: Rowman and Littlefield, 1980.

Goodlad, J., Soder, R. and Sirotnik, K., *The Moral Dimensions of Teaching*, San Francisco: Jossey-Bass, 1990.

Goodman, P., *Growing Up Absurd*, London: Gollancz, 1960.

——*Compulsory Miseducation*, Harmondsworth: Penguin, 1971.

Grace, G., *School Leadership: Beyond Educational Management*, Lewes: Falmer Press, 1995.

Gretton, J. and Jackson, M., *William Tyndale: Collapse of a School or a System?*, London: George Allen and Unwin, 1976.

Gribble, J. (ed.), *Matthew Arnold*, London: Collier-Macmillan, Educational Thinkers Series, 1967.

Halstead, M., 'Voluntary apartheid? Problems of schooling for religious and other minorities in democratic societies', *Journal of Philosophy of Education*, 29, 1995, pp. 257–72.

Hamilton, E. and Cairns, H. (eds), *Plato: The Collected Dialogues*, Princeton: Princeton University Press, 1961.

Hare, R.M., *The Language of Morals*, Oxford: Oxford University Press, 1952.

Hargreaves, D., *The Future of Teacher Education*, Cambridge: Hockerill Educational Foundation, 1990.

Hartley, D., *Reschooling Society*, London: Falmer, 1997.

Hirst, P.H., *Knowledge and the Curriculum*, London: Routledge and Kegan Paul, 1974.

——'Educational theory', in P.H. Hirst (ed.), *Educational Theory and its Foundation Disciplines*, London: Routledge and Kegan Paul, 1983.

——'The theory and practice relationship in teacher training', in M. Wilkin, V.J. Furlong and M. Booth (eds), *Partnership in Initial Teacher Training: The Way Forward*, London: Cassell, 1990.

Hirst, P.H. and Peters, R.S., *The Logic of Education*, London: Routledge and Kegan Paul, 1970.

Hodgkinson, C., *Educational Leadership: The Moral Art*, Albany, NY: SUNY Press, 1991.

Hollis, M., 'Education as a positional good', *Journal of Philosophy of Education*, 16, 1982, pp. 235–44.

Honderich, T., *Punishment: The Supposed Justifications*, Harmondsworth: Pelican, 1971

Hostetler, K.D., *Ethical Judgement in Teaching*, Boston: Allyn and Bacon, 1997.

Hoyle, E, 'Professionality, professionalism and control in teaching', *London Education Review*, 3, 1974, pp. 13–19.

Hudson, W.D., *Modern Moral Philosophy*, London: Macmillan, 1970.

Hume, D., *A Treatise of Human Nature*, Harmondsworth: Penguin Books, 1969.

Humes, W., *The Leadership Class in Scottish Education*, Glasgow: Bell and Brain Ltd, 1986.

Hyland, T., 'Competence, knowledge and education', *Journal of Philosophy of Education*, 27, 1993, pp. 57–68.

——*Competence, Education and NVQ's: Dissenting Perspectives*, London: Cassell, 1994.

Illich, I., *Deschooling Society*, Harmondsworth: Penguin, 1973a.

——*Celebration of Awareness*, Harmondsworth: Penguin, 1973b.

——'Disabling professions', in I. Illich, *Disabling Professions*, London: Marion Boyars, 1977.

Jackson, A.J. (ed.), *Professions and Professionalisation*, London: Cambridge University Press, 1970.

Jackson, P.W., Boostrom, R.E. and Hansen, D.T., *The Moral Life of Schools*, San Francisco: Jossey-Bass, 1993.

Jessup, G., 'The evidence required to demonstrate competence', in H. Black and A. Wolf (eds), *Knowledge and Competence: Current Issues in Training and Education*, Sheffield: Careers and Occupational Information Centre, 1990.

Johnson, J.T., *Professions and Power*, London: Macmillan, 1981.

Johnson, S., 'Skills, Socrates and the Sophists: learning from history', *British Journal of Educational Studies*, 46, 1998, pp. 201–14.

Jonathan, R., *Illusory Freedoms: Liberalism, Education and the Market*, Oxford: Blackwell, 1997.

Kant, I., *Groundwork of the Metaphysic of Morals*, in H.J. Paton (ed.), *The Moral Law*, London: Hutchinson, 1948.

——*The Critique of Pure Reason*, trans. N. Kemp Smith, London: Macmillan, 1968.

Kirk, G., *Teacher Education and Professional Development*, Edinburgh: Scottish Academic Press, 1988.

Koehn, D., *The Ground of Professional Ethics*, London: Routledge, 1994.

Kohlberg, L., *Essays on Moral Development: Volumes I–III*, New York: Harper Row, 1984.

Kultgen, J., *Ethics and Professionalism*, Philadelphia: University of Pennsylvania Press, 1988.

Lane, H., *Talks to Parents and Teachers*, London: Allen and Unwin, 1954.

Larson, M.S., *The Rise of Professionalism: A Sociological Analysis*, London: Marion Boyars, 1977.

Lawlor, S., *Teachers Mistaught*, London: Centre for Policy Studies, 1990.

Luntley, M., *Reason, Truth and Self: The Postmodern Reconditioned*, London: Routledge, 1995.

Lyotard, J-F., *The Post-Modern Condition: A Report on Knowledge*, trans. G. Bennington and B. Massumi (eds), Manchester: Manchester University Press, 1984.

MacIntyre, A.C., *After Virtue*, Notre Dame: Notre Dame Press, 1981.

——'The idea of an educated public', in G. Haydon, *Education and Values: The Richard Peters Lectures*, London: Institute of Education, University of London, 1987a.

——*Whose Justice, Which Rationality?*, Notre Dame: Notre Dame Press, 1987b.

——*How to Appear Virtuous Without Actually Being So*, University of Lancaster: Centre for the Study of Cultural Values, 1991.

——*Three Rival Versions of Moral Enquiry*, Notre Dame: Notre Dame Press, 1992.

McKeon, R. (ed.), *The Basic Works of Aristotle*, New York: Random House, 1941.

McNiff, J., *Action Research: Principles and Practice*, London: Routledge, 1988.

Martin, M.W., 'Rights and the meta-ethics of professional morality', *Ethics*, 91, 1981, pp. 619–25.

Milton, J., *Paradise Lost*, in *Paradise Lost and Other Poems*, New York: Mentor Books, 1961.

Nagel, T., *The View From Nowhere*, New York: Oxford University Press, 1986.

National Council for Vocational Qualifications (NCVQ), *General National Vocational Qualifications*, London: National Council for Vocational Qualifications, 1991a.

——*Criteria for National Vocational Qualifications*, London: National Council for Vocational Qualifications, 1991b.

National Curriculum Council (NCC), *Spiritual and Moral Education: A Discussion Paper*, National Curriculum Council, UK, 1993.

Neill, A.S., *Summerhill*, Harmondsworth: Penguin Books, 1968.

Ofsted, *Spiritual, Moral, Social and Cultural Development: An Ofsted Discussion Paper*, Office for Standards in Education, UK, 1994.

O'Hear, A., *Who Teaches the Teacher?*, Research Report 10, London: Social Affairs Unit, 1988.

Parsons, T., *The Structure of Social Action*, London: The Free Press, 1949.

——'Professions', in D.L. Sills (ed.), *International Encyclopedia of the Social Sciences*, New York: Free Press, 1968.

Passmore, J., *The Philosophy of Teaching*, London: Duckworth, 1980.

Pendlebury, S., 'Practical reasoning and situational appreciation in teaching', *Educational Theory*, 40, 1990, pp. 171–9.

——'Practical arguments, rationalization and imagination in teachers' practical reasoning', *Journal of Curriculum Studies*, 25, 1993, pp. 145–51.

Perry, L. (ed.), *Four Progressive Educators*, London: Collier-Macmillan, Educational Thinkers Series, 1967.

Peters, R.S., *The Concept of Motivation*, London: Routledge and Kegan Paul, 1958.

——*Authority, Responsibility and Education*, London: George Allen and Unwin, 1959.

——*Ethics and Education*, London: George Allen and Unwin, 1966.

——'Reason and habit: the paradox of moral education', in R.S. Peters, *Moral Development and Moral Education*, London: George Allen and Unwin, 1981.

Phillips, M., *All Must Have Prizes*, London: Little, Brown and Company, 1996.

Piaget , J., *The Moral Judgement of the Child*, New York: Free Press, 1932.

——*The Psychology of Intelligence*, London: Routledge, 1950.

Popper, K.R., *Conjectures and Refutations*, London: Routledge and Kegan Paul, 1969.

Postman, N. and Weingartner, C., *Teaching as a Subversive Activity*, Harmondsworth: Penguin, 1971.

Pring, R., *Closing the Gap: Liberal Education and Vocational Education*, London: Hodder and Stoughton, 1995.

Quine, W.V.O., *From a Logical Point of View*, New York: Harper and Row, 1953.

Rawls, J., *Theory of Justice*, Cambridge: Harvard University Press, 1985.

Raz, J. (ed.), *Practical Reason*, Oxford: Oxford University Press, 1978.

Reader, W.J., *Professional Men: The Rise of the Professional Classes in Nineteenth Century England*, London: Weidenfeld and Nicolson, 1966.

Reimer, E., *School is Dead*, Harmondsworth: Penguin, 1971.

Reznek, L., *Evil or Ill: Justifying the Insanity Defence*, London: Routledge, 1997.

Rousseau, J-J., *The Social Contract and Other Discourses*, London: Dent, 1973.

——*Emile*, London: Dent, 1974.

Ryle, G., *The Concept of Mind*, London: Hutchinson, 1949.

Sandel, M., *Liberalism and the Limits of Justice*, New York: Cambridge University Press, 1982.

Scheffler, S. (ed.), *Consequentialism and its Critics*, Oxford: Oxford University Press, 1988.

Schon, D.A., *The Reflective Practitioner: How Professionals Think in Action*, New York: Basic Books, 1984.

Schools Curriculum and Assessment Authority (SCAA), *Spiritual and Moral Development*, Schools Curriculum and Assessment Authority, UK, Discussion Paper No. 3, 1995.

——*Education for Adult and Moral Life*, Schools Curriculum and Assessment Authority, UK, Discussion Paper No. 6, 1996.

Scottish Education Department (SED), *Primary Education in Scotland*, Edinburgh: SED, 1965.

Scottish Office Education Department (SOED), *Using Ethos Indicators in Primary/Secondary School Self-Evaluation: Taking Account of the Views of Pupils, Parents and Teachers*, Edinburgh: SOED, March 1992.

——*Guidelines for Teacher Training Courses*, Edinburgh: SOED, 1993.

Sergiovanni, T.J., *Moral Leadership: Getting to the Heart of School Improvement*, San Francisco: Jossey-Bass, 1992.

Smith, R., 'Theory: an entitlement to understanding', *Cambridge Journal of Education*, 22, 1992, pp. 387–98.

Smith, R. and Standish, P. (eds), *Teaching Right and Wrong: Moral Education in the Balance*, London: Trentham Books, 1997.

Sockett, H., *The Moral Base for Teacher Professionalism*, New York: Teacher's College Press, 1993.

Soltis, J.F., 'Teaching professional ethics', *Journal of Teacher Education*, 37, 1994, pp. 2–4.

Strike, K.A. and Soltis, J., *The Ethics of Teaching*, New York: Teacher's College Press, 1985.

Strike, K.A. and Ternasky, P.L. (eds), *Ethics for Professionals in Education: Perspectives for Preparation and Practice*, New York: Teacher's College Press, 1993.

Strom, S.M., 'The ethical dimension in teaching', in M.C. Reynolds (ed.), *Knowledge Base for the Beginning Teacher*, Oxford: Pergamon Press, 1989, pp. 267–76.

Taylor, C., *The Explanation of Behaviour*, London: Routledge and Kegan Paul, 1964.

——*Sources of the Self: The Making of the Modern Identity*, Cambridge: Cambridge University Press, 1989.

——*Multiculturalism: Examining the Politics of Recognition*, edited by A. Gutmann, Princeton, N.J.: Princeton University Press, 1994.

Warnock, M. (ed.), *Utilitarianism*, London: Collins, The Fontana Library, 1970.

——'The neutral teacher', in M. Taylor (ed.), *Progress and Problems in Moral Education*, Slough, Berks: NFER Publishing, 1975, Section II.

White, J.P., *Education and the End of Work*, London: Cassell, 1997.

Wiggins, D., 'Deliberation and practical reason', in J. Raz (ed.), *Practical Reason*, Oxford: Oxford University Press, 1978.

Williams, B., *Ethics and the Limits of Philosophy*, London: Fontana Press/Collins, 1985.

Wilson, J., 'Teaching and neutrality', in M. Taylor (ed.), *Progress and Problems in Moral Education*, Slough, Berks: NFER Publishing, 1975, Section II.

Winch, C., 'Education needs training', *Oxford Educational Review*, 21, 1995, pp. 315–25.

Winch, P., *The Idea of a Social Science and its Relation to Philosophy*, London: Routledge and Kegan Paul, 1958.

Wiseman, S. (ed.), *Intelligence and Ability*, Harmondsworth: Penguin Books, 1967.

Wittgenstein, L., *Philosophical Investigations*, Oxford: Blackwell, 1953.

——'A lecture on ethics', *Philosophical Review*, 74, 1965, pp. 3–26.

Young, M.F.D. (ed.), *Knowledge and Control*, London: Collier-Macmillan, 1971.

# INDEX